Contemporary Gender Issues in India

Contemporary Gender Issues in India:
Some Reflections

Edited by

Asha Mukherjee
Shahnaz Begum

GYAN

Published, 2021

Published by

Gyan Publishing House
5, Ansari Road
Daryaganj, New Delhi-110002
Phone: 011-47034999, 9811692060
www.gyanbooks.com
E-mail: books@gyanbooks.com

Printed at: Gyan Press, Delhi.

Cataloging in Publication Data—DK
Courtesy: D.K. Agencies (P) Ltd. <docinfo@dkagencies.com>

Contemporary gender issues in India : some reflections / [edited] by Asha Mukherjee, Shahnaz Begum.
pages cm
Contributed articles.
Includes bibliographical references.
ISBN 9788121219815

1. Feminism—India. 2. Women's rights—India. 3. Women—India—Social conditions. I. Mukherjee, Asha, editor. II. Shahnaz Begum (Scholar of gender studies), editor.

LCC HQ1742.C66 2021 | DDC 305.420954 23

Contents

Section - III
Women's Movements

Preface

My involvement with Women Studies for almost last four decades is both academic and existential. It received a sharp focus during 2009-2012 when I worked as Founder Director with Women's Studies Centre, Visva-Bharati. Ever since, I attended Professor Martha Nussbaum's lectures during her visit to the Department of Philosophy, Visva-Bharati in 1982, I got particularly engaged with the issues related with Capability Approach for Development that takes gender seriously.

In my various essays since then, I have been dealing with the problems of Gender Justice, women rights, tradition, culture and religion analysing and questioning in Indian context; "Women, Rights and Religion in India: Questioning the Tradition", (2020) "Women, *Dharma* and Social Justice in India: Utopia and Reality" (2016), Introduction of the the Edited volume of ***Labrys,*** *Feminisms in India*, 2015 are some of the recent writings.

In my early edited book *Conditioning and Empowerment of Women,* (jointly with Kumkum Bhattacharya), 2004, I dealt with the multidimensional approach towards empowerment of women.

The present book *Contemporary Gender Issues in India: Some Reflections* traces and focuses on the study and approach to some of the major issues that need critical reflection, analysis and practice.

For the preparation of this book, we owe more than we can express the gratitude to the contributors and reviewers for their patience and fine scholarship, for their tireless work on the papers and for the understanding for the expert handling of the final draft.

We also express our gratitude to Professor Rekha Pande for the gracious Foreword.

This book is dedicated with faith and hope to the cause of betterment of women in India.

Nov. 3, 2020

Asha Mukherjee & Shahnaz Begum
Santiniketan

Foreword

Indeed, it is a privilege and a great pleasure to write the foreword to the book, *Contemporary Gender Issues in India: Some Reflections,* edited by, Asha Mukherjee and Shahnaz Begum, two well-known scholars in the area of gender studies. This is a perfectly well-timed book. The new challenge before the country today as we face the twenty first century is to become a developed society which requires not only a vibrant economy driven by knowledge, but one where justice and human values prevail and women achieve gender equality. Women's place in every society is vital to the well-being of that society, for without their work in the formal and informal sector and in the family, most communities could not survive. A fundamental women's right is to bring in equality and remove all kinds of discriminations against women across the world. Unfortunately, the existing pandemic has also put a hurdle in achieving many of these goals.

Indian society has always been patriarchal. Yet through history in the centuries of patriarchal control women have mediated several layers and levels of existence and carried out various ways of resistance across different media that have often gone unnoticed. One such medium that was open to women was bhakti. Since religious space was one of the few spaces accessible to women in early India, many women embraced bhakti that gave them the space to define their own truths in voices that revised culture, politics, relationships and religions (Pande, Rekha, 2010). Women's status again came to the forefront in the social reform movement in the 19th century. At this time, our educated elite was imbibing the western concept of democracy, equality and fraternity through English education and contact with the west. This western liberalism was applied to the issue of women, and transformed into a movement for social change. The reform movements were not homogeneous, and differed considerably in terms of the proposals and improvements to be promoted. However, they expressed a common desire to weed out the social evils, partially in reaction to the colonial rulers' allegations of barbarity. This was a time in which imperial ideology had hegemonic power and influence. This was a period of transition, a bourgeois society emerging, and the values of new ways of thinking.

In this period, the foreign influence was no longer limited to the market or politics alone, but was creeping into areas of our cultural life and community, and this could affect change in Indian society's social fabric. At this juncture, the Indian intellectual reformer responsive to the influence of colonial rule on the one hand also pursued ways and means to combat this colonial domination and this they did by what K N Panniker refers to as Cultural defence.(Panniker, PIHC, 1975).

This resulted in a paradoxical situation. Inspired by new ideas of rationalism and developments in Europe, the reformers tried to establish a new culture, modern but rooted in Indian tradition. They started a critical evaluation of Indian culture in an effort to establish a modern paradigm which was devoid of any kind of social aberrations such as polytheism, polygamy, casteism, sati, child marriage, illiteracy, purdah, all of which they believed were impediments to women's advancement. All the social reformers in the 19th century shared a common belief as in many parts of the world that if their women were backward, no society could progress. The role of Indian women, as it was in the 19th century, was abysmally low to the reformers and thus their efforts were geared towards an overall improvement in women's status through legislation, political action and propagation, education. This was largely brought on by Western first wave feminism and focused on women's human rights (Pande, Rekha, 2009, 22).

The reform movements was not homogeneous and varied in its agendas in terms of the ideas and changes that were to be brought about. However, it was very much concerned with the position of women in Indian society and to remove the social evils such as illiteracy of women, the purdah system (covering and screening off of women), child marriages, widow remarriage, and women's status as second-class citizens, as a response to charges of barbarity from the colonial rulers (Pande, 2015). The movement for social reform did not radically challenge the existing patriarchal structure of society or question the relationship between sexes. Only those things that the British pointed out as signs of degeneration in Indian society were picked up for change. At this juncture, the Indian intellectual reformers like Raja Ram Mohan Roy, Dayanand Saraswathi, Ishwar Chandra Vidyasagar, and Govind Ranade, sensitive to the power of colonial domination and responding to the Western ideas of rationalism, liberalism, and civilised society, also sought ways and means of resisting this colonial hegemony (Pande, et.al, 2020, 17). Even the organisations and organisations of women that arose during this time had no distinct agenda but just took off from what the men said. It is understandable, as the creation of such organisations was initiated largely by the reformers' wives and sisters. Without doubt, the women's organisations embraced the course and scope of change as set by the reformers. As a consequence even when women talked for themselves they spoke only men's language, determined by male criteria.

Women were seen as passive beneficiaries of a more humane care for western-educated male elite to provide. So there was an effort to reform the individual, instead of changing the social structures that opposed her. There were no attempts to alter the system of power and the relationship between man and woman within society. This was but inevitable, because the shift of woman's status was only pursued within the context of the family and not challenging patriarchy itself. The attempt was to establish a new Indian woman, truly Indian and yet adequately educated and tutored in the values of the nineteenth century to match the evolving society. Thus, girls' education was not intended to equip them to be self-sufficient, independent, and emancipated, and to train them to follow some profession, but to be good housewives, home and home mistress (Pande and Kameshwari, 1987, PIHC).

All this created a very paradoxiacal situation for women. On the one hand, there was a desire to imitate, assimilate or reject western values, on the other hand there was also the dimension of revivalism or the need to reassert and uphold a cultural identity distinct from the British colonisers. In addition to implementing changes through legislation, education was seen as an important tool for improving the condition of women (Forbes, 1981). Women's education, which saw its start, was now visualised to establish suitable wives for the newly emerging westernised elite men (Mazumdar, 1972). Women also participated in the fight against colonialism, but although leaders such as Gandhi urged them to participate, their involvement in the struggles was merely an extension of their housework. Very few women were allowed to enter the front ranks with men, and those who did talk of the alienation they often felt (Kumar, 1993, 4). Women's roles were being moved to a more conventional way of life as a sort of reaction against those new ideas that colonialism brought against India. Traditionally, women have become the carriers of tradition and conventional and reworking is often carried out by discussing women's rights and status in society (Sangari, 1989, 90). Regardless of this prevalent image of women, women are enforced to remain in more conventional positions if society is confronted with an immediate response.

One definitely isn't belittling the social reform movement's efforts. Despite its shortcomings, it can not be denied that the movement for social change has helped to eliminate biases toward women's education and created a democratic space for women in the public sphere. Earlier, the only room available to a woman was in the religious sphere and this room was created by Buddhism and Jainism in the ancient era, but women had to choose between this and the family and if they chose religion they had to step out of the families by being part of the Sangha. In medieval times, the bhakti movement proclaimed that God dwells in each person and that one could attain God through faith, and many of the bhakti saints took religion to the oppressed sections of society and women. Bhakti offers a place for women to step out of the everyday life of patriarchal domination and get their freedom in the process. For all these bhaktas women, the rejection of the power of the male figure to whom they were bound in subordinate relationship became the terrain of struggle, self-assertion, and alternative quest. Yet the saintly women had to choose between marriage and a domestic life and their love for the supreme God (Pande, 2005, 281-82).

All these efforts from the end of 19th century have created a contradictory situation in contemporary India. On paper we as women are equal to men in all spheres. Yet, as in the case of other socially deprived groups these legal guarantees are completely undermined and made ineffective by the powerful socio-cultural and ideological milieu which subordinates women. In the euphoria of the post-independence period it was believed that women's status would dramatically improve when we would become the masters of our own destiny. Ideals of equal status for women and important provision for the welfare of women were incorporated into the Indian constitution. The constitution guaranteed equal rights to both the sexes. Article 15 and Article 16(2) of the constitution forbids discrimination, accepted as being equal in the eyes of the law (Article 14) and the franchise is granted to men and women above 21 years of age. Article 15(3) authorises the State to implement special provisions for women. There were also a lot of policy papers that followed. In the early 1950's a number of legislations such as the Hindu marriage act, Hindu succession act, Dowry prohibition act and equal remuneration act were passed and women achieved an equal status with men at least legally. It was mainly because of women's efforts and their role in the fight for independence that women got the right to vote and full equality in the Indian constitution.

India has had to deal with a number of issues shortly after independence. The sorrow of partitioning and displacement of a vast number of people and the outbreak of communal violence in Punjab and Bengal have tempered the joy of Independence. This was followed by the war in Kashmir, the danger of territorial division, the dispersal of power between 600 princely states, and last but not least, the economic dislocation that was to have the most effect on women. Years of colonial rule had wiped out our indigenous skills and exhausted our natural wealth. Industrialisation, changing technology, lack of mobility all resulted in women being unable to cope with the new world. Once their labour was considered insignificant in the productive market, their role in the family also became marginal, giving them a raw status that became abysmal over time.

During the first few decades post-independence period, the main concern was over all economic development. This was immediately followed by another decade, experiencing a increasing concern for justice and alleviating poverty. Female problems were subsumed in poverty-related questions, and no other unique initiatives targeting women existed (Women in India, 1985). Women were involved in such movements as the anti-price, anti-law, and anti-famine relief movement during this period but did not begin to pick up issues involving their oppression as women until the 1970's. After this there was more and more emphasis placed on promoting women's development by Non-Governmental, grassroots level organisations (NGO's). Some of these organisations have varied in scope; aims and vision, but overall they have provided outlets for women to communicate their concerns collectively. Such grass root groups have challenged women's approach to welfare, whereby they are seen mainly as beneficiaries or service providers and instead implement a participatory approach to empowerment. While questions about the success of these organisations are often raised, women exposed to some amount of mobilisation often show great potentialities, receptivity and capacity-defining (Banerjee, 1992).

The path breaking, Study of 1974 (Towards Equality) shattered the illusion of freedom for women. It pointed out the fact that despite many progressive social legislation and constitutional protections, the status of women has not necessarily changed significantly. Women have continued to have a lower status in many areas such as political, economic and social. The report pointed out a sad fact that society has not yet succeeded in defining the required norms and structures to allow women to fulfill the requirements. The growing incidence of custom such as dowry, suggests a further reduction in women's status. They also point to a cycle of regression from some of the norms established during the movement of independence. The study also pointed out that in the last two decades there has been a decrease in the concern for women and their issues that have gained traction since the free movement.

Suggested interventions in the fields of education, health, family planning and nutrition, employment, social security and legal status and provisions to operationalise the recommendations of the CSWI "A Blue Print of Action Points and National Action Plan for Women 1976." In the sixth five year plan, a separate chapter on "Women and Growth 1980-85" culminated in women being viewed as important contributors to the national economy. The seventh five-year plan had a chapter on "socio-economic services for mothers" (1959) that shifted further away from a more constructive holistic approach to welfare. The Indian parliament adopted a 1986 national education policy which included a chapter on women's equality education. In October 1988 a national women's perspective plan was issued. The action plan for the SAARC decade focussed on the girl child 2000.

There was no dearth of records or legislation relating to women in the post-independence period. There has been a change from welfare to growth to women's participation in growth, from earlier decades to empowerment in these. The 73rd and 74th 1993 amendments to Indian constitution providing for women's seats in panchayats and municipalities is a giant step in empowering women. And we are also witnessing the hurdles and obstacles put in passing the Bill providing for quotas in the Parliament. The creation of the National Commission has also helped to create an atmosphere for achieving equality amongst women. Moreover, higher education issues are no longer just centric nation-wide. They have already achieved global dimensions, especially after trade in services has been brought under the WTO regime's remit. (Report 2003, India's Higher Education: Issues, Concerns and New Directions).

Today we can see some very important trends as a result of globalisation. There is a lot of commodification — the use of information as a product that can be bought and sold, and it becomes an alternate supplier with a profit motive. In the global economy, marked by increasing income inequalities, economic growth inequalities, disparities in human capital (life expectancy, nutrition, infant and child mortality, adult literacy, enrolment ratio, etc.), disparities in the distribution of global economic resources and opportunities, the disturbing question arises as to who will protect the rights of the poor and under privilege The supremacy of developed nations, multinational companies, and foreign capital over developing countries' economies, energy, and labour through trade, aid, and technology transfer has significantly undermined nation states and governments' ability to support human development and provide security to the poor. Should the global resources were to be distributed unevenly, the effects of the most pressing issue, poverty, will gradually overflow national boundaries (Human Development Report, 1999). Unorganised market, marked by income inequality and dominated by the poor and underprivileged, is the hardest affected in this transition. Gender violence and trafficking of women and children for sexual exploitation, has emerged as a new threat to security, is one of the grossest and most outrageous human rights violations in the world today and is unacceptable (Pande, 2014, 277).

Market free play, liberalisation, privatisation and competition have become the key words on the road to globalisation. The three pillars of neo liberalism i.e. Privatisation, liberalisation and restructuring have impact on the daily lives of women. Women have been pushed into free trade zones to work under exploitative conditions. Thousands of families have been displaced and forced to migrate in search of better livelihood. In this rapidly shifting paradigm, the state, instead of helping the poor, marginalised and socially disadvantaged people, has gradually withdrawn from essential sectors like healthcare, education, power and water (Pande, 2001,1). This is followed by the withdrawal of the state from more and more welfare oriented activities and south Asia is no exception. However, the response of different countries has varied substantially with reference to the length of adjustment period, intensity of adjustment and the component of the adjustment package. Since there was already a disparity existing in the world, the reduction in the social sectors undermined the quality of human resources thereby jeopardising the countries prospects for achieving sustained economic development in the future. Complementing the forces of global capital is technology, which has given a new meaning to the speedy exchange of information. Simultaneously, we see is a flow of ideas, culture, people and images across borders.

Hence, with these various developments taking place around the world and India also being affected by these, it is a right time to taker stalk of the gender issues as they emerge today. The book is divided into contains three parts. Part one "Women and Religion" has three essays dealing with the issues involved in basically the two most important traditions -Hinduism and Islam. The second part of the book "Women in Literature, Film and Theatre" has four chapters. The third part of the book "Women's Movements" in its next four chapters deals with issues related to women moments for justice and gender equality. All the ten papers in this book present the various ways in which a limited part of Indian society has been trying to change the social and cultural norms in a significant way. The articles cover philosophic-religious grounds for gender equality and the socio-cultural aspects of women rights as well as the legal aspects. Some papers are also devoted on the literary and audio-visual (film) representation of struggle for women rights in Indian society, women in Indian myth and their modern appropriation of gender equality in the literary arena and issues related to mainstreaming of women police. Other papers deal with legal issues addressing the domestic violence act, the legal war against the mining in Odisha, the issue of triple *talaq* and other Muslim laws for the gender equality.

These essays written by well-known scholars of Women's studies, span different cultures, and regions to convey a holistic message and validate the generalisations and also to account for the diversity of experiences. Some of the issues that are focused in this book include exploring the foundations of culture of violence and oppression and examine the structural supports in the social, political and legal systems that are supposed to provide protection to the victims in reality. Some other explore the foundations through literature and films. The book would be very useful to anyone interested in knowing about the recent trends in women's status. It is intended for a wide range of readership, college students (undergraduate and graduate), scholars, journalists, and interested general audiences who will use the book as a reference. This book will be extremely beneficial to scholars of religion, media and women's studies interested in gender questions in contemporary India.

Rekha Pande

Head, Centre for Women's Studies, Professor,
Department of History, School of Social Sciences,
University of Hyderabad, Indian Institution of Eminence,
Prof. C.R.Rao Road, P.O. Central University,
Hyderabad- 500 046, Telangana, INDIA

References

Banerjee, Narayan 1992, *Grassroots empowerment,* mimeograph, New Delhi, Center for Women's Development Studies.

Forbes, Geraldine, 1981, "The Indian Women's Movement: A struggle for Women's rights or National Liberation?" in Gail Minault (Ed), *The Extended Family,* New Delhi, Chankya Publication, pp. 49-82.

Human Development Report, 1999, New York, Oxford University Press.

Kumar, Radha, 1993, *History of Doing,* New Delhi. Kali for Women.

Mazumdar, Vina, 1972, *Education and social change: three studies in 19th century Bengal,* Shimla, Indian Institute of Advanced Studies.

Pande, Rekha, Wen Liu, and Hsunhui Tseng, 2020, Feminist Theory and Methodologies Crossing Disciplinary Boundaries, Fanny M. Cheung and Diane F. Halpern (Ed), *The Cambridge Handbook of the International Psychology of Women,* U.K. Cambridge University Press, pp. 14-26.

Pande, Rekha, 2014, Human Security, Globalisation, and Trafficking of Women and Children in South Asia", in, *Globalisation, Development and Security in Asia,* (ed) Zhquin Zhu, Foreign Policy and Security in an Asian Century: Threats, Strategies and Policy choices, Vol. 1, (ed), Benny The Cheng Guan, New Jersey, USA, World Scientific. Hackensack, pp. 277-296.

Pande, Rekha, 2015, Indology and the Women's Question- Discourses on women's status - Traditional past and continuing modern discourses, *Manas, Studies into Asia and Africa.* Electronic Journal of the Centre for Eastern Languages and Cultures Sofia University "St. Kliment Ohridski" Issue No. 2.

Pande, Rekha, 2010, *Divine Sounds from the Heart,* United Kingdom, Cambridge Scholars Publishing.

Pande, Rekha, 2009, "Feminism and the Women's Movement in India- a historical perspective", *Journal of Women's Studies*, Vol. 1, No. 1, Bangalore, pp. 22-39.

Pande, Rekha, 2005, Solidarity, Patriarchy and empowerment- Women's struggle against attack in India, in Luciana Ricciutelli, Angela Miles, Margaret M.Mcfadden(ed) *Feminist Politics, Activism and Vision,- Local and Global Challenges,* New York, Zed Publications, pp. 212-226.

Pande, Rekha, 2001, The Social costs of Globalisation : Restructuring Developing World Economies, *Journal of Asian Women's Studies,* Vol. 10, December, Japan, Kitakyushu Forum, pp.1-14.

Pande, Rekha and Kameshwari, J. 1987, "Women's Discourse on Education" (a preliminary readings of the speeches delivered at the Annual Conferences of the Andhra Mahila Sabha, (1913 & 1914) *Proceedings of Indian History Congress*, PIHC, Goa, 1987, pp. 390-396.

Panikkar, KN, 1975, Presidential Address: Section III, Proceedings of the Indian History Congress, *PIHC*, thirty-sixth session, Aligarh.

Report, 2003, *Higher education in India:* Issues, Concerns and New Directions. Issues, Concerns and New directions, University Grants Commission https://www.ugc.ac.in/oldpdf/pub/he/heindia.pdf Accessed, 6th July, 2016 and 29th May, 2020.

Sangari, Kumkum and Vaid, Suresh (ed), 1989, *Recasting Women: essays in Colonial history,* New Delhi. Kali for Women.

Towards Equality, 1975, Report of the Committee on the status of women India, Government of India, New Delhi, Ministry of Education and Social Welfare.

Women in India- A country Paper, 1985, Department of Women and Child Development, Ministry of Social Welfare, Government of India.

Introduction

The status of women in India has undergone considerable change in last three decades. Though, Indian women in cities are now far more independent and aware of their legal rights, such as right to work, equal treatment, property and maintenance, still a majority of women in India remain unaware of these rights especially in rural set-up and even if they are aware, hardly exercise these opportunities. There are other factors that affect their quality of life such as age of marriage, extent of literacy, role in the family, culture, tradition and so on. In many of the Indian families, women still do not have a voice in most of the decision making. The gender disparity is also a cause for worry due to unbalanced development taking place in India.

The status of women has become a matter of serious concern in India and the traditional role of a woman as mother and nurturer needs to be reviewed; this has been insisted by the feminist in India just as anywhere else. The family for a women matters a lot in India (even today) and so does women for a family. The woman of the family binds everyone, looks after every member of the family, provides care, solves money problems in crisis but what she gets in return? Does she have any right to demand care for herself? Does she have a right to a dignified living within her family? Does she get due respect, love and affection in return from her family members and from the larger society? As an ideal wife of the house (*grihalakshmi*) she is not supposed to raise any voice whatever conditions she lives in and suppose to submit to everything and be tolerant. She has no rights, no dignity, no voice and no choice of her own. Many Non-Governmental Organisations (NGOs), empowerment programmes by the government, social work departments through extension programmes, Women Studies programmes and Self-Help-Groups are trying to help women in making them aware of these problems but are women aware of the rights provided to them by Indian constitution and law? Do women exercise the rights given to them by law and by the government? We perhaps at the best can create awareness of laws and recent amendments but do we have any supportive social system which is conducive to the woman who chooses to exercise the rights? Even the people who are working or helping in such organisations, often do not extend the favourable environment so that the women can exercise their rights. One wonders what could be the compulsions, deep rooted reasons? By and large, it is argued in the book, that it is due to their own and society's deep rooted patriarchal convictions coming from their own traditions and cultures. The situation in cities may be a little better than the villages due to the awareness programmes and education. In such scenario, the role of society and its obligations becomes most important. In a village setting the social pressure is visible. The attitudinal change is much more needed and if the rights of women are recognised as valid and some obligations towards betterment for women are recognised by the society at large, the change of status of women would be faster.

The eleven papers in this book present the various ways in which a limited part of Indian society has been trying to change the social and cultural norms in a significant way. The articles cover philosophic-religious grounds for gender equality and the socio-cultural aspects of women rights as well as the legal aspects. Some papers are also devoted on the literary and audio-visual (film) representation of struggle for women rights in Indian society, women in Indian myth and their modern appropriation of gender equality in the literary arena and issues related to mainstreaming of women police. Some other will deal with legal issues addressing the domestic violence act, the legal war against the mining in Odisha, the issue of triple *talaq* and other Muslim laws for the gender equality.

The chapters in this book are contributed by some of the competent writers on women's issues basically exploring the foundations of culture of violence and oppression and examine the structural supports in the social, political and legal systems that are supposed to provide protection to the victims in reality. Some other explore the foundations through literature and films.

The book contains three parts. Part one "Women and Religion" has three essays dealing with the issues involved in basically the two most important traditions -Hinduism and Islam. The second part of the book "Women in Literature, Film and Theatre" has four chapters. The third part of the book "Women's Movements" in its next four chapters deals with issues related to women moments for justice and gender equality.

The first chapter by Asha Mukherjee "Women Rights and Religion in India: Exclusive or Inclusive?" argues that it is often suggested that human rights and duties are two sides of the same coin and yet in Indian context traditionally (in almost all the traditions of Indian origin) we have *dharma* discourse (obligation based) and the issue of human rights has never been the center of discussion nor it has been a 'problem' for Indian masses. In modern India, human rights and women rights have been reconciled or discovered within Hinduism and its caste system which necessarily generates tension and conflict due to the complexity and multilayered structure and also since opportunities are not in abundance.

The author argues that in India today we face the most difficult question - how to include the excluded and how to exclude the included. The other important question is 'who deserves what and who decides?'. At the core of the Women's Rights debate there lies a need to interrogate the very being of individual, person, self and "other" for accommodating the claims and the counter claims of rights to be creatively human, the promise of mankind which gets threatened by any destructive self of the few in power either political or social or economic or religious.

What we find in India today is more and more divide between the 'self' and the 'other' on the name of democracy and secularism. There is no automatic guarantee of success by the mere existence of democratic institutions, democratic institutions like that of all other institutions depend on the activities of human agents in utilising opportunities for reasonable realisation.

Further, Indian civilisation based on *Dharma* often been claimed as creative and communicative and to be understood as human dignity and worth in terms of justice, unity and benevolence as virtue for human fulfillment along with its theological insights and metaphysical doctrines. *Dharma* has both descriptive and prescriptive contents; the way things are and the way things ought to be- the nature of man and the obligations or duties.

The concern for gender justice and women rights has also been extremely important area in Indian Constitution right from the Independence. While examining how *dharma* is practiced in Indian society as part of gender justice, one finds a paradox between an urge to change and accept Western progressive and democratic values and yet this change has to be rooted in the past glory of Indian society. This paradox influences to a large extent the way the women's questions are developed and we find two conflicting images of women in India *devi* (goddess) or *dasi* (servant). Author argues further that it is difficult for the middle class, educated working women to be either of the two, she wants some space to be treated as human being, a dignified person who would have power to decide *to be* and *to do* and for this she would have to constantly face a struggle, often very difficult. The article focusses on the different layers of struggles women in India have to face to negotiate freedom and dignity.

The second chapter by Shahnaz Begum "Islamic Feminism: A Liberating force or a Religious Constraint?" explores Islamic Feminism which is a postcolonial phenomenon having its root in Muslim women's consciousness in 1990's. It stresses on the socio-religious practices prevalent in Muslim societies as well as the interpretation of the Quran that is intrinsically patriarchal. Therefore, Islamic feminists claim that they need to unread the patriarchal interpretation of the Quran to establish gender equality already embedded in this sacred text. Since, Islamic Feminism receives challenges and attacks from various corners, the paper interrogates whether it really succeeds in breaking the constraints and acts as a liberating force. The paper also addresses the issues plaguing the rights of Muslim Women in India.

The third chapter by Chandreyi Alam Gupta "Abolition of Arbitrary Triple *Talaq*- A Landmark Judgement on Rights of Women: Legal and Social Dimension" focuses on the most controversial verdict regarding the abolition of arbitrary Triple *talaq,* an issue that has been plaguing the life of Indian Muslim women. Arbitrary triple *talaq* has already been banned in many Muslim countries. But it continues to persist in India as approved by Muslim Personal Law board. The verdict conferred victory to the struggles of women rights activists of India. The paper critically discusses all the legal cases related to the issue of arbitrary triple *talaq* and the success that came finally.

The chapter by Himadri Lahiri "Return of the Myth: Gender and the Politics of Rewriting" examines how the feminist concern for foregrounding women's 'bodies' (in the sense of material existence) and voices recalls important mythic figures to address some contemporary issues related to women's lived experience. These issues are raised against the backdrop of overwhelming amnesia about women's rights in general. This 'recall' goes well with the overall trends in postcolonial discourses which have retrieval and restoration of forgotten voices as one of their important projects. Women writers' penchant for going back to the mythic female figures is in fact an *anamnesic* effort to bring to the fore the continuing 'colonial' practice of forgetting and erasing women's voices. They scour the depth of myths and legends in search of appropriate female figures as their models. Naturally, there has been a proliferation of myth-based creative works where mythic female figures are retrieved. Article does not analyse any text in particular—some texts are rather invoked briefly to seek a connection between archetypal mythic characters and some contemporary feminist issues. Two such figures — Sita and Draupadi — constitute the focus of the discourse in the article.

The chapter by Anindita Bandyopadhyay "Women's Movements in 19th Century and as it reflected in Bengali Women's Writings" traces the history of women rights movement in the 19th century Bengal with special references to writings by women such as *Chittabilasini* (1856) by Krishnakamini 'Which Superstitions are to be Eradicated to Ensure for the Prosperity of the Country?' (1861), a pamphlet by Bamasundari Devi, *Hindu Mohilaganer Hinabastha* (1863) by Kailasbasini Debi, Usha by Kaminisundari Debi and "Apurbasati" by Sukumari Dutta.

Chapter six by Amitayu Chakraborty "Decoding the Ideal Woman: A Reading of Rituparno Ghosh's *Unishe April*" studies Rituparno Ghosh's *Unishe April* from feminist perspective and explores the central conflict of the film: the tussle between the mother who allegedly has no time for her family and the daughter who seeks refuge in her deceased father's memory. By analysing the ways in which the film addresses the issue of working/ celebrity woman's role in her family, the chapter argues that Mithu/Aditi, the daughter, has a longing for a 'traditional' mother, a *grihalakshmi* (the Lady of the Bengali middle-class household), and this longing is predicated upon patriarchal discourses on ideal womanhood. The conclusion brought home by the chapter is that Ghosh's women-centric film aspires to challenge the gender stereotypes that gain prominence in the contemporary Bengali middle-class society vis-à-vis the role of women in family, but ends up yielding to the patriarchal ideology that it aspires to destabilise.

Debayan Deb Barman in Chapter seven "Theatre as Forum for Women's Rights Activism in India: The Case of Tendulkar's *Silence! The Court is in Session* (1968) and Jana Natya Manch's *Aurat* (1979)" shows how Gender discrimination has received much critical attention from mid-twentieth century onwards in theatre. International legal and social welfare organisations have focussed in this area and have been probing for answers. Similarly, theatre, as a political weapon has been very effective and potent in voicing protests against social injustice. Increasingly, in the twentieth century, theatre has emerged as not merely a source of entertainment, but also a medium of voicing agitation and propaganda. Matters of injustice, discrimination, violence and suppression against women has been a neglected area that found protesting voices among feminist activists and thinkers, and these matters found voice and representation in theatre also. In India, post-Independence theatre saw the emergence of theatre activists like Rati Bartholomew, Maya Krishna Rao, Neelam Man Singh Choudhury, Usha Ganguli, Moloyasree Hashmi, Shaonli Mitra to name a few. Similarly, playwrights like Vijay Tendulkar, Mahesh Dattani or Girish Karnad were scrutinising modern Indian society through pathbreaking plays. Keeping in mind the political intent of modern theatre both in the West and in India, in various forms. The author presents a comparative analysis of two phenomenal plays in modern Indian theatre that have contributed much in building a feminist theatre of protest against patriarchal attitudes. One is the hugely successful proscenium play *"Silence the Court is in Session!"* by Vijay Tendulkar and the other is the street play *Aurat* by Janam. After a detailed study the author presents the modus operandi of each play in critiquing and protesting against oppressive patriarchal attitudes.

Rakesh Chandra in his chapter "Claim for Equal Justice and Universalistic Hopes" engages with questions of multiculturalism and stand point from epistemology with reference to women's gendered identities and claim for equal justice. He considers some claims of multiculturalism against modernity and enlightenment and suggests that Descartes position as a splendid isolationist is misconstrued. He also tries to examine the idea of women's self alienated serial identities within the framework of civic reciprocity. A practical, philosophic and a meta-philosophic question is raised to the multicultural positions. The stand point of epistemology is examined and attention is drawn to some of its peculiar anthropomorphic constructions of logic. He also suggests that objectivity in science must not necessarily be conflated with 'a view from nowhere' but could be taken as an approximation arrived at through inter subjective criticism similar to the idea of Longino's maximal minimisation of the subjective.

Rakesh Chandra in conclusion argues that knowledge as engagement and interaction is a much favoured view but may not necessarily constrain universalistic hope for boundaryless communication. Liberal feminist and some *dalit* voices seeking inclusion may be universalistic without being hegemonic reflecting the hopes of Bulle Shah-"Let us move to the land where everyone is blind. No one recognizes my caste and no one minds me."

Urmimala Das in ninth chapter "Vanguardship of Women in Vedanta Movement- Laljigarh, Odisha" focusses on gender issues in displacement, development and livelihood issues in Odisha. She draws attention to the consequences of the development projects. The lives and livelihoods of nearly Ten million people across the globe are affected by forced displacement due to infrastructure projects such as dams, mines, factories and roads and emerging research shows that this number is likely to increase, rather than decrease. Forced displacement leads to new social and economic benefits in some cases. Largely, however, it is a traumatic event that leads to a decline in the standard of living and a diminished sense of wellbeing for those displaced. Lanjigarh has been the site of tremendous resistance and the protest movement has influenced anti-mining struggles in Odisha. Communities living in south-west Odisha in eastern India – already one of the poorest areas of the country – are at threat from the expansion of an alumina refinery and plans for a new bauxite mining project. Her case study shows how the women of Lanjigarh took the leading role in the protest movement against Vedanta Bauxite mining in the area.

The tenth chapter by Tumpa Mukherjee "Mainstreaming of Women in Kolkata Police" while pointing out the contradictions, argues and suggests the ways of mainstreaming of women in police that can help in solving gender issues as an alternative model taking into account the social structure and cultural values of contemporary Indian society.

Generally, policing is considered one of the world's most masculinised occupations dominated not only by men, but also by male values. The institution of police has been heavily influenced by army corps or militia, adopting a military model for its training, uniform, promotional structure, formal work culture and informal cultural ethos. Culturally ascribed and stereotyped masculine traits such as boldness, risk-taking, aggression, competitiveness, assertiveness, commanding voice, assertion of autonomy, and authoritative expertise are regarded as quintessential attributes to be successful in this profession. The 'cult of womanhood' emphasising the role of women as wives, mothers, nurturing families, and submissiveness dominates the imagination and consciousness of women, generation after generation, as a result of gendered socialisation. The masculine attributes are antithetical to the feminine qualities women acquire due to cultural, ideological and psychological gender conditioning. But women have entered the institution of police considered to be a male bastion. The paper traces the socio-historical growth and expansion of women in Kolkata Police and discusses the problems women in police confront at their workplace. Jennifer Brown, after an in-depth study of the evolution and growth of women police in the western world (the U.S.A. and the U.K.), has identified a sequence of stages through which women in the police have gone through with the ultimate goal of total integration with mainstream police culture and structure. This chapter examines such a model of gender mainstreaming in the context of Kolkata Police and suggests an alternative model.

The concluding chapter by Rupa Biswas "Understanding Justice Delivery System from the Perspective of Survivors of Intimate Partner Violence in the Context of Protection of Women from Domestic Violence Act 2005" examines through case studies the effects of Intimate Partner Violence Act and Domestic Violence Act.

Of all the forms of violence that women face, intimate partner violence remains the least reported and differs from other forms of violence against women is that it occurs within the framework of private sphere and in intimate relationships. Thus, reporting of incidences, access to support services and legal aid becomes difficult task for the survivors. Intimate partner violence especially domestic violence against women is a significant phenomenon in India. Almost 30% of married Indian women between the ages of 15 and 49 years reported experiencing spousal violence at least once in their lifetime (National Family Health Survey-4, 2015-2016). The majority of cases categorised as crimes against women were reported under 'Cruelty by husband or his relatives' (32.6%), followed by 'Assault on woman with intent to outrage her modesty' (25%), 'Kidnapping and abduction of women' (19%) and 'Rape' (11.5%) (NCRB, 2016). West Bengal (19,302), Rajasthan (13,811) and Uttar Pradesh (11,156) have reported the highest number of incidents of 'cruelty by husband'. The article reports the research findings conducted on survivors of intimate partner violence in the Barddhaman district of West Bengal conducted on the 200 married women who had registered cases under the Protection of Women from Domestic Violence Act, 2005. Research is based on simple random sampling technique followed by in-depth interviews. Most of the survivors (83.50%) found that legal provisions were hardly detrimental to combat intimate partner violence. The study findings indicate the barriers in socio-legal system which contributed in attaining justice.

We hope that the readers will enjoy reading the book, reflect on the issues and also will make some real changes in the life of the Indian women.

Asha Mukherjee
Shahnaz Begum

Section - I
Women and Religion

1

Women Rights and Religion in India: Exclusive or Inclusive?

Asha Mukherjee

It is often suggested that human rights and duties are two sides of the same coin. Yet in Indian context traditionally, we have *dharma* discourse (obligation based) and the issue of human rights has never been the centre of serious discussion nor, it has been a 'problem' for Indian masses. In modern India human rights and women rights have been reconciled or discovered within Hinduism and its caste system which necessarily generates tension and conflict due to the complexity and multilayered structure and also since opportunities are not in abundance. Therefore, who deserves what and who decides are extremely important questions. I would argue that in India today, we face the most difficult question - how to include the excluded and how to exclude the included. At the core of the Women's Rights debate there lies a need to interrogate the very being of woman as individual, person, self and "other" for accommodating the claims and the counter claims of rights to be creatively human, the promise of mankind which gets threatened by any destructive self of the few in power- political, social, economic or religious. What we find in India today is more and more divide between the 'self' and the 'other' on the name of democracy and secularism. The women are divided in as many as 7500 groups on the basis of caste, religion, class, backward class and tribe using Indian Constitution itself and any objective of the women right's movement gets defeated on the way. There is no automatic guarantee of success by the mere existence of democratic institutions. Democratic institutions like that of all other institutions depend on the activities of human agents in utilising opportunities for realisation.

Most of the thinkers of modern India before independence and around independence were concerned with the idea of India and the future of India.

Gandhi's "Hind Swaraj", Tilak's *Gita Rahasya* and Tagore's critique of narrow nationalism are expressions of ideas beyond India's Independence. 'What model of development to be adopted in India' was as relevant a question as it is today. The basic question is the same even today 'what direction we should adopt to realise our cherished dream of all round development in the lives of our countrymen, including women.

Even after 75 years of Independence, there is hardly any ideological conscientious on Socialism, Marxism, Liberalism, Capitalism, and Welfare State with democratic values, yet some aspects of these ideologies have been integrated in Indian constitution and followed-up with interpretation and reinterpretations. Can Indian Constitution be taken as representing all the citizens of India or integrating all Human irrespective of caste, religion and gender?

All polarities like modern versus ancient, foreign versus indigenous, west versus east and *our* versus *their,* individual versus society, mind versus body, intellect and soul, microcosm and the macrocosm can be dissolved or integrated in principles termed in "Dharma", laws of life- a foundation all the religions of Indian origin 'All those principles which bring about harmony, peace and progress in the life of mankind are included in this "Dharma". On the sound basis of "Dharma" then, we must proceed with the analysis of life as an integral whole; dharma should be the guiding principle for our thoughts and actions. What it means to insist that Dharma sustains the cosmos, regulates the cosmic process and helps in realisation of allround development? How one realises of *dharmika* individual, *dharmika* society, *dharmika* nation and *dharmika* world? Is the new paradigm of world order with a spirit of spiritual globalisation often been suggested by contemporary thinkers, only an ideal- a demand of spirituality and rationality or this is also practically feasible and can be actualised in the daily life of an Indian woman? These are some of the questions, we need to look for answers.

In this paper I will make an attempt to critically understand these ideas and the foundation of "Dharma" as often interpreted and look for the relevance in the present crisis Indian women are facing specially from the human right's discourse perspective.

A long debate between the scholars has been and still continuing whether the concept of human rights/women rights can be consistently developed within the caste system. B.R Ambedkar who himself was born as untouchable, played the vital role in drafting the Indian Constitution which include the Right of Equality, Right to Freedom, Right Against Exploitation, Right to Freedom of Religion, Right to Property, and Right to Constitutional Remedies challenging all forms of inequalities prominent in India including gender inequality making it much wider than "fundamental rights". He was of the opinion that human rights/women rights cannot be reconciled within Hinduism with its caste system and he converted himself to Buddhism. Other scholars like S. Radhakrishnan, thought that 'if democracy is to be seriously implemented, then caste and untouchability should go.' (Radhakrishnan, S.: 1960 :163). Pandit Deen Dayal Upadhyaya says that 'the definition of democracy, to say that it is a government of the people is not enough. It has to be for the good of the people. What constitutes the good of the people? Dharma alone can decide. Therefore, a democratic Government "Jana Rajya" must also be rooted in Dharma i.e. a "Dharma Rajya". In the definition of 'Democracy' viz. "government of the people, by the people and for the people", of stands for independence, 'by' stands for democracy and 'for' Indicates Dharma. Therefore, the true democracy is only where there is freedom as well as Dharma encompasses all these concepts. (Upadhyaya: 2016)

There is another approach which suggests rather than doing away with caste, the human rights can be derived from the caste system itself. Among these the most well-known was Mahatma Gandhi although he asserted that human rights are in opposition to the caste system while he was campaigning against untouchability. He accepted the *varna* system based on birth and by implication the caste system but denounced untouchability. He did not see caste system as advocating inequality. A number of other scholars R. Panikkar, J.B. Carman, Klaus K. Klostermaier and others have been trying to work out a restricted idea of caste duty or caste rights as the basis for universal rights, and universal duties like *satya* (truth telling) and *ahimsa* (not harming living beings). But the important point that these scholars were making was that Hindu thought draws our attention to the human rights discourse as 'rights and duties as an integrated whole'.

Basham argues that the word caste is not of Indian origin. (Basham: 1954:148) It was first used by Portuguese who came to India in the 16th century and found Hindu community divided into many separate groups which they called *castas* meaning tribes, clans or families, later it became common for Hindu social groups. This word is also used confusingly to refer to *Varna* and *Jati* both. Originally we find word *varna* referring to the fourfold division of society into *Brahmanas, Ksatriyas, Vaisyas* and *Sudras* referring to priestly, warriors, agriculturists and trading and serving classes respectively. According to Daya Krishna, *Sudras* in fact happen to be treated as a residual category and not much attention has been paid to them in Indian thought. (Daya Krishna: 1997) *Jati* refer to the people who did not fall under anyone of these categories. It seems when the Indo-Aryans, with their *varna* system intermingled with the indigenous people and were mostly characterised by *jati* after entering India referring to tribal people. We also find a conglomeration of units the category of untouchables, who virtually formed a separate group at the bottom, and any contact with them was considered polluting. They also have *jatis* among them as well. Moreover, the birth of an individual to be born in a Jati is also determined by his karmas (actions) of this life and previous life as accepted by more or less by every philosophical school and religion of Indian origin- Hinduism, Buddhism, Jainism and Sikhism. Other religions who found their roots in Indian soil later like Islam, Sufism and Christianity etc. also by way of conversion unfortunately, assimilated some form of the casteism within their religion.

Untouchability was legally abolished in 1950 and today's India and all discourse on India is the end result of *Varna, Caste* and *Jati*. This complex and multi layered *varna-jati* system is referred as caste system and is significant for our discussion on Human rights in India. It is worth mentioning that Manu and Kautilya dealt with these divisions but in different ways, the former in the context of society and the latter in the context of polity and the nature of social reality as expressed through the caste system is heavily odd with the spiritual nature of human being as understood within Hinduism. (K. Satchitananda Murty: 1993: 14)

The Constitution of India provides ample space for reforms based on democratic principles of human liberty and dignity and is the most rights based Constitution in the world. It was heavily influenced by the Universal Declaration of Human Rights guarantees the fundamental principles of human rights. The Constitution of India guarantees to all Indian women equality under Article 14, no discrimination by State Article 15 (1), equality of opportunity Article 16, equal pay for equal work Article 39(d) and Article 42. Political rights such as women reservation in panchayats. It is true that Indian Constitution provides a solid foundation for equality except in terms of providing reservation clause 3 of Article 15, Article 46 in providing educational and economic interests of the weaker section of the society and getting government jobs for section of people who have been marginalised and are called scheduled castes and scheduled tribes as they belong to the lower castes which is unique due to the social and cultural conditions of India. Some important changes an Human Rights Acts are passed : SC and ST reservation at all levels under Preservation of Atrocities Act in 1989, one-third seats to women reserved in *panchyat* (Local Council level) 1992, Human rights commission is established in 1993 which is protection of Human rights act, Right to Food, 2001, Right to Information 2005, National Rural Employment Guarantee Act in 2005 and National Commission for Women in 1990.

It is important to note that the concern for gender justice and women rights has also been extremely important area in Indian Constitution right from the Independence. While examining how *dharma* is practiced in Indian society as part of gender justice, one finds a paradox between an urge to change and accept Western progressive and democratic values and yet this change has to be rooted in the past glory of Indian society. This paradox influences to a large extent the way the women's questions are developed and we find two conflicting images of women in India *devi* (goddess) or *dasi* (servant). But it is difficult for the middle class, educated working women to be either of the two. She wants some space to be treated as human being, a dignified person who would have power to decide *to be* and *to do* and for this she has to go through constantly a struggle, often very difficult. Women in India have to negotiate freedom and dignity at almost every moment.

The status of women has been a focus of attention in India from four decades or so. The traditional role of a women as mother and nurturer is a 'social construct' and it needs to be reviewed, this has been insisted by the feminists. The women of the family binds everyone, looks after every member of the family, provides care, solves money problems in crisis but what she gets in return? Does she have any right to demand care for herself? Does she have a right to a dignified living within her family? Does she get due respect, love and affection in return from her family members and from the society? As an ideal wife of the house (*grah vadhu*) she is not supposed to raise any voice and has to submit to everything. She has no rights, no dignity, and no choice of her own. Many NGO's, empowerment programme by the government, social work departments through extension programmes, and forming self-help groups are trying to help women in making them aware of these problems but do women exercise the rights provided to them by law? Creating awareness of laws and making constant amendments law is surely a positive aspect but do we have any supportive social system which is conducive to the women who choose to exercise their rights? Even the people who are working in public offices and are supposed to help women often do not extend the favourable environment so that the women can exercise their rights. The situation in cities and villages is more or less the same. The role of society and its obligations is of fundamental importance. In a village, social pressure is visible. The attitudinal change is much easier and if the rights of women are recognised as valid and some obligations towards betterment for status of women are recognised by the society at large, the change would be faster. Cities are more individualistic, people in general do not care much about others, therefore change in the status of women is slow.

This cultural defence resulted in a paradoxical situation. Rooted in new European ideas of rationalism and progress, the reformers tried to create a new society, modern yet rooted in Indian tradition. They began a critical appraisal of Indian society in an attempt to create a new ethos devoid of all overt social aberrations like polytheism, polygamy, casteism, sati, child marriage, illiteracy- all of which they believed were impediments to progress of women. All the social reformers shared a belief common to many parts of the world in the 19th century that no society could progress if its women were backward. To the reformers, the position of Indian women, as it was in the 19th century was abysmally low and hence their efforts were directed at an overall improvement in the status of women through legislation, political action and propagation, of education. This was mainly spurred by the first wave feminism of the west and concentrated on basic rights for women (Pande, 2009, 27). Nandita Dhavan in her essay "'Hindutva Feminism'? Challenges to the Indian Women's Movements" raises very interesting questions in Indian context -What happens when the opportunities of well-being are being denied by the state, due to particular religious belief- Christianity, Islam or Hinduism? The question of justice becomes extremely important in this context- 'How the good and bad things in life should be distributed among the members of a human society, given how other members of the society in question are faring?' Theories of justice do not cover the entire spectrum of moral and religious issues; they generally agree that some components of morality and religiosity fall outside the scope of justice. Justice is a property that has been ascribed to both individuals and institutions: justice is a virtue of individuals in their interactions with others, but justice is also a virtue of social institutions.

The History of Women Rights Movement

If we look at the historical development of women rights movements in India, we note different phases. Before and during Independence movement women participated in large number but their participation was, in a way, a role of subordination required by the sheer contextual necessity. These movements can hardly be considered as women rights movements. It is only around 1970's that 'gender' was recognised as a category and was asserted. Feminism was seen as a tool for transcending sphere of knowledge, production and feminism as critical perspective to various disciplines was added. It took the form of an academic movement as well as a political movement and as a result greater inclusion of women and women's experience in every inquiry was felt. Women got engaged in transforming every branch of knowledge by using gender as a category of understanding, examining the relation of theory to political questions and argued that there is a close relation between theory and politics. It was realised that a particular theory either entails a mode of politics or the mode of politics engenders a theory. Feminists argue that notions such as reason, laws of thought, logical forms, objectivity, selfhood-construction, and self-identity are in need of major revision. Feminist concepts of relational-self, care, distributive justice, etc. need to be recognised as legitimate concepts. During this time the 'privileged' feminists reached out to, and identified with their distant sisters to avail social, economic and gender justice, for 'all' women and exercised women rights as a crucial part of human rights.

Women rights are recognised as human rights during the world conference on human rights held in Vienna in 1993. It declared the full and equal participation of women in civil political, economic, social, and cultural life, at the national, regional, and international levels, and the eradication of all forms of discrimination on grounds of sex as priority objectives of the international community. Indian constitution also prohibits any discrimination on grounds of religion, race, caste, sex, or place of birth. The convention on the Elimination of All Forms of Discrimination Against Women, 1976 (CEDAW) acknowledges that discrimination against women violates the principles of equality or rights and respect for human dignity, and is an obstacle to the participation of women on equal terms with men, in the political, social economic and cultural life of their countries. This in turn affects the development of family and society as a whole. This convention has been ratified by India and utilised by the Indian judiciary in order to direct the state to take action.

There has been much more organised movements recently based on demands for women rights, such as the right of a girl child to school education, the right to food (and, in particular, to midday school meals), the entitlement to basic healthcare, guarantees of environment preservation and the right of 'employment guarantee' they also 'provide a politically harder edge to socially important demands'. (Sen: 2009: 351)

But during 1980-90 one can notice significant change in political questions especially when Mondal Commission recommendations took place, *mandir-masjid* (temple-mosque) debates and free-bank policies were implemented. The issues of caste, religion and economic liberalisation started creating new problems and contexts, 'a reconfigured hegemonic culture' when the knower and the known were both feminist forcing feminists to re-introspect their immediate world (Tharu and Niranjan: 1994 and John, 1996 a). Tharu and Niranjan expressed their serious concern and dissatisfaction with the Hinduism becoming hegemonic and the discourse of 'new Indian Women' a new hegemonic subject: The shift in feminist issues is perceptible as the issues of 'gender and development' which were primarily economic issues, started becoming the social issues as well. Women are treated by the state as self-sacrificing and political centers of family, taking back to their traditional roles within the feminist agenda. Women were empowered to act as agents within the development agenda of the state, with Govt. officials preparing to use the term 'women's empowerment' for feminism. Women's movements as empowerment programmes have also been able to achieve to a certain extent, intellectual, institutional and political transformation perceived by the founders of women's studies centers in education system in India during this decade.

In recent times women's protests have, in the whole country, gained a distinct voice in the context of eco-feminism and in the area of development. The problems related to development, mal-development and the 'subsistence perspective' are major issues. It is believed that the marginalised rural women's participation and their lived experience at the grass root level can transform feminist epistemology making space for women's ways of knowing and women's consciousness. They are recognised as "experts" due to their intellect and close association with nature. Further, women's work is recognised not only as 'producers' but also as 'home makers'. Women contribute most to the family and all their domestic work is not considered as 'work'. (María Mies, Vandana Shiva:1993) Later, women's movements are taking shape of NGOs. Completing specific projects without fresh thinking on what constitute feminism and the notion of 'self' and 'identity' (Menon: 2004). They depend mostly on foreign funding who dictates the terms and conditions of the project for 'gender issues' such as HIV or AID or trafficking without any focus on feminist concern.

Rekha Pande in her essay "Mapping the terrain of activism in the Feminist and the Women's Movement in India" maps the terrain of activism in the feminist movements in India. The diversity of Indian women's movement covers the cultural, historical, geographical, religious, political and regional factors that make it very difficult to analyze all the movements in general. She stresses that the women's movements in India is not a homogeneous group or federation of different groups. (Pande: 2015) Feminist movements represent social, cultural and political movements, theories and moral philosophies are concerned with gender inequalities and equal rights for women. Tracing the history, Pande says 'In the pre-independent era, the Women's Movement began as a social reform movement in the 19th century. At this time, the western idea of liberty, equality and fraternity was being imbibed by our educated elite through the study of English and the contact with the west. This western liberalism was extended to the women's question and was translated into a social reform movement. The reform movements were not homogeneous and varied a lot in terms of the ideas and changes that was to be fostered. ..This was a period of the hegemonic control and influence of colonial ideology. At this juncture, the Indian intellectual reformers were sensitive to the power of colonial domination. They were responding to the western ideas of rationalism, liberalism and civilised society on one hand also sought ways and means of resisting this colonial hegemony by resorting to what Panniker refers to as Cultural defence'. (Panniker :1975).

What are Women Rights and what is their concern?

Modern thinkers seem to be concerned with mainly four ways of looking at rights: Rights as liberties, Rights as claims, rights as entitlement and rights as trumps. (When in conflict negotiate to reduce the tension but not absolute) and they have been integrally related with discourse on duties and discourse on rights. These two discourses are not only comparable but also to a certain extent convertible, this does not mean that both have the same extension. For Kant for example, 'a rationally based concept of self-respect… breaks free of a notion of rights'. Rights are claims against others (individuals, state or group) whereas the obligations of human beings pertain both to 'man-as-such towards himself and others'. Thus, duties discourse, theoretically provides a broader base and goal for human development. But does it make any sense in the real life of the women?

While the women rights movements in India has been successful in mitigating some serious forms of oppression and has kept alive the spirit of democracy in India but with limitations. Social and women rights movements are voluntary in nature and depend on individual or collective enthusiasm for special interests. There are women rights groups advocating numerous social causes, but most of them with narrow focus and with the result have failed to make significant changes in society. The expansion of Non-Governmental Organisations (NGO's) across India, whose funding comes either from the government or from international agencies, cannot be considered as strong women rights movement. Most of them are politicised and they have a large network to fight one another by proxy through NGO's and they do not provide legitimate criticism of the government, leaving a vacuum for true social movement. Various civil liberties movements to change economic and social inequalities and gender discrimination through violent methods often take place, a huge number of political leaders, trade unions leaders and social activists take interests to divert the movement.

One needs to interrogate the very being of person and "other" for accommodating the claims and the counter claims of rights to be creatively human, the promise of mankind which gets threatened by any destructive self of the few in power either political or social or economic or religious. The history of the world has witnessed to such threats again and again. India in spite of the unity in diversity through the ages has been accused of the land of denying the basic women rights to the citizens basically due to the caste religion and gender discrimination. Women rights discourse is meaningful only in the context of the "other" which presupposes that there is self and the 'other' which is also a self, and the self must relate to the other self. If the self is relating to the other, then only social relationship becomes meaningful. The question is how to relate with the other- a woman? The relation with the other could be of cohesive, peaceful, cooperative, and dutiful or it could be of antagonistic, demanding, claiming and counter-claiming. In society the other as woman exists, whether we like it or not. And the existence of the other is a requirement for our existence in the society. What kind of requirement it is? Is it just a social need or it is deeper than that? These are important questions that need serious attention, I would not discuss them here. But the other can exist as human- a dignified person and demands reciprocity on the part of every individual as Kant would say 'Treat Humanity as an end and never as a means only'(Kant: 1871). It is the inter-subjectivity, the relation with the other which is the corner stone that makes my world and society meaningful.

Indian Feminism and Women Rights

Using the formulation by Mohanty (Mohanty:1986) and Mary John (John:1996a) one could say that 'no non-contradictory' or 'pure' feminism is possible in India. The women with their identities become especially important in the present context because of the fragmentation of the universal category of 'woman', which makes it impossible to speak of women without reference to their class, caste, religion and community. India today is facing the biggest challenge posed by 'Hindutva Feminism' to the Indian women's movements and the limited space provided within 'Hindutva Feminism'. One has to seriously look into the answers of the questions such as 'If Hinduism is also full of diversity and plurality as argued by Balagangadhara, Pannington and Lorenzen, is there any grand narrative of Indian Hindu tradition?' 'Is there any change in the trajectory of feminism and it's politics from the 1990's?' and 'Does Western feminism object to the institution of marriage as such?' Granting that gender is naturalised in an individual (due to faith in a particular tradition and culture, in this case Hindutva) in such a way that she and others cease to see the distinction between just and unjust, how do we implement the idea of justice? The big and foundational question 'how do we get justice in a society like India' remains unanswered that seems to be the prime concern in India today.

I have argued in my paper "Indian Feminism: Challenges and Dynamics" (Mukherjee: 2015) that the primarily objective for feminist is to end sexual oppression and injustice as moral imperative at the level of thought as well as practice, one needs to carefully analyze the social reality of gender and the patriarchal mode of dominated culture in Indian context. At the level of thought we need to understand ourselves well enough as human beings as normal females as a reality. Subjects as well as collectivities are necessarily dynamic agent(s) and not simply a passive victim of religious traditions and culture. Thus, feminist by implication is committed to redressing perceived male bias in Indian culture and religion, not as an emancipatory agenda but taking women as subjects and their collectivities. It examines relation between theories of political questions in ethics such as justice, equality and rights. Feminism as method of questioning and critiquing questions the presuppositions and concepts that are based on either an overt or a covert male bias. Feminist emphasise on recognising women's lived experiences.

If we look at the women's struggles in India during the last three decades, we notice that we have come a long way and the divisive/globalisation factors within the women rights movements have added a new dimension. The "New Indian Women" is the result of the complexities, we face today in India. But perhaps we need to ask some of the fundamental questions such as are there two distinct categories such as Western Feminism and Indian Feminism? No doubt the differences and complexities exist in both the traditions, still the question always remains how western is the western feminism? The category of Western Feminism itself is not a homogeneous category. Yet, the category of "Indian Feminism" has an inbuilt paradox so as to how much Indian Feminism be based on Indian values of self-sacrifice, care giver, surrender, supportive, submissive, cooperative, traditional and culture based and how much it would be within the spirit of the Western concept of liberal, democratic, rights, justice and equality based? How does an Indian woman balance the two so as to keep her identity as an Indian woman rooted in her values, can fight for her legitimate rights?

In India, today we face the most difficult question how to include the exclusive and how to exclude the inclusive. Our policies must give ample space to develop the *shudra* consciousness not as *shudra* but as person and must revise our mind set towards the 'other' to accommodate them as persons. Citizens of our democracy must exhibit the culture of tolerance of difference and understanding of the other as co-human. Unfortunately, the political leadership is patterned mainly on the basis of caste along with other factors and the doctrine of 'equality and social justice' makes no sense in political democracy like India democracy is only limited to vote politics. People in public sphere are always judged and voted on the basis of their castes and seldom on the basis of their merits. Mandal Commission and the reservation policies also have a very limited success. 27% reservation for OBC and 50% reservation for Women at all levels also require meritocratic justification. The debates in parliament go on and on without any result often resulting in walk-outs. The liberal political democratic ideal to provide equality of opportunities to all through suitable reforms is a utopia.

Indian woman, if at all it makes any sense, must have a balance of the two- a tight rope walk, balancing and facing often the danger of being stamped either of "Propagating Hindutva" or "Western Woman"- to be rejected straight away within Indian society. The issues of oppression, gender bias, and discrimination are neither Indian nor western they are issues related to humanity- based on morality. If women are recognised as human beings having equal opportunities and equal choices then one has to realise that the way the girl child is treated in a family in India has to be changed, she needs much more dignified treatment not only after birth but also before she is born.

References

Balagangadhara, S.N. 2005. *"The Heathen in His Blindness..." Asia, the West and the Dynamics of Religion,* Manohar. New Delhi.

Basham, A.L. 1954. *The Wonder that Was India*, Rupa. New Delhi.

Chaudhuri, Maitrayee. 2004. Ed. *Feminism in India,* Kali for Women. New Delhi.

Daya Krishna. 1997. "Socio-Political Thought in India", in *Indian Philosophy: A New Approach.* Satguru Publications. Delhi.

Dhavan, Nandita. 2015. "'Hindutva Feminism'? Challenges to the Indian Women's Movements" in *Feminism in India.* Ed. Asha Mukherjee, *Labrys.* Vol. 28.

John, Mary. 1996. "Gender and Development in India, 1970-1990s," *Economic and Political Weekly.* Vol. XXXI, No. 47, November 23, pp. 3071-77.

John, Mary. 1996a. *Discrepant Dislocations: Feminism, Theory and Postcolonial Histories.* Delhi: Oxford University Press.

Kant, I. *Groundwork of the Metaphysics of Morals.*Edinburgh. 1871.

Lorenzen, David. 2006. *Who Invented Hinduism: Essays on Religion in History.* New Delhi. Yoda Press.

María Mies, Vandana Shiva. 1993. *Ecofeminism*, Fernwood Publications.

Menon, N. 2004. *Recovering Submersions: Feminist Politics and Beyond the Law.* Delhi: Permanent Black.

Mohanty, Chandra. 1986. "Under Western Eyes: Feminist Scholarship and Colonial Discourses" in *Third World and the Politics of Feminism.*Talpade, C.M., Rush, A. and Torres, L. eds., Bloomington: Indiana University Press.

Mukherjee, Asha, 2003. Bhattacharya Kumkum. Eds. *Conditioning and Empowerment of Women: A Multidimensional Approach.* New Delhi: Gyan Publishing House.

Mukherjee, Asha. 2015. "Indian Feminism: Challenges and Dynamics" in *Feminism in India. Labrys,* Vol. 28.

Mukherjee, Asha. 2020. "Women, Rights and Religion in India: Questioning the Tradition" in *Explorations in Women, Rights and Religions.* Ed. Morny Joy. Equinox. Bristol. 260-278.

Murty, K. Satchitananda. 1993. *Vedic Hermeneutics.* Delhi: Motilal Banarasidass.

Pande, Rekha. 2009. "Feminism and the Women's Movement in India- a historical perspective" in *Journal of Women's Studies.* Vol. 1, No. 1. Bangalore. 22- 39.

Pande, Rekha, 2015. "Mapping the terrain of activism in the Feminist and the Women's Movement in India" in *Feminism in India. Labrys.* Vol. 28.

Panikkar, K.N. 1975. *Presidential Address:* Section III, Proceedings of the *Indian History Congress.* PIHC. Thirty-sixth Session. Aligarh.

Pannington, B.K. 2005. *Was Hinduism Invented?.* Oxford University Press.

Radhakrishnan, S. 1960. *The Brahma Sutra: The Philosophy of Spiritual Life*, London: George and Unwin.

Sen, A.K. 2009. *Idea of Justice.* Allen Lane & Harvard University Press.

Sharma, Arvind. 2004. *Hinduism and Human Rights, A Conceptual Approach* Oxford University Press.

Tharu, S. and Niranjan, T. 1994. "Problems for a Contemporary Theory of Gender" in *Social Scientist.* 22, 3/4. 93-117.

Upadhyaya, Pandit Deendayal. 2016. *Integral Humanism: An Analysis of Some Basic Elements,* Delhi.

2

Islamic Feminism: A Liberating Force or a Religious Constraint?

Shahnaz Begum

Introduction

Women's rights, emancipatory movements, migration and legal-judicial provisions are increasingly available in the post-60s, more recently from the 1990s. In the context of fast developing technological communication, particularly emails and social networking, and availability of education to women in general, articulations about their selves and their community have gained solid ground. Miriam Cooke in her book, *Women Claiming Islam: Creating Islamic Feminism through Literature* (Cooke: 2001: vi) informs us that the declaration of the 'Decade for Women' (1975-1985) by the United Nations in 1975 encouraged the growth of anti-patriarchal attempts all over the world. Many Muslim women took this opportunity to cross the threshold of the domestic boundary. Cooke considers two factors which helped this regeneration: revival of Islamic discourse and the advancement of information technology. At the beginning of the twenty first century, there was a reawakening of Muslims. They wanted the reformation of Islamic ideologies so that they can address newer challenges of life. Thus, the Muslim people embarked on the project of implementing Islamic modernity that is to reinterpret Islam in the light of contemporary contexts. These Islamic modernists realised that development of women's condition is prerequisite for achieving their mission. They put emphasis on the unorthodox roles women can play. Being encouraged, these women take up the task of *ijtihad* or independent reasoning on their own. They use their critical reasoning to identify the cause of sexual/textual oppression. The latter point mentioned by Cooke helped these women in creating a worldwide network among the activists.

Feminist writers assert that the socio-religious practices prevalent in Muslim societies are intrinsically patriarchal. Margot Badran, a well known scholar in this field, popularised the term 'Islamic Feminism'. She identified this to be an academic exercise to reinterpret the Qur'an from a gender-egalitarian perspective. According to Badran, the nomenclature gained circulations among the Muslim activists in 1990s. It was widely used by Iranian scholars including Nayereh Tohidi[1] in *Zanan*, a Tehran based women's journal. Later when Badran visited South Africa in 1999, she found the term 'Islamic Feminism' very much in use among the progressive Muslims such as Shamima Shaikh and her co-activists. (Badran: 2009: 28).

The Muslim scholar-activists challenge patriarchal interpretations and envision women's rights, gender equality and social justice as enshrined in the sacred text. They encourage questioning of patriarchal forms of Islamic teachings made through use of the *Qur'an*, the holy book, *Hadith* (sayings of Muhammad) and *Shar'ia* (law). Although rooted in Islam, the Islamic feminist activists appropriate secular and non-Muslim feminist discourses. They recognise Islamic feminism as part of an integrated global feminist movement. They also contest the myth that feminism is exclusively a 'Western' phenomenon. Scholars such as Fatima Marnissi of Moroccan origin, Amina Wadud, an Afro-American scholar, Leila Ahmed, an Egyptian American scholar, Asma Barlas, a Pakistani American scholar, Sa'diyya Shaikh, South African scholar and Kecia Ali try to foreground the glorious past of the Muslim world where women used to enjoy social liberty.

An important roundtable on "Identity Politics and Women" was organised by social scientist, Val Moghadam at the United Nations University World Institute for Development Economics Research (UNU-WIDER) in Helsinki in 1990. It was pointed out there that "Muslim women were subverting patriarchal Islamist projects through what appeared to be a new form of feminism-in-the-making which Muslim women in different parts of the world would soon call Islamic feminism" (Badran :2008: 26). In the same Roundtable, Iranian sociologist Nayereh Tohidi mentioned how some women in the Islamic Republic of Iran were growing increasingly defiant under gender restrictions imposed on them by the State. These women were re-reading the Qur'an in order to claim rights accorded to them by Islam. Discussion was also held on how some new 'religious women' in Egypt, initially close to or affiliated with the Muslim Brothers[2], were embarking upon a re-examination of the Qur'an to work out a new "feminist" paradigm grounded in scripture (Badran: 2009: 26).

A Liberating Force or a Constraint?

The popularisation of the term 'Islamic feminism' by Margot Badran in 1990s to designate the works of some Muslim gender activists working within the periphery of religion generated heated debates. It receives attack both from Muslims and non-Muslims. Maulana Waris Mazhari seemed quite unaware of the precepts of Islamic feminism. He alleged that many advocates of Islamic feminism "have no independent world-view of their own and that they simply follow the dominant Western feminist discourse, which they seek to propagate in an Islamic guise" (Schneider: 2017: 58). On the other hand, secular feminists attacked Islamic Feminism calling it a covert, divisive project of America (since most of the activists are immigrants in the U.S.) to weaken the force of feminism in general.

Even some Muslim activists abhorred the term "feminism," while acknowledging their indebtedness to the works of some feminists. Yet they were in search of a satisfactory alternative. There is a long debate between Asma Barlas, who calls herself a 'believing woman' instead of a 'feminist' and Margot Badran who is in favour of the term Islamic Feminism. Badran feels that the term 'Islamic Feminism' "focuses on the process of unmasking these principles from the confines of patriarchal traditions; as an extension of the faith position instead of a rejection of this position" (Kynsilehto: 2008: 10). But Barlas contends that her position is strikingly different from those of other feminists. She says that all feminists consider that religious texts are sexists by nature whereas Barlas has complete faith in the *Qur'an* as an egalitarian book. She also does not want to be equated with other Muslim feminists like Fatima Mernissi who thinks that Islam has put a "sacred stamp onto female subservience" (Barlas: 2008: 17). She further adds:

> In contrast to such feminists, my own stance is that Muslims read Islam as a patriarchy partly because of how they read the Qur'an, who reads it, and the contexts in which they read it. In other words, I believe that texts are always read from and within specific material and ideological sites and that we need to be aware of these sites when attempting to understand readings of scripture. (Barlas: 2008: 17)

The debate between Margot Badran and Asma Barlas is well-known. In an international seminar on "Islamic Feminism: Current Perspectives", held in Tampere, Finland in August 2007, both Asma Barlas and Margot Badran agreed to talk on the same topic "Engaging Islamic Feminism" from their own ideological positions. There, Barlas argues that by 'provincializing feminism as master narrative', the westerners erase 'fundamental epistemic differences between feminists':

> In part, my resistance was a displacement of frustration with real, live, feminists, all of them white. Although I'm sure they were and remain well-meaning, many of them seemed utterly blind to the racial politics of speaking for women of colour like myself and that too in our presence, as if we didn't exist. (Barlas: 2008:17)

Barlas, nonetheless, does not reject the idea of Islamic feminism completely. She acknowledges that Islamic feminism endorses gender equality. She also admits 'the very real political necessity of certain feminisms', but she thinks, the term, feminism proves to be a close-ended discourse as it precludes 'the possibility of theorising sexual equality from within alternative paradigms' (Barlas: 2008: 21).

We find here that Badran is unwilling to accept feminism as a western discourse. She categorically states that history establishes the fact that feminism is created and empowered by 'both easterners and westerners, of Muslims and those of other religions, of the colonised and colonisers, and of women of different races and ethnicities' (Badran: 2008: 25). Calling feminism a western or white phenomenon is the negation of history and perpetuation of myths. In *Women Claim Islam*, author Miriam Cooke offers similar reflections. She informs that throughout the twentieth century Muslim gender activists have searched for an alternative jargon:

> However, whether they name themselves *unthawiyat, nassawiyat* (Al-Ali 1997:174), "womanists" (Zuhur 1993:32), or "remakers of women" (Abu Lughod 1998:5–6), these educated, privileged, and engaged women are all struggling to improve the situation for women. While I too have tried to find synonyms for the word "feminism," I found myself compelled to define the synonym in such a way that it would serve the same function as "feminism". (Cooke: 2001: viii)

Cooke quotes cultural critic Anne McClintock who says "If all feminisms are derived as a pathology of the West, there is a very real danger that Western, white feminists will remain hegemonic, for the simple reason that such women have comparatively privileged access to publishing, the international media, education and money" (Cooke:2001:384). Cooke remarks that she believes feminism to be neither a 'culturally specific term' nor 'restricted to a narrow notion of public action' but it is a powerful name.

According to Badran, Islamic feminism, unlike secular feminism and Islamism, caters to the need of maximum number of Muslim women where they need not discard their religion for attaining gender equality, neither do they need to accept the paternalistic model of women empowerment promoted by the political Islamists. By claiming gender equality through reinterpretation of the Quran and other sacred texts, they exert their agency and break through the western stereotypes of Muslim women as meek subdued community. Badran also insists that Islamic feminism is more radical than other forms of feminisms practised by Muslim women. The agenda of 'Muslims' foundational secular feminism' are not comprehensive. Their struggle was to achieve gender equality in the public domain only, for example, in the sphere of education, job, voting rights etc. But they excluded the religious space such as mosques, graveyard et al from the public space. Moreover, their silence about the private space, insinuates that they fail to identify gender inequity there and accept the 'patriarchal model of the family'. But the Islamic Feminists specially Asma Barlas has used Islamic hermeneutics and has successfully debunked patriarchy as un-Islamic both in the familial space and the public space:

> Islamic feminists not only connected the public and private as the indivisible terrain of gender equality but also elucidated the necessary linkage of gender equality and social justice. Gender equality is integral to the Islamic feminist notion of equality of all *insan* or humankind transcending tribe, class, ethnicity, and race. (Barlas: 2008: 33)

Raja Rhouni seconds Badran's formulation. She adds that Islamic Feminists may have two types of positions. One is the position of deep faith on 'the *Qur'an*'s egalitarian global ethics.' The second one is the scholarly or academic position to critically engage with the religio-cultural construction of 'Islamic gender norms'. Rhouni says:

> 'Strategic' should not always be distrusted as denoting an opportunistic, hypocritical, attitude that participates in the instrumentalisation of religion. Strategy can also be dictated by a given situation and can actually emanate from the beneficial position of scholars, who we might designate as "organic intellectuals," in the broad sense of the Gramscian phrase, and who, to continue influencing their societies, cannot but follow its moves and engage in its issues, while refusing to stay in the elitist ivory tower of 'enlightened secularist intellectuals'. (Rhouni: 2010: 23)

Islamic feminism is an on-going project since it has yet to negotiate many gender related issues that crop up in recent times and to apply their gender sensitive *ijtihad* to those problems. For example, one may think of same-sex intimacy which Kecia Ali has discussed in her book, *Sexual Ethics and Islam: Feminist Reflections on Qur'an, Hadith, and Jurisprudence*. She also warns the Islamic feminists that they should not fall prey to romanticisation or essentialisation. Ali says, as the Islamic Feminists require involving profoundly with the centuries old Islamic epistemology, one may end up romanticising with the rich heritage. She also cautions that one should be extremely optimistic about radical changes prescribed by them:

> Most importantly, as we expose reductive and misogynist understandings of the Qur'an and [H]adith, refusing to see medieval interpretations as coextensive with revelation, we must not arrogate to our own readings the same absolutist conviction we criticize in others. We must accept responsibility for making particular choices — and must acknowledge that they are interpretative choices, not merely straightforward reiterations of "what Islam says." (Ali: 2016: 195)

She urges the Islamic feminists to demand the equality as a component of justice not simply affirm it as Qur'anic. She also stresses "the freedom to treat the *Qur'an* and *Hadith* not as repositories of regulations to be applied literally in all times and places but as sources of guidance". These religious texts, according to her, should be treated just as the base or foundation both for 'the ethical development of the human being', and for 'the transformation of human society' (188). Following Ali, Rhouni talks about 'post-foundationalist Islamic gender critique'. This would mean engaging in dialogue with the tradition and applying contextual approach in order to expand the methodologies of exegesis, rather than undermining foundations and traditions. Along with rethinking gender in Islamic thought, Rhouni argues that the contextual approach would aid in complicating 'political and ideological instrumentalisations of religious texts' (Rhouni: 2008: 114).

Badran thinks that theoretical corpus of Islamic Feminism has reached a level where it can be claimed to be an established genre. Now it needs more and more praxis both in the private domain (such as family) and in the public sphere (such as society and the state). Here one needs to probe into the Muslim women's lived experience in India in the light of Islamic Feminist exegesis. An attempt should be made whether the 'contextual approach' that Rhouni speaks of in terms of progression of Islamic Feminism as an ideology is applied by the Indian Muslims; whether Indian Muslim women can apply the basic tenets of Islamic Feminist discourses to subvert patriarchy and establish gender equality in their lives. The Shariyat

Application Law 1937, enacted by the British ruler stressed that Muslim lives in India will be governed by the Muslim law not by the customary law. Since then only three laws were implemented for betterment of Muslim women. The Dissolution of Muslim Marriages Act 1939 which allowed Muslim women to seek Divorce on nine specific grounds. Next comes the Protection of Rights on divorce Act 1986 which was the result of the famous Shah Bano case. The case championed the Muslim women's fight for justice on the right to claim alimony. The last one came recently. Instant Talaq, Triple Talaq or *Talaq e Biddat* was banned the Supreme Court of India on 22 August 2017. All India Muslim Personal Law Board which was established to monitor Muslim lives, criticised this law. In spite of the fact that many Muslim countries and our neighbouring countries such as Pakistan, Bangladesh and Sri Lanka had abolished Verbal *Triple Talaq*, the Personal Law Board condemns the law:

> We women/men followers of Islam believe in Shariat of Islam/ Islamic Shariyat and Talaq is part of Shariyat in Islam on which imposing boundations/ regulations are encroachment of our rights. Hence the freedom that has been protected to follow Muslim Personal Law be continued/retained. We understand that change in it by the Supreme Court or the Parliament is wrong. (Resolution)

This is heartening to see that the Personal Law Board has implemented the aforementioned 'contextual approach' selectively. It has rejected or modified many Islamic laws in order to negotiate modern days requirement such as photographs of human being for official purpose, giving interest in case of loan from the bank etc. But interestingly the board pays no attention to the claims made by the Islamic Feminists all over the world. Their Patriarchal as well as orthodox mindset for normative Islam is the root cause of gender discrimination. Furthermore, it could not ensure the implementation of Quranic rights of women in reality. Consequently, general condition of Muslim women in India beggars description. In 2013, the Bharatiya Muslim Mahila Andolan conducted an extensive study on the Muslim women's condition in various states of India. This field study also asks women to express their views on reforms in Muslim personal law. 4,710 Muslim women from the 10 states of Bihar, Gujarat, Jharkhand, Karnataka, Maharashtra, Madhya Pradesh, Odisha, Rajasthan, Tamil Nadu and West Bengal were contacted and the revelations were quite shocking as well as alarming. An overwhelming 82% women said they did not have any property in their name and 83.9% women confirmed that their current residence was not in their name. They did not own any property despite ownership of property being a Quranic right.

Mehr is an important Quranic right given to a Muslim woman that she can demand from her groom. It can be in the form of cash or any other form such as gold, property, etc, and it should be given to her at the time of marriage. The findings suggest that this important affirmative measure favouring women has been diluted in practice. More than 40% women had received less than Rs 1,000 as *mehr* while 44% women did not receive *mehr* at all. Most respondents were not aware of the empowering provisions about *mehr* and that it is their right to decide the amount. The majority or 85.7% women wanted *mehr* to be given at the time of marriage while 83.9% of respondents wanted equivalent of the annual income of the husband to be the minimum *mehr* amount.

Since Muslims in India are socially, economically and educationally poor (Sachar committee report bears testimony of it) and they do not know Arabic in which the holy *Quran* is written, Shariat courts, qazis, muftis (religious clerics), jamaats (sect arbitration councils) control their lives with patriarchal interpretation of Islam. Few educated Muslim families that exist in India focus more on secular social issues than the rights of Muslim women. Kecia Ali has mentioned that accepting Islamic life is more an ethical choice than a legal compliance for this diasporic Muslim women in America and in other Western countries. This also happens with Indian Muslims since India is a secular country. Now this is high time for all Muslims of India to take the situation of Muslim women seriously and try to implement the contextual approach to Quranic exegesis for the betterment of Muslim lives.

Notes

1. Tohidi at first used the term 'Islamist Feminism' in the article "Modernisation Islamisation and Gender in Iran" (1994) to identify the reformist activities done by the Muslim women of aristocratic society. Later she changed it to 'Islamic Feminism' as she realised that the term 'Islamist' is more related to the Modernist Islamist propaganda of Political Islam, an extension of orthodox patriarchal faith position.
2. Muslim Brothers is an Islamic group established in Egypt in 1928. Hasan al- Banna, an Egyptian school teacher is the founder of this organisation. The aim of this organisation was to employ the traditional *Shar'ia* in every walk of life. It encouraged Political Islam as they wanted Islam to be a political affair. In other words, they thought the state law should be guided by the Islamic law. This organisation achieved huge popularity as its members reached 2.5 million. The new religious women were initially affiliated to the Muslim Brothers but later on, they drifted away from them because of ideological difference.

References

Ali, Kecia. 2016. *Sexual Ethics and Islam: Feminist Reflections on Qur'an, Hadith, and Jurisprudence*. Oneworld Publications: London.

Badran, Margot. 2008. "Engaging Islamic Feminism." *Islamic Feminism: Current Perspectives*. Ed. Anitta Kynsilehto. Tampere Peace Research Institute: Tampere. 25-36.

—. 2009. *Feminism in Islam: Secular and Religious Convergences*. Oneworld: London.

Barlas, Asma. 2008. "Engaging Islamic Feminism: Provincializing Feminism as a Master Narrative". *Islamic Feminism: Current Perspectives*, Ed. Anitta Kynsilehto. Tampere Peace Research Institute: Tampere.15-24.

Cooke, Miriam. 2001. *Women Claim Islam: Creating Islamic Feminism through Literature*. Routledge: New York.

Kynsilehto, Annita ed. 2008. *Islamic Feminism: Current Perspectives*. Tampere Peace Research Institute: Tampere.

"*Muslim Women's Views on Muslim Personal Law*". https://bmmaindia.com/2016/01/03/muslim-womens-views-on-muslim-personal-law/ January 2016.Web. accessed on 17/09/2020.

"Resolution.pdf." http://www.aimplboard.in/Resolution.pdf. Web. accessed on 17/09/2020.

Rhouni, Raja. 2008. "Rethinking 'Islamic Feminist Hermeneutics': the Case of Fatima Mernissi", *Islamic Feminism: Current Perspectives*. Ed. Anitta Kynsilehto. Tampere Peace Research Institute: Tampere. 103-116.

—. 2008. *Secular and Islamic Feminist Critiques in the Work of Famita Mernissi*. Brill: Leiden.

Schneider, Nadja-Cristina.2009. "Islamic Feminism and Muslim Women's Rights Activism in India: From Transnational Discourse to Local Movement- or Vice Versa?" *Journal of International Women's Studies*. 11.1 (Nov. 2009). 56-71. Web. 25 Jan. 2017. http://vc.bridgew.edu/cgi/viewcontent.cgi?article=1148&context=jiws

3

Abolition of Arbitrary Triple *Talaq* - A Landmark Judgement on the Rights of Women Legal & Social Dimension

Chandreyi Alam

Women's rights are a matter of regular discussion, consideration, review by the society and the march of times have proved that no right has been bestowed upon her automatically and she has had to fight tooth and nail to secure her rights which include right to education, rights in the family, her economic and political rights and last but not the least her right to live with dignity.

Since a very long time it was the universal thought of society that women were inferior to men. According to the Chinese civilisation "A woman without ability is normal" Aristotle saw the virtue of a woman in obeying, being less complete, less courageous, weaker and more impulsive than men "Plato accepted that women could be philosophers and had admitted then in his academy. But he was of the opinion, that learning did not give any improvement. Dante had observed that "books destroy women's brains and it was not safe for a women to learn Latin". True, that all religions accept the universal right to education but all insist that the women must obey, be silent and remain without ability.

We now consider universal education to be a normal phenomenon but only a couple of centuries ago women's education was practically unheard of. In India, the concept of a good woman was that she will remain under the care of her father during her maidenhood, under her husband during her married days and thereafter under her son. She was not entitled to any freedom – na stree swatantramarhati. So much so that the stridhan she received during her wedding was not her sole properly she did not have the right to dispose of stridhan her if the occasion so arose. In fact society had taught its women that education, independent thinking would result in widowhood and so it was best if the women remained as the chattels of the men. Society was more comfortable with the woman who obeys and remain silent. Hence, when the call for women's education was raised, the most common apprehension of the conservatives were that women were too weak to stand the strain of serious mental labour. In India too, the conservative society resisted women's education on the plea that education would not be a forte for Indian girls as they did not have the intellect to be educated. "Have you ever tested a girls intellect?" Raja Rammohan Roy and countered the conservatives and it was much later in 1849 the first official school for women was established in Calcutta.

With education, the girls showed how their intellect blossomed. Very soon women made their presence felt in society. Women saw through the societal bondage and there were many who identified the factors of bondage and laboured to free society of the same.

Begum Rokeya Sakhawat Hussain had thought of liberating women from such bondage. Born in 1880 she had, while her family slept, surreptiously, under the light of a candle, received the first light of education from her brother. In 1911, Rokeya had started the Calcutta Muslim Female School. She had dreamt that women too would become Magistrates, Judges, Doctors earning members in the family. It was her argument that women were no less than men. Rokeya argues "do not we have hand, foot or mind? The energy that we spend out in household affairs of our husband's house, cannot that energy be successfully utilised in our business?"

Rokeya's dream is now being fulfilled. Today a woman is free to pursue any line of education. Careers that were out of bounds for her are now within her access. So to day we do have women judges, magistrates, lawyers, police, pilots, astronauts, doctors and various professions who have all successfully, utilised the energy-that their mothers and grandmothers had spent after their household, for the society.

While the universal access to education might make us complacent about the equality between the sexes but in reality we have a long way to go in order to achieve social equality. While education has ushered in a sea change in the lives of the woman, but does she really have the right to live with dignity? As early as in 1904, Begum Rokeya Sakhawat had questioned the oppressive religious injunctions imposed on women. In her essay "Amadiger Abanati" she has, without mincing any words, stated as follows:-

"Due to our degraded status we have not been able to raise our heads against bondage. The main reason is that whenever a sister has tried to raise her head in protest her head has been crushed with stern warnings of religious texts which fell upon like the stunning blows of a rock. Men have created the religious texts to keep us in darkness. All theological texts are therefore nothing but restrictive regulations created by men."

Even in the 21st Century she is still subjected to illogical discriminations that are practiced in the name of religion. The issue of arbitrary Triple *Talaq* is a sore point in the life of a Muslim. The woman apprehends the danger of becoming a victim while men, as fathers or brothers of the victim, also have a feeling of helplessness - but all surrender to their destiny. In 1985, after the verdict of the Supreme Court in the Shah Bano case was pronounced, the women's movement was proactive in spreading awareness. There was a sustained movement amongst women informing them what Islam actually ordains in social issues and what is actually practiced in the name of Islam. Victims had, across the country raised such social issues in Court, but were not always successful. Those who were successful, mostly kept their success to themselves since to much publicity could result in social problems that frustrated their success. The fortunate occasionally gained some publicity but that was not enough to ring the bell of awareness throughout the Muslim community.

As stated earlier the practice of arbitrary Triple *Talaq* is a burning issue amongst the Muslim Community and also amongst socially conscious people of our country. It is a matter of great pride that the sustained awareness programmes throughout the country yielded positive results. Not only did five victims challenge the dissolution of their marriage by prouncing arbitrary Triple *Talaq*, but the Supreme Court also directed that two articles – the Muslim Women's Quest for Equality by Vandana Shukla published *the Tribune* dated 24.09.2015 and "in her court" by Dipti Nagpaul D' Souza published in *the Sunday Express Magazine* dated 04.10.2015 be treated as Public Interest Litigations and hence Suo Moto, or, the Court on its own motion, registered the PILs and placed before the Hon'ble Chief Justice.

The Suo Moto Pil Wp (C) No. 2 of 2015 The Muslim Women's Quest For Equality Vs Jamiat Ulama, Hind, Wp (C) No. 118 of 2016 Shyara Bano Vs Union Ministry of Women and Child Development Secretary, Wp (C) No. 288 of 2016. Afreen Rehman –Vs–Union of India Wp (c) No. 327 of 2016 Gulshan Parveen Vs Union of India Represented by the Secretary,

W p. (C) No. 665 of 2016 Ishrat Jahan Vs Union of India, Ministry of Women and Child Development and Wp (C) No. 43 of 2017 Atiya Sabri Versus Union of India challenging dissolution of marriage by the arbitrary Triple *Talaq* and praying that such form of *Talaq* be declared void abinitio were placed before a Constitutional Bench of the Supreme Court comprising of 5 Judges. Out of whom 3 Judges held that *Talaq–e-Biddat* or arbitrary Triple *Talaq* as unislamic and could not be given any protection as a right of religious practice under Article 25 of the Constitution of India and hence was unconstitutional. The minority judgement held Triple *Talaq* to be a valid practice and India can introduce appropriate legislation to do away with *Talaq-e-biddat* and granted an injunction, on arbitrary Triple *Talaq* initially for six months to enable the Union of India to enact appropriate legislation.

All the writ petitions before the Hon'ble Supreme Court had challenged the longstanding practice of arbitrary triple *Talaq* against Muslim Women. These women were granted Triple *Talaq* by their husbands at one go. According to the petitioners, the Holy *Quran* has ordained a definite procedure for dissolution of marriage:-The initial procedure is of reconciliation and thereafter the process of *Talaq* involves three menstrual cycles. The verses in the Holy *Quran* are as follows:-

11. Sura II contains the following verses pertaining to divorce:

"226. For those who take
An oath for abstention
From their wives,
A waiting for four months
Is ordained;
If then they return,
God is Oft.-forgiving;
Most Merciful.
227. But if their intention Is firm for divorce, God heareth
And knoweth all things.
228. Divorced women
Shall wait concerning themselves
For three monthly periods.
Nor is it lawful for them
To hide what God
Hath created in their womb,

If they have faith
In God and the Last Day.
And their husbands
Have the better right
To take them back
In that period, if
They wish for reconciliation.
And women shall have rights
Similar to the rights
Against them, according
To what is equitable;
But men have a degree
(of advantage) over them.
And God is Exhalted in Power, Wise."
229. A divorce is only
Permissible twice: after that,
The parties should either hold
Together on equitable terms.
Or separate with kindness.
It is not lawful for you,
(Men), to take back
Any to your gifts (from your wives),
Except when both parties
    Fear that they would be
    Unable to keep the limits
Ordained by God.
If ye (judges) do indeed
Fear that they would be
Unable to keep the limits
Ordained by God.
There is no blame on either
Of them if she give
Something for her freedom.
These are the limits
Ordained by God;

So do not transgress them
If any do transgress
The limits ordained by God.
Such persons wrong
(Themselves as well as others).
230. So if a husband
Divorces his wife (irrevocably),
He cannot, after that,
Re-marry her until
After she has married
Another husband and
He has divorced her.
In that case there is
No blame on either of them
If they re-unite, provided
They feel that they
Can keep the limits
Ordained by God.
Such other limits
Ordained by God,
Which He makes plain
To those who understand.
231. When ye divorce
Women, and they fulfill
The term of their ('Iddat),
Either take them back
On equitable terms
Or set them free On equitable terms;
But do not take them back
To injure them, (or) to take
Undue advantage;
If anyone does that,
He wrongs his own soul.
Do not treat God's Signs
As a jest,

But solemnly rehearse
God's favours on you,
And the fact that He
Sent down to you
The Book
And Wisdom,
For your instruction.
And fear God.
And know that God
Is well acquainted
With all things".

It is evident from the Holy book that the marriage cannot be dissolved at one go. The process involves the initial reconciliation between the parties. If that fails then the husband will abstain from the wife during three courses of purity or three menstrual cycles. If cohabitation is resumed even after the second cycle, then the process of dissolution of marriage ceases and the spouses can live together. But if cohabitation between the spouses are not resumed then, after three menstrual cycles the *Talaq* becomes irrevocable and the marriage ties are thus dissolved.

The Holy book ordained a definite course where there was scope for reconciliation and reflection before *Talaq* reaching finality. But what was the origin of the Triple *Talaq* or *Talaq –e - Biddat*? The land mark judgement provides the history of the practice of Arbitrary *Talaq* as provided by the Learned Senior Counsel.

"(a) Caliph Umar, finding that the checks imposed by the Prophet on the facility of repudiation interfered with the indulgence of their caprice, endeavoured to find an escape from the strictness of the law, and found in the pliability of the jurists a loophole to effect their purpose.

(b) When the Arabs conquered Syria, Egypt, Persia, etc. they found women there much better in appearance as compared to Arabian women and hence they wanted to marry them. But the Egyptian and Syrian women insisted that in order to marry them, they should divorce their existing wives instantaneously, by pronouncing three divorces in one sitting.

(c) The condition was readily acceptable to the Arabs, because they knew that in Islam divorce was permissible only twice in two separate period of tuhr and its repetition in one sitting was considered un-Islamic, void and not effective. In this way, they could not only marry these women, but also retain their existing wives. This fact was reported to the second Caliph Hazrat Umar.

(d) The Caliph Umar then, in order to prevent misuse of the religion by the unscrupulous husbands decreed, that even repetition of the word '*talaq*, *talaq*, *talaq*' at one sitting, would dissolve the marriage irrevocably. It was, however, a mere administrative measure of Caliph Umar, to meet an emergency situation, and not to make it a legally binding precedent permanently."

Talaq-e-Biddat was introduced during the reign of the Ummayid Dynasty. This shortcut instant mode renders the measures provided for in the Holy *Quran* against any hasty action ineffective, and, according to the Hon'ble Supreme Court, "thereby deprives people of a chance to change their minds, to retrieve their mistakes and retain their wives".

The illegal and arbitrary process of instant Triple *Talaq* spread amongst the World Muslim community like wild fire. People found the instant form much more convenient than the Quranic injunctions. So religious bodies, clergy-et al-advocated this practice. It is not difficult to infer the plight of the victim women. Marriage meant the risk of being dumped at the drop of a hat. Very often post marriage, the paternal home was not welcomed for the abandoned wife and family. Hence internationally there was resentment amongst the Muslim women against this arbitrary practice and ultimately countries have enacted legislation that ended arbitrary practice of Triple *Talaq*.

In its landmark judgement, Supreme Court had recorded the Abrogation of the practice *Talaq-e-Biddat* by legislation, the world over in Islamic as well as non-Islamic states. The Hon'ble Supreme Court had divided the countries into Arab States, South East Asian States and Sub-continental States. The following countries with sizeable Muslim populations have through legislations abrogated the practice of Triple *Talaq* which are as follows:

A. Laws of Arab States

151. Algeria: Is a theocratic State, which declares Islam to be its official religion. Muslims of the Sunni sect constitute its majority. On the issue in hand, it has enacted the following legislation :

Code of Family Law, 1984

Law 84-11 of 1984 as amended in 2005.

49. Divorce cannot be established except by a judgement of the Court, proceeded by an attempt at reconciliation for a period not exceeding three months".

152. Egypt: Is a secular State. Muslims of the Sunni sect constitute its majority. On the issue in hand, it has enacted the following legislation:

Law of Personal Status, 1929

Law 25 of 1929 as amended by Law 100 of 1985

1. A *talaq* pronounced under the effect of intoxication or compulsion shall not be effective.
2. A conditional *talaq* which is not meant to take effect immediately shall have no effect if it is used as an inducement to do some act or to abstain from it.
3. A *talaq* accompanied by a number, expressly or impliedly, shall not be effective except as a single revocable divorce.
4. Symbolic expressions of *talaq* i.e. words which may or may not bear the implication of a divorce, shall not effect a divorce *unless the husband actually intended it*." (emphasis supplied).

153. Iraq: Is a theocratic State, which declares Islam to be its official religion. The majority of Iraq's Muslims is Shias. On the issue in hand, it has enacted the following legislation:

Code of Personal Status, 1959

Law 188 of 1959 as amended by Law 90 of 1987

35. No divorce shall be effective when pronounced by the persons mentioned below:

(a) one who is intoxicated, insane or imbecile, under duress, or not in his senses due to anger, sudden calamity, old age or sickness;

(b) a person in death-sickness or in a condition which in all probabilities is fatal and of which he actually dies, survived by his wife.

37. (1) Where a *talaq* is coupled with a number, express or implied, not more than one divorce shall take place.

(2) If a woman is divorced thrice on three separate occasions by her husband, no revocation or remarriage would be permissible after that.

39. (1) When a person intends to divorce his wife, he shall institute a suit in the Court of Personal Status requesting that it be effected and that

an order be issued there for. If a person cannot so approach the court, registration of the divorce in the court during the period of *iddat* shall be binding on him.

(2) The certificate of marriage shall remain valid *till it is cancelled by the court*." (emphasis supplied)

154. Jordan: Is a secular State. Muslims of the Sunni sect constitute its majority. On the issue in hand, it has enacted the following legislation:

Code of Personal Status, 1976 Law 61 of 1976

88. "(1) *Talaq* shall not be effective if pronounced under intoxication, bewilderment, compulsion, mental disorder, depression or effect of sleep.

(2) "Bewildered" is one who has lost senses due to anger or provocation, etc., and cannot understand what he is saying.

90. A divorce coupled with a number, expressly or impliedly, as also a divorce repeated in the same sitting, will not take effect except as a single divorce.

94. Every divorce shall be revocable except the final third, one before consummation and one with consideration.

98. Where an irrevocable *talaq* was pronounced once or twice, *renewal of marriage with the consent of parties is not prohibited*." (emphasis supplied)

155. Kuwait: Is a theocratic State, which declares Islam to be the official religion. Muslims of the Sunni sect constitute its majority. On the issue in hand, it has the following legislation in place:

Code of Personal Status, 1984

Law 51 of 1984

102. *Talaq* may be effected by major and sane men acting by their free will and understanding the implications of their action. Therefore *talaq* shall not take effect if the husband is mentally handicapped, imbecile, under coercion, mistake, intoxication, fear or high anger affecting his speech and action.

109. If a *talaq* is pronounced with a number (two, three) by words, signs or writing, *only one talaq shall take effect*." (emphasis supplied)

156. Lebanon: Is a secular State. Muslims constitute its majority, which is estimated to be 54 percent (27 percent Shia and 27 percent Sunni). On the issue in hand, it has enacted the following legislation:

Family Rights Law, 1962

Law of 16-7-1962

104. A divorce by a drunk person shall have no effect.

105. A divorce pronounced under coercion shall have no effect."

157. Libya: Is a theocratic State, which declares Islam to be its official religion. Muslims of the Sunni sect constitute its majority. On the issue in hand, it has enacted the following legislation:

Family Law, 1984

Law 10 of 1984 as amended by Law 15 of 1984

28. Divorce is termination of the marriage bond. No divorce will become effective in any case except by a decree of a competent court and subject to the provision of Article 30.

29. Divorce is of two kinds — revocable and irrevocable. Revocable divorce does not terminate the marriage till the expiry of *iddat*. Irrevocable divorce terminates the marriage forthwith.

30. All divorces shall be revocable except a third-time divorce, one before consummation of marriage, one for a consideration, and those specified in this law to be irrevocable.

31. A divorce shall be effective only if pronounced in clear words showing intention to dissolve the marriage. Symbolic or metaphorical expression will not dissolve the marriage.

32. A divorce pronounced by a minor or insane person, or if pronounced under coercion, or with no clear intention to dissolve the marriage, shall have no legal effect.

33. (1) A divorce meant to be effect on some action or omission of the wife shall have no legal effect.

(2) A divorce given with a view to binding the wife to an oath or restrain her from doing something shall have no legal effect.

(3) A divorce to which a number is attached, by express words or a gesture, shall effect only a single revocable divorce, except when it is pronounced for the third time.

35. The marriage may be dissolved by mutual consent of the parties. Such a divorce must be registered with the court. If the parties cannot agree on the terms of such a divorce, they shall approach the court and it will appoint arbitrators to settle the matter or reconcile them.

47. A divorce must be pronounced in a court and in the presence of the other party or his or her representative. *The court shall before giving effect to a divorce exhaust all possibilities of reconciliation*." (emphasis supplied)

158. Morocco: Is a theocratic State, which declares Islam to be its official religion. Muslims of the Sunni sect constitute its majority. On the issue in hand, it has enacted the following legislation:

Code of Personal Status, 2004 Law 70.03 of 2004

"79. Whoever divorces his wife by *talaq* must petition the court for permission to register it with the Public Notaries of the area where the matrimonial home is situate, or where the wife resides, or where the marriage took place.

80. The petition will mention the identity of spouses, their professions, addresses, number of children, if any, with their age, health condition and educational status. It must be supported by a copy of the marriage agreement and a document stating the husband's social status and financial obligations.

81. The court shall summon the spouses and attempt reconciliation. If the husband deliberately abstains, this will be deemed to be withdrawal of the petition. If the wife abstains, the court will notify her that if she does not present herself the petition may be decided in her absence. If the husband has fraudulently given a wrong address for the wife, he may be prosecuted at her instance.

82. The court will hear the parties and their witnesses in camera and take all possible steps to reconcile them, including appointment of arbitrators or family reconciliation council, and if there are children such efforts shall be exhausted within thirty days. If reconciliation takes place, a report will be filed with the court.

83. If reconciliation attempts fail, the court shall fix an amount to be deposited by the husband in the court within thirty days towards payment of the wife's post-divorce dues and maintenance of children.

90. No divorce is permissible for a person who is not in his senses or is under coercion or provocation.

92. Multiple expressions of divorce, oral or written, shall have the effect of a single divorce only.

123. Every divorce pronounced by the husband shall be revocable, *except a third-time divorce, divorce before consummation of marriage, divorce by mutual consent, and divorce by khula or talaq-e-tafweez.*" (emphasis supplied)

159. Sudan: Is a theocratic State, which declares Islam to be its official religion. Muslims of the Sunni sect constitute its majority. On the issue in hand, it has the following legislation in place:

Law on *Talaq*, 1935

"Judicial Proclamation 4 of 1935

1. A divorce uttered in a state of intoxication or under duress shall be invalid and ineffective.
2. A contingent divorce which is not meant to be effective immediately and is used as an inducement or threat shall not have effect.
3. A formula of divorce coupled with a number, expressly or impliedly, shall effect only one divorce.
4. Metaphorical expressions used for a divorce shall have the effect of dissolving the marriage only if the husband actually meant a divorce." (emphasis supplied)

160. Syria: Is a secular State. Muslims of the Sunni sect constitute its majority. On the issue in hand, it has enacted the following legislation:

Code of Personal Status, 1953

Law 59 of 1953 as amended by Law 34 of 1975

89. No divorce shall take place when the man is drunk, out of his senses, or under duress. A person is out of his senses when due to anger, etc. he does not appreciate what he says.

90. A conditional divorce shall have no effect if not actually intended and used only as an inducement to do or abstain from doing something or as an oath or persuasion.

92. If a divorce is coupled with a number, expressly or impliedly, not more than one divorce shall take place.

94. Every divorce shall be revocable except a third-time divorce, one before consummation, a divorce with a consideration, and a divorce stated in this Code to be irrevocable.

117. Where a person divorces his wife the court may, if satisfied that he has arbitrarily done so without any reasonable cause and that *as a result of the divorce the wife shall suffer damage and become destitute, give a decision, with due regard to the husband's financial condition and the amount of wife's suffering, that he should pay her compensation* not exceeding three years' maintenance, in addition to maintenance payable during the period of *iddat*. It may be directed to be paid either in a lump sum or in installments as the circumstances of a case may require." (emphasis supplied)

161. Tunisia: Is a theocratic State, which declares Islam to be its official religion. Muslims of the Sunni sect constitute its majority. On the issue in hand, it has enacted the following legislation:

Code of Personal Status, 1956

"Law 13-8 of 1956 as amended by Law 7 of 1981

31. (1) A decree of divorce shall be given:

(i) with the mutual consent of the parties; or

(ii) at the instance of either party on the ground of injury; or

(iii) if the husband insists on divorce or the wife demands it.

The party causing material or mental injury by the fact of divorce under clauses (if) and (in) shall be directed to indemnify the aggrieved spouse.

(2) As regards the woman to be indemnified for material injury in terms of money, the same shall be paid to her after the expiry of *iddat* and may be in the form of retention of the matrimonial home. This indemnity will be subject to revision, increase or decrease in accordance with the changes in the circumstances of the divorced wife until she is alive or until she changes her marital status by marrying again. If the former husband dies, this indemnity will be a charge on his estate and will have to be met by his heirs if they consent to it and will be decided by the court if they disagree. They may pay her in a lump sum within one year from the former husband's death the indemnity claimable by her.

32. (1) No divorce shall be decreed except after the court has made an overall inquiry into the causes of rift and failed to effect reconciliation.

(2) Where no reconciliation is possible the court shall provide, even if not asked to, for all important matters relating to the residence of the spouses, maintenance and custody of children and meeting the children,

except when the parties specifically agree to forgo all or any of these rights. The court shall fix the maintenance on the basis of all those facts which it comes to know while attempting reconciliation. All important matters shall be provided for in the decree, which shall be non-appealable but can be reviewed for making additional provisions.

(3) The court of first instance shall pass orders in the matters of divorce and all concerning matters including the compensation money to which the divorced wife may be entitled after the expiry of *iddat*. The portions of the decree relating to custody, maintenance, compensation, residence and right to visit children shall be executed immediately."

162. United Arab Emirates: Is a theocratic State, as the Federal Constitution declares Islam to be the official religion. The Constitution also provides for freedom of religion in accordance with established customs. Muslims of the Shia sect constitute its majority. On the issue in hand, it has the following legislation in place:

Law of Personal Status, 2005

Federal Law 28 of 2005

" 140. (1) If a husband divorces his wife after consummation of a valid marriage by his unilateral action and without any move for divorce from her side, she will be entitled to compensation besides maintenance for *iddat.* The amount of compensation will be decided with due regard to the means of the husband and the hardship suffered by the wife, but it shall not exceed the amount of one year's maintenance payable in law to a woman of her status.

(2) The *Kazi* may decree the compensation, to be paid as a lump sum or in instalments, according to the husband's ability to pay.

163. Yemen: Is a theocratic State, which declares Islam to be the official religion. Muslims of the Sunni sect constitute its majority. On the issue in hand, it has the following legislation in place:

Decree on Personal Status, 1992

"Decree 20 of 1992

61. A divorce shall not be effective if pronounced by a man who is drunk, or has lost his senses, or has no power of discernment, if this is shown by his condition and action.

64. A divorce to which a number is attached, whatever be the number, will effect only a single revocable divorce.

65. The words saying that if the wife did or failed to do something she will stand divorced will not effect a divorce.

66. The words that if an oath or vow is broken it will effect a divorce will not dissolve the marriage even if the said oath or vow is broken.

67. A divorce can be revoked by the husband during the *iddat* period. After the expiry of iddat, a direct remarriage between them will be lawful.

71. If a man arbitrarily divorces his wife without any reasonable ground and it causes hardship to her, the court may *grant her compensation* payable by the husband not exceeding maintenance for one year in accordance with her status. The court may decide if the compensation will be paid as a lump sum or in instalments." (emphasis supplied)

B. Laws of Southeast Asian States

164. Indonesia: The Constitution of Indonesia guarantees freedom of religion among Indonesians. However, the Government recognises only six official religions—Islam, Protestantism, Catholicism, Hinduism, Buddhism and Confucianism. Muslims of the Sunni sect constitute its majority. On the issue in hand, it has the following legislation in place:

"(a) Law of Marriage, 1974

Law 1 of 1974

38. A divorce shall be effected only in the court and the court shall not permit a divorce before attempting reconciliation between the parties. Divorce shall be permissible only for sufficient reasons indicating breakdown of marriage.

41. In the event of a divorce both the parents shall continue to be responsible for the maintenance of their children. As regards custody of children, in case of a dispute between them the court shall take a decision. Expenses of maintenance and education shall be primarily the father's liability, but if he is unable to discharge this liability the court may transfer it to the mother. The court may also direct the former husband to pay alimony to the divorced wife.

(b) Marriage Regulations, 1975 Regulation 9 of 1975

14. A man married under Islamic Law wanting to divorce his wife shall by a letter notify his intention to the District Court seeking proceedings for that purpose.

15. On receiving a letter the court shall, within thirty days, summon the parties and gather from them all relevant facts.

16. If the court is satisfied of the existence of any of the grounds mentioned in Article 19 below and is convinced that no reconciliation between the parties is possible it will allow a divorce.

17. Immediately after allowing a divorce as laid down in Article 16 above the court shall issue a certificate of divorce and send it to the Registrar for registration of the divorce.

19. A divorce may be allowed on the petition of either party if the other party:

(a) has committed adultery or become addict to alcohol, drugs, gambling or another serious vice;
(b) has deserted the aggrieved party for two years or more without any legal ground and against the said party's will;
(c) has been imprisoned for at least five years;
(d) has treated the aggrieved party with cruelty of an injurious nature;
(e) has been suffering from a physical deformity affecting conjugal duties, or where relations between the spouses have become too much strained making reconciliation impossible."

165. Malaysia: Under the Constitution of Malaysia, Islam is the official religion of the country, but other religions are permitted to be practised in peace and harmony. Muslims of the Sunni sect constitute its majority. On the issue in hand, it has the following legislation in place:

"Islamic Family Law Act, 1984

Act 304 of 1984

47. Divorce by *talaq* or by order.—(1) A husband or a wife who desires a divorce shall present an application for divorce to the court in the prescribed form, accompanied by a statutory declaration containing—

(a) particulars of the marriage and the names, ages and sex of the children, if any, of the marriage;
(b) particulars of the facts giving the court jurisdiction under Section 45;
(c) particulars of any previous matrimonial proceedings between the parties, including the place of the proceedings;
(d) a statement as to the reasons for desiring divorce;

(e) a statement as to whether any, and if so, what steps have been taken to effect reconciliation;

(f) the terms of any agreement regarding maintenance and habitation of the wife and the children of the marriage, if any, and the division of any assets acquired through the joint effort of the parties, if any, or where no such agreement has been reached, the applicant's proposals regarding those matters; and

(g) particulars of the order sought.

(2) Upon receiving an application for divorce, the court shall cause summons to be served on the other party together with a copy of the application and the statutory declaration made by the applicant, and the summons shall direct the other party to appear before the court so as to enable it to inquire whether or not the other party consents to the divorce.

(3) If the other party consents to the divorce and the court is satisfied after due inquiry and investigation that the marriage has irretrievably broken down, the court shall advise the husband to pronounce one *talaq* before the court.

(4) The court shall record the fact of the pronouncement of one *talaq* and shall send a certified copy of the record to the appropriate Registrar and to the Chief Registrar for registration.

(5) Where the other party does not consent to the divorce or it appears to the court that there is reasonable possibility of a reconciliation between the parties, the court shall as soon as possible appoint a Conciliatory Committee consisting of a Religious Officer as Chairman and two other persons, one to act for the husband and the other for the wife, and refer the case to the Committee.

(6) In appointing the two persons under sub-section (5) the court shall, where possible, give preference to close relatives of the parties having knowledge of the circumstances of the case.

(7) The court may give directions to the Conciliatory Committee as to the conduct of the conciliation and it shall conduct it in accordance with such directions.

(8) If the Committee is unable to agree or if the court is not satisfied with its conduct of the conciliation, the court may remove the Committee and appoint another Committee in its place.

(9) The Committee shall endeavour to effect reconciliation within a period of six months from the date of it being constituted or such further period as may be allowed by the court.

(10) The Committee shall require the attendance of the parties and shall give each of them an opportunity of being heard and may hear such other persons and make such inquiries as it thinks fit and may, if it considers it necessary, adjourn its proceedings from time to time.

(11) If the Conciliatory Committee is unable to effect reconciliation and is unable to persuade the parties to resume their conjugal relationship, it shall issue a certificate to that effect and may append to the certificate such recommendations as it thinks fit regarding maintenance and custody of the minor children of the marriage, if any, regarding division of property and other matters related to the marriage.

(12) No advocate and solicitor shall appear or act for any party in any proceeding before a Conciliatory Committee and no party shall be represented by any person, other than a member of his or her family, without the leave of the Conciliatory Committee.

(13) Where the Committee reports to the court that reconciliation has been effected and the parties have resumed their conjugal relationship, the court shall dismiss the application for divorce.

(14) Where the Committee submits to the court a certificate that it is unable to effect reconciliation and to persuade the parties to resume the conjugal relationship, the court shall advise the husband to pronounce one *talaq* before the court, and where the court is unable to procure the presence of the husband before the court to pronounce one *talaq*, or where the husband refuses to pronounce one *talaq*, the court shall refer the case to the Hakams [arbitrators] for action according to Section 48.

(15) The requirement of sub-section (5) as to reference to a Conciliatory Committee shall not apply in any case—

(a) where the applicant alleges that he or she has been deserted by and does not know the whereabouts of the other party;

(b) where the other party is residing outside West Malaysia and it is unlikely that he or she will be within the jurisdiction of the court within six months after the date of the application;

(c) where the other party is imprisoned for a term of three years or more;

(d) where the applicant alleges that the other party is suffering from incurable mental illness; or

(e) where the court is satisfied that there are exceptional circumstances which make reference to a Conciliatory Committee impracticable.

(16) Save as provided in sub-section (17), a *talaq* pronounced by the husband or an order made by the court shall not be effective until the expiry of the *iddat*.

(17) If the wife is pregnant at the time the *talaq* is pronounced or the order is made, *the talaq or the order shall not be effective until the pregnancy ends*." (emphasis supplied).

166. Philippines: Is a secular State. Christians constitute its majority. On the issue in hand, it has the following legislation in place:

Code of Muslim Personal Law, 1977

Decree 1083 of 1977

"46. (1) A divorce by *talaq* may be effected by the husband in a single repudiation of his wife during her Tuhr [non-menstrual period] within which he has totally abstained from carnal relations with her.

(2) Any number of repudiations made during one Tuhr [non-menstrual period] shall constitute only one repudiation and shall become irrevocable after the expiration of the prescribed *iddat*.

(3) A husband who repudiates his wife, either for the first or second time, shall have the right to take her back within the *iddat* period by resumption of cohabitation without need of a new contract of marriage. Should he fail to do so, the repudiation shall become irrevocable.

85. Within seven days after the revocation of a divorce the husband shall, with the wife's consent, send a statement thereof to the Circuit Registrar in whose records the divorce was previously entered.

161. (1) A Muslim male who has pronounced a *talaq* shall, without delay, file with the Clerk of the Shariat Circuit Court of the place where his family resides a written notice of such facts and the circumstances attending thereto, after having served a copy to the wife concerned. The *talaq* pronounced shall not become irrevocable until after the expiration of the prescribed *iddat*.

(2) Within seven days from receipt of notice the Clerk of the court shall require each of the parties to nominate a representative. The representatives shall be appointed by the court to constitute, with the Clerk of the Court as Chairman, an Agama [religious scholars] Arbitration Council which shall try and submit to the court a report on the result of arbitration on the basis of which, and such other evidence as may be allowed, the court will pass an order.

(3) The provisions of this article will be observed if the wife exercises right to *Talaq-e-Tafweez*.

183. A person who fails to comply with the requirements of Articles 85, 161 and 162 of this Code shall be *penalised by imprisonment or a fine of two hundred to two thousand pesos, or both*." (emphasis supplied).

C. Laws of Sub-continental States

167. Pakistan and Bangladesh: Are both theocratic States, wherein Islam is the official religion. In both countries Muslims of the Sunni sect constitute the majority. On the issue in hand, it has the following legislation in place:

Muslim Family Laws Ordinance, 1961

Ordinance 8 of 1961 amended in Bangladesh by Ordinance 114 of 1985

(Bangladesh changes noted below relevant provisions)

"7. *Talaq*.—(1) Any man who wishes to divorce his wife shall, as soon as may be after the pronouncement of *talaq* in any form whatsoever, give the Chairman a notice in writing of his having done so, and shall supply a copy thereof to the wife.

(2) Whoever contravenes the provision of sub-section (1) shall be punishable with simple imprisonment for a term which may extend to one year, or with fine which may extend to [five thousand rupees]*, or with both.

(3) Save as provided in sub-section (5), a *talaq* unless revoked earlier, expressly or otherwise, shall not be effective until the expiration of ninety days from the day on which notice under sub-section (1) is delivered to the Chairman.

(4) Within thirty days of the receipt of notice under sub-section

(1) The Chairman shall constitute an Arbitration Council for the purpose of bringing about reconciliation between the parties, and the Arbitration Council shall take all steps necessary to bring about such reconciliation.

(5) If the wife be pregnant at the time *talaq* is pronounced, *talaq* shall not be effective until the period mentioned in sub-section

(3) or of pregnancy, whichever is later, ends.

(6) Nothing shall debar a wife whose marriage has been terminated by *talaq* effective under this section from *remarrying the same husband without any intervening marriage with a third person, unless such termination is for the third time so effective.*" (emphasis supplied)

168. Sri Lanka: Is a secular State. Buddhists constitute its majority. On the issue in hand, it has the following legislation in place:

Muslim Marriage and Divorce Act, 1951

Act 6 of 1951 as amended by Act 40 of 2006

"17. (4) Save as otherwise hereinafter expressly provided, every marriage contracted between Muslims after the commencement of this Act shall be registered, as hereinafter provided, immediately upon the conclusion of the *Nikah* ceremony connected therewith.

(5) In the case of each such marriage, the duty of causing it to be registered is hereby imposed upon the following persons concerned in the marriage;

(a) the bridegroom,
(b) the guardian of the bride, and
(c) the person who conducted the *Nikah* ceremony connected with the marriage.

27. Divorce by husband.—Where a husband desires to divorce his wife the procedure laid down in Schedule II shall be followed.

28. Divorce by wife.—(1)

(2) Where a wife desires to effect a divorce from her husband on any ground not referred to in sub-section (1), being a divorce of any description permitted to a wife by the Muslim Law governing the sect to which the parties belong, the procedure laid down in Schedule III shall be followed so far as the nature of the divorce claimed in each case renders it possible or necessary to follow that procedure."

The Triple *Talaq* case was heard by a Constitutional Bench comprising of five Judges. Chief Justice Jagdish Singh Khehar and Justice S Abdul Nazeer delivered the minority view that since the different countries had enacted legislations to do away with the practice of *Talaq-e-Biddat*, hence the Court found "No reason, for an independent India to lag behind". Till such time the legislation in the matter was considered Muslim husbands were in juncted from "Pronouncing *Talaq-e-Biddat* as a means of severing their matrimonial relationship". The majority view, of Justices Kurian

Joseph, Rohintan Fali Nariman and Uday U Lalit had held *Talaq-e-Biddat* to be unconstitutional. Therefore, the order of the Court, by a majority of 3:2 held that the "practice of *Talaq-e-Biddat*" Triple *Talaq* is set aside".

The five courageous writ petitioners had the immense grit to challenge the arbitrary practice of *Talaq-e-Biddat* that has paved the way for a better future for the Muslim community. This legal battle is very significant. The otherwise quiet, submissive Muslim women had all raised there voices against the arbitrary practice. The tremor of the voices of the voiceless women could be sensed throughout the length and breadth of this country. While the case was pending, the social media went viral with divergent opinions. Even the Hon'ble Supreme Court could not, but take judicial notice of the strong social reaction. Therefore, in the minority view the Supreme Court observed:

"384. The whole nation seems to be up in arms. There is seemingly an overwhelming majority of Muslim women demanding that the practice of *Talaq-e-Biddat*, which is singful is theology, be declared as impermissible in law. The Union of India has also participated in the debate. It has adopted an aggressive posture, seeking the invalidation of the practice by canvassing that it violates the fundamental rights enshrined in Part III of the Constitution, and by further asserting that it even violates constitutional morality. During the course of hearing, the issue was hotly canvassed in the media. Most of the views expressed in crudete articles on the subject, hugely affirmed that the practice was demeaning. Interestingly even during the course of hearing, the learned Counsel appearing for the rival parties, were in agreement and described the practice of *Talaq-e-Biddat* differently as, unpleasant, distasteful and unsavoury. The position adopted by otherwise was harsher, they considered it as disgusting, loathsome and obnoxious. Some even described it as being debased, abhorrent and wretched..."

"It is evident that the All India Muslim Personal Law Board to served the mood and decided to be sympathetic to the cause and evolve some reform. Even through they pitched a serious battle in Court, admitting that the practice was not recognised either by the Holly *Quran* or *Hadith*, but the practice is in existence for the last 1400 years and thereafter there is no reason or abrogation, but in their affidavit filed before the Supreme Court stated :-

I, the Secretary of All India Muslim Personal Board, will issue an advisory through its website, publications and social media platforms and thereby advise the persons who perform '*nikah*' (marriage) and request them to do the following:

(a) At the time of performing *nikah* (marriage), the person performing the *nikah* will advise the bride groom/man that in case of differences leading to *talaq* the bridegroom / man shall not prounce three divorces in one sitting since it is an undesirable practice in *Shariat* ;

(b) That at the time of performing *nikah* (marriage), the person performing the *nikah* will advise both the bridegroom / man and the bridge / woman to incorporate a condition in the *'nikahnama'* to exclude resorting to pronouncement of three divorces by her husband in one sitting.

3.1 I say and submit that, in addition, the Board is placing on record, that the Working Committee of the Board had earlier already passed certain resolutions in the meeting held on 15.04.2017 & 16.04.2017 in relation to divorce (*talaq*) in the Muslim community. *Thereby it was resolved to convey a code of conduct / guidelines to be followed in the matters of divorce particularly emphasising to avoid pronouncement of three divorces in one sitting.* A copy of the resolution dated 16.04.2017 along with the relevant translation of Resolutions Nos. 2, 3, 4 and 5 relating to *talaq* (divorce) is enclosed herewith for the perusal of this Hon'ble Court and marked as Annexure A-1 (Colly) pp r4 to 12, to the present affidavit."

(emphasis supplied)

A perusal of the above affidavit reveals that AIMPLB has undertaken to issue an advisory through its website, they advice those who enter into a matrimonial alliance to agree in the *nikahnama*, that their marriage would not be dissolve by *Talaq – e – Biddat*. AIMPLB has sworn an affidavit to prescribe guidelines to be followed in matters of divorce emphasising that *Talaq-e- Biddat* be avoided. It would not be incorrect to assume that event AIMPLB is on board, to assuage the petitioner's cause.

Unfortunately, the above mentioned stand of All India Muslim Personal Law Board seems to be confined to its affidavit and there is really no concerted effort to impress upon the community against arbitrary Triple *Talaq*. On the contrary, Ishrat Jahan, one of the petitioners hailing from West Bengal was subjected to severe social ostracisation from the community on her so called audacity to challenge a religious practice. Even though we find such practices loathsome but the reaction is not surprising. Any social change, any reforms that give space to the woman or the marginalised section of society have always been treated with scorn, belligerence, indignity. In case of other social vices, inspite of legislation to the contrary e.g. prohibition of child marriages or dowry prohibition or Prevention of sex selection the community at large turns a blind eye and proceeds to act according to its own habits and economic considerations and cares little for the woman's right to live with dignity.

In abeyance to the judgment of the Hon'ble Supreme Court, the Muslim Women Protection of Rights on Marriage Bill, 2018 was tabled in the Lok Sabha. As expected, it generated the usual noisy opposition – Every attempt was meticulously made to stall its passing. The Opposition members of the House were unable to accept the clause that pronouncement of arbitrary Triple *Talaq* would amount to a cognizable offence, and render a punishment of 3 years. In the guise of protecting the wife the opposition members threw their weight behind the erring husband – making it very apparent that they do not want any legislation. The Bill has been sent to the Select Committee. It is hoped that the legislation shall, someday overcome all the hurdles and see the light of the day so that independent India, like other countries can do away with this barbaric practice.

The historic judgement of the Supreme Court, the attempt to table legislation banning arbitrary Triple *Talaq* have ushered in a fresh breeze in the otherwise claustrophic social mileau. Inspite of the commitment of the *Jamiat-Ulema-i-Hind*, the Organisation of the Maulanas before the Hon'ble Supreme Court that the *nikahnama* shall contain the clause that the husband shall not pronounce three *Talaqs* at one sitting, yet the news media is replete with news items on the pronouncement of arbitrary Triple *Talaq* or *Talaq-e-Biddat*.

In fact after pronouncement of the judgement, one of the writ petitioners, Ishrat Jahan was subjected to severe social Ostracisation. In a television discussion aired after pronouncement of the judgement where a leader of the *Maulanas* and Ishrat were both present, she was publicly reprimanded by the representative of her community as being a "bad wife". We are proud of her grit as she unhesitatingly described the occasions when she bound to hit back. What else can the wife do when her husband decided to trample upon her? Ishrat's narration on Television enraged her neighbours and the community. Thereafter, there were reports of her being brutally assaulted and subjected to various forms of violence by her relatives and neighbours.

Begum Rokeya Sakhawat, more than a century ago, in 1904 had identified the cause of the degraded status of women and why they were not allowed to raise their heads against bondage. We admire Begum Rokeya's progressive thoughts which she articulated so long ago. From 1904 to 2017 – Women's continuous combat with a patriarchial society, yielded a great honour in the form of the judgement in the arbitrary Triple *Talaq* case. From 2017 her new fight begins – to implement the judgement in its true letter and spirit. Our fight for equality will continue – the fight to live with dignity, to obtain equal opportunities will continue. We are still waiting for the "Muslim Women Protection of Rights on Marriage Bill, 2018" to be enacted and pressure must be mounted so that the Bill is not left to freeze in a cold storage. We hope that the Select Committee, considering the welfare of the Muslim Community, will reconsider the issue and the political parties opposing the Bill will keep gender justice and the direction of the Supreme Court as their prime consideration. For a change, political opposition urgency needs to give way to social interest.

We, the people of India, are thus waiting for the legislature to enact the "Muslim Women Protection of Rights on Marriage Bill, 2018" so that it can be a concrete step towards securing Justice ; social, economic, political and Equality of status and opportunity that the people of India, in 1950, had pledged to secure to all its citizens.

References

1. Encyclopedia Britannica
2. Chattopadhyay, Basabi. *Womens Studies: Various Aspects,* Urbee Prakashan, 2014. Pages 110, 129, 602.
3. 2017 (4) *Calcutta High Court Notes* – SC 299
4. 2017 (4) *Calcutta High Court Notes* – SC 314
5. (2017) 9 *Supreme Court Cases Para* – 9, 149, 150, 156-168, 198, 384 391.

Section - II
Women in Literature, Film and Theatre

4

Return of the Myth: Gender and the Politics of Rewriting

Himadri Lahiri

About a year back, while riding a taxi on a busy Kolkata street, I caught, at an important street junction, a bill board displaying the words "What would have Sita told? A talk by Navaneeta Dev Sen." Although I could not view the details of the programme on the display board from the running taxi, I could realise that Dev Sen, while discussing the female character of the *Ramayana,* would be talking about a very important thrust of feminist discourses. This 'would have been told' motif runs through not only around the character of Sita but also around Draupadi or Panchali. The authors who re-write the old mythic narratives detect supposedly untold aspects of women characters which they foreground. In the 'Author's Note' in *The Palace of Illusion* (2008), Chitra Banerjee Divakaruni argues that "Panchaali (also known as Draupadi), King Drupad's beautiful daughter, who has the unique distinction of being married to five men at the same time" remained in some way "shadowy figures" (xiv). She maintains that their emotions were "portrayed only when they affected the life of male heroes, their roles ultimately subservient to those of their fathers or husbands, brothers or sons" (xiv). Divakaruni thought of placing "the women in the forefront of action," of 'uncover[ing] the story that lay invisible between the lives of the men's exploits' (xv). She would have women characters telling their stories in their own voices (xv). Visibility and audibility are thus two important challenges that women face down the ages as they go on fighting against the attempts that aim to erase them from history and other forms of narratives.

In this article I shall focus on how the feminist concern for foregrounding women's 'bodies' (in the sense of material existence) and voices recalls important mythic figures to address some contemporary feminist issues. These issues are raised against the backdrop of overwhelming amnesia about women's rights in general. This 'recall' goes well with the overall trends in postcolonial discourses which have retrieval and restoration of forgotten voices as one of their important projects. Women writers' penchant for going back to the mythic female figures is in fact an *anamnesic* effort to bring to the fore the continuing 'colonial' practice of forgetting and erasing women's voices. They scour the depth of myths and legends in search of appropriate female figures as their models. Naturally, there has been a proliferation of myth-based creative works where mythic female figures are retrieved. This article does not intend to analyse any text in particular — some texts are rather invoked briefly to seek a connection between archetypal mythic characters and some contemporary feminist issues. Two such figures — Sita and Draupadi — constitute the focus of the discourse in this article.

The core issue at hand is 'rewriting', or more appropriately 're-visioning'. A text created long ago is re-invented and the characters found there are appropriated to conform to the norms of the new ideology which, in all likelihood, is counter-memorial in nature. The texts re-worked are usually the widely read and widely valued ones. These are canonical texts and sites of conventional socio-cultural and moral values. Some characters there assume archetypal dimensions and are cited as statements of conventional wisdom. Through repetitions of these statements, the texts and their characters acquire sediments of 'truth' values. Under particular regimes of 'truth' specific social norms are constructed and imposed. Devdutt Pattanaik, a popular mythologist, observes that "[f]rom myth comes beliefs, from mythology customs. Myth conditions thoughts and feelings" (xvii). But he also points out, "People outgrow myth and mythology when myth and mythology fail to respond to their cultural needs. So long as Egyptians believed in the afterworld ruled by Osiris, they built pyramids. So long as Greeks believed in Charon, the ferryman of the dead, they placed copper coins for him in the mouth of the dead. Today…there are new funeral ceremonies spawned by new belief systems, new mythologies based on new myths, each one helping people cope with the painful inevitability and mystery of death" (xvii-xviii).

Creative works show the dynamics of social changes. With change of time, the sediments of values contained in the old texts are challenged ideologically. The old textual contents and motifs are re-situated in changed time and contexts to make new statements suitable for the new temporal and social order. Since many of these texts assume mythic stature and/or considered to be sacred, and hence 'unchangeable' in popular perceptions, any transformation in the storyline or ideological content is likely to face hostility. This has exactly happened in the case of Sanjay Leela Bhansali's yet-to-be-released film "Padmavati," starring Deepika Padukone as Padmavati, an imaginary queen of extraordinary beauty, and Ranveer Singh who plays the role of Alauddin Khilji. Some radical groups and political leaders have alleged that the film has distorted history. Indeed the very idea of a beautiful Rajput woman falling in love with Alauddin Khilji is repulsive to many who want to 'protect' a Hindu woman's purity. That a Rajput-Hindu woman will not commit self-immolation (*jauhar*) to protect herself from religious and cultural pollution and that she would fall prey to the 'lust'of a *bidharmi* (one who belongs to a different religion/culture) are beyond their imagination. But the film obviously seeks to rework and re-vision the traditional story. The allegations as to the distortion of history does not stand as the film is based on the epic *Padmavat* (1540), written in Awadhi language by Malik Muhammad Jayasi, a Sufi poet. He closes his *masnavi* (an extensive poem) *Padmavat* by saying that he has "made up the story and related it" (*Scroll* Thursday, 23 November, 2017). Padmavati is an imaginary character which in popular imagination has acquired sediments of historical 'truth.' Re(-)visionary works thus pose threats to traditional value systems. Questions are raised not only about the 'historiography' of new cultural constructions but also about the limits of poetic license. These controversies feed the business of contemporary politicians as well. *Padmavati* as a representation is 'political' in its contestations of the value-laden mindset of the conservatives. Mukul Kesavan even suggests that the Hindutva leaders now in power have subtly launched an ideological programme to "read Hindus like Bhansali, Padukone and Singh as floating signifiers of Muslim hegemony over the medieval past" (16).

Such disruptive, and hence 'political,' changes basically suggest that the 'politics of representation' lead to materialisation of an alternative mindset actualised through contestations. The deviations may be radical in the sense that they are *transformative*. These are indeed re-orientations, and often reversal, of Laws – the Laws of Manu or of any authoritative, hegemonic source. Revision affects the smooth flow of cultural memory. Rewriting is, according to Leidake Plate, "a technology of cultural memory" (30) which changes perspectives of old memories. They provide counter-memories in favour of new formations.

The mythic narratives make the past revitalised and look forward to the future in a reparative spirit. Creative writers look for themes and characters in epic sources because they have become mythicised in the cultural lives of communities and the values they represent are validated by continuous repetitions at familial and public spaces. Mythic sources are foundational and are widely believed to be true mainly because they are usually associated with a religious belief system structured around binaries like the Good/ the Evil and the Moral/the Immoral. Myths are narratives that are "[c]ounter-factual in featuring actors and actions that confound the conventions of routine experience" (McDowell 80). In the altered time of the present, myths may not be as strongly associated with religion as they used to be but they are now being re-worked in other categories like gender and class because the motif of marginalisation is strongly found in the old myths. And the association of old canonicity makes the new renderings both powerful and subversive — they draw our attention to the injustice done during the old times and at the same time make them appealing, based as they are on familiar figures and themes, albeit altered by deviant models and social values. The reworked cultural texts foreground new ground realities. Return of the myths is mostly return of the repressed. Draupadi's humiliation, for instance, is a recurrent theme as is that of Sita. These characters serve as motifs for new assertions, even in unexpected contexts. They may be projected in a futuristic manner as well, bringing out some particular aspects of mythic existence. I would like to mention in this connection a Bengali mini-story entitled "Kuri Shobder Kolpobigjan" ("A Science Fiction Written in Twenty Words") written by Nibedita Halder Ganguly. It centres around the theme of a woman having multiple husbands in the zone of possibilities. It is quite a different way of re-writing. My translation of the mini-story reads like this:

> 'Draupadi' [who is the speaker here]
>
> The sex-ratio has increased terribly. I have five husbands, everyone is happy. I have been depriving four. In four different families, four of my *clones* are discharging their duties. (8; emphasis added)

This story originally appeared in the web magazine *Kolpobiswa* and was later published in a book. It has its focus on a possible critical imbalance of sex ratio in future when the solution will be provided by technology. The dilemma of having five husbands and rotating wifely duties to all of them is considered to be a near-impossible task, thereby critiquing the mythic absurdity and underscoring human limitations. Technology comes in handy here because creation of Draupadi's clones will solve the problem. Draupadi's image has been re-positioned here in the structure of a science fiction. So the mythic image of the iconic, deviant female figure of Draupadi is reconfigured in a futuristic re-vision. However, in Mahesweta Devi's celebrated story, "Draupadi," the female protagonist (Dopti) is tribalised and imagined as a revolutionary who was disrobed and raped by the agents of the state power as part of the strategy to put down a revolutionary movement. The gender aspect is foregrounded and disrobing is used by the tribal woman as a weapon against the patriarchal structure which invents and regulates a strict code of 'honour' and of sartorial compulsions for women. Disrobing and raping at the behest of the agents of the State to humiliate her and to violate her honour is conceived as permissible when patriarchal agents consider it necessary. However, when the table is turned and the woman accepts her disrobing as a weapon and uses it to confront the perpetrators face to face, the masculine agents do not know how to cope with the female nudity they themselves have created. 'Robing' and 'disrobing' in Mahasweta Devi's stories are strong metaphors taken from the epic source. Draupadi is re-born here as anti-patriarchal and anti-authoritarian instrument.

The State, as the fate of Dopti (tribal form of Draupadi) in Devi's story indicates, is held responsible for the gendered nature of the torture inflicted on women. The mythic name of Draupadi as the recipient of injustice resonates throughout the story. In a similar fashion, the character of Panchali, another name of Draupadi, takes the centrestage in Rudrani Sarma's Assamese novel *Damitar Dastaves* (2014). She refashions herself in the contemporary insurgency-ridden situation of Assam as a fighter against the State and the society at large. Panchali, raped by the marauding members of the anti-insurgency State forces who raided her house in search of her brother who had become an insurgent, takes her battle to the wider social and political space. The naming of the major characters is crucial in the text as it reverberates with the echoes of the Mahabharata, although the characters are transplanted in the recent times. Her boyfriend whom she is to marry is Partha (Arjun of the epic) who is born in a wealthy family and is far higher in social status. As they come closer to each other, they decide to meet at Partha's house to seek the consent of his parents. Panchali is humiliated in the meeting place just as Draupadi was humiliated in public in the epic. Partha can hardly come to her rescue. Panchali comes out of his house and decides to sever all her relations with Partha. Partha is shown as 'effeminate' as his original in the epic (in the episode of the game of dice). The context is different spatio-temporally but nothing indeed has really changed. It is no wonder that Panchali mourns the absence of any 'devaki-nandan' (Krishna) around who can come to her rescue.

Interestingly, as I have pointed out in my article mentioned earlier,[1] Panchali takes upon herself the task of compiling a list of women who have suffered like her throughout history. She links her own sufferings to thousands of innocent women victimised during wars and other forms of political crises. There are references to history – to the World War, to Genghis Khan, to Partition history, to Assam movement. These references generate feminist discourses encompassing the history of human beings. Panchali surveys and reviews the whole range of the history of suppression of women. The meaning of 'damita' ("the dominated one") in the title of the novel, as I have pointed out in my article referred to earlier, takes a wider range – Panchali is 'damita' but there are thousands of 'damitas' in history and mythical stories. These stories are either told or referred to, like the real life event of Mukhtar Mai's rape in Pakistan and her retaliation to the oppressive forces. The motto of the ravagers in any war is: "The greatest pleasure in life is to defeat your enemies, and to ravage their wives and daughters" (Sarma 12). The author refers to Amrita Pritam's novel *The Skeleton*, Rajanikanto Bordoloi's "Monomoti" and Lakshikanto Bezbarua's "Kasibasi" to exemplify how women become victims in wars, partitions and communal riots. The warring parties construct binaries like "our women/their women," and by raping "their women" one community takes revenge on another community. So women are imagined as the representative of a nation, community and religion; a war (and even in a game of chess) is fought on women's bodies. I maintained in my article mentioned earlier that "[b]y referring to works by Amrita Pritam, Rajanikanto Bordoloi and Lakshikanto Bezbarua, Sharma's text in effect weaves a network of events, stories, literary narratives and feminist discourses — it in fact creates an archive of oppositional ventures. *Damitar Dastaves* itself is a gesture towards that goal, the word '*dastaves*' itself suggesting archival possibilities and historiographical renovations."

In this respect I shall refer to an interview entitled "The Diary of Sita: Nilima Devi and A.K. Ashby in Conversation" published in the book *In Search of Sita* edited by Malashri Lal and Namita Gokhale to indicate the innovative ways in which new creative works are structured on the female characters taken from myths. Gokhale, in her own essay "Sita: A Personal Journey" included in the volume, rightly maintains, "Indian myth is never static, it is constantly in the process of reinterpreting and revalidating itself, and the society that it defines. Perhaps it is time to seek a new image of Sita — one who does not have to return to the Earth, but can resolutely reclaim it" (xvii). Nilima Devi, a noted choreographer and classical dancer, speaks of her dance performance "From the Diary of Sita" where Sita enters the pristine earth but does not hesitate to 'speak up'(113). Her Sita presents a new image of Sita in transnational perspectives. Nilima Devi notes Sita's agency in two specific moments of the protagonist's life: her decision to accompany her husband to the *vanavasa* (exile in the forest) and her act of entering into the refuge of Mother Earth. In her dance performance she used poems composed by herself and her daughter Anila, the main thrust in it being Sita's agency and freedom. The poem which is 'a condensed narrative' and 'a nuanced interpretation' (115) may be quoted here:

> Born of Mother Earth
> I dance to the pulse of my gurus,
> Vast oceans, venerable trees,
> Rama, archer prince, pierced my heart
> I followed him into exile
> Abducted by Ravana
> Rama came to my rescue
> Not me but his pride
> I walked through flames to prove my chastity
> But not my love
> Yet Rama abandoned me to the forest
> These mute memories
> These tears of stone
> Mother Earth called me
> 'Return Daughter'
> I entered her depthless embrace
> Everyone calls me 'Sita'
> But I have other names too
> Seema, Sara, Sophie.
> O my mother
> I shall be born again and again
> And in every breath
> In every voice
> In every woman
> I manifest
> For I am free. (114-5)

This is what Sita feels towards the end, according to Devi's rendition?[2] The poem is read and a dancer enters the stage announcing, "My name is Sita" in English and then retreats. This is both a vocal assertion of the female self and a means of making her visibility an important point. Another dancer comes with the same assertion "My name is Sita," this time in Hindi: "*Mera naam Sita hai.*" The third one announces the same in French. "Sita is thus depicted as a woman of the universe by making her speaking different languages" (116). Interestingly, the fourth dancer employs martial art behind a backlit panel to create plunging shadows. This is interesting because the image of the fighter, the 'woman warrior,' is suggestive of the ground reality which necessitates courage and resources on the part of the woman. This image recurs in the legends and history. One of the most prominent examples is that of the Chinese chant of Fa Mu Lan who came out of her family confines to lead an army against the invaders. Maxine Hong Kingston weaves this narrative into her fiction *The Woman Warrior* where women fight patriarchal norms both in the diasporic space (racism and sexism) and the domestic space (deeply entrenched patriarchal norms both in China and the family/community space in the United States of America). The shadows of the fighting woman in Nilima Devi's presentation both remembers this tradition and anticipates/rehearses fights in the context of the contemporary gender violence and discrimination all over the world. The last dancer storms into the stage and announces in a loud voice, "She has other names too." Nilima Devi comments, "I wanted to suggest that beyond geography and language, Sita exists within every woman" (116). She thus suggests that women go through similar experiences all over the world and underneath all differences womanhood merges into 'larger tapestry' suggesting the existence of 'an efflugent universal sisterhood'(117). Divakaruni's novel *The Palace of Illusion* also uses an epigraph which underscores this sisterhood in generational context: "Who is your sister? I am she./Who is your mother? I am she./Day dawns the same for you and me" (ix). By using an extract from *Innana's Journey to Hell* (3rd Millennium BCE, translated from Sumerian by N.K. Sanders), Divakaruni not only makes inter-spatial connection but also speaks of trans-temporal association to underscore the need for a broad-based sisterhood but also for an inter-textual coalition across time and space.

Rewriting the mythic stories is thus a re(-)visionary act which puts emphasis on the play of memory. It is an act of remembering the cultural past. It makes the past 're-usable' for purposes of communicating new meanings and to create unique perspectives related to the present. Through the re-visioning, a different present is produced. Liedeke Plate rightly comments:

> As each age rewrites the past in its own image, rewriting is the process and product of cultural remembrance and can thus be viewed as

> emblematic, representative, and characteristic of cultural memory conceived as a 'realm of traditions, transmissions, and transferences' (Assmann 2008: 110). *Rewriting is marked by a dynamics of storing and retrieving, inscribing and obliterating, remembering and forgetting, that is productive of memory as shared and formative of collective, cultural identity* (3; emphasis added).

In this "dynamics of storing and retrieving, inscribing and obliterating, remembering and forgetting" lies the politics of representation, the politics of writing back to those in charge of hegemonic historiography. Plate refers to Milan Kundera who comments: " 'Rewriting comme esprit de l'époque' – 'Rewriting as the spirit of the times'" (qtd. in Plate 3). Considering re-writing as the 'central technology of memory,' Plate confirms its emancipatory potential, specially in the field of women's writings. Moreover, as he reiterates, myths offer the scope of mending and reshaping because in its very nature lies an in-built structure providing re-tellers a 'liquid' time.

> Myth can be taken as a non-linear mode of understanding liquid time. As a narrative form, myth brings the past into the present in a movement that remains open to a future in becoming. Characterised by cyclical return (Eliade, 1969), myth is traditionally defined as an oral story whose distinguishing feature is that it presupposes retelling: it needs to be told and retold to achieve the status of myth (Kirk 1974). Myth works according to the principle of repetition with a difference. This built-in reproduction mechanism makes that myth is never fixed but is in permanent flux, changeable and changing with every telling, part of 'a long tradition of borrowings and mendings' (Sellers, 2001: 7). Does this make myth particularly suited to the spirit of the present, 'liquid' age? I would suggest so: the narrative dynamics of mythical retelling appear adapted to its fluid character, resonating with the sense of a memory culture as marked by a 'secondary orality', as Walter Ong suggested in *Orality and Literacy* (1982). (29)

In this sense, retelling of myths ensures a continuous play of contestations, giving way to the construction of an archive that goes through ceaseless renewals. Rewriting of myths becomes 'a field of negotiation,' a kind of 'hostile takeover' and a space of continuing dialogue. In this process of 'archive making,' there is, to borrow Huyssen's words, no signs of 'memory fatigue'. The 'seduction of the archive'(Huyssen) sucks the creative authors into the alleys of history and myth.

Adrienne Rich was one of the first proponents of the concept of 're-vision.' Speaking from a feminist position, she spoke of the need for writing back to tradition by authoring innovative texts of their own from their own perspectives. The absence of women's perspectives in traditional literature haunted her. The existing literature offers no 'guides, maps, possibilities.' It offers no model for upcoming women writers. Re-writing is, for her, a 're-vision'. She observes, "Re-vision — the act of looking back, of seeing with fresh eyes, of entering an old text from a new critical direction – is for us more than a chapter in cultural history: it is an act of survival. Until we can understand the assumptions in which we are drenched we cannot know ourselves. And this drive to self-knowledge, for woman, is more than a search for identity: it is part of her refusal of the self-destructiveness of male-dominated society" (18). Women's writing, she opines, must be a motor of cultural change and re-writing, a means of opening the past to alternative stories, which in turn meant opening the future to new possibilities. (5-6)

If we accept Julie Sanders' distinction between 'adaptation' and 'appropriation,' we must consider the 'revisionary' writings more as an 'appropriation' than an 'adaptation'. Adaptation, she asserts, is "an inherently conservative genre" (8) and it "signals a relationship with an informing source text or original" (26). Appropriations, on the contrary, "frequently affects a more decisive journey away from the informing source into a wholly new cultural product and domain" (26). The texts we have discussed briefly have mostly appropriated the names of the characters and reshaped the themes and environments radically to produce new cultural texts/domains. They have de-mythicised the earlier texts, keeping the core intact but changing the texture and the borderlines, thereby creating re-mythicised texts. These creative texts have recourse to a 'hostile takeover' (Sanders, 9) of the archive, driving anti-establishment messages home. Using the memory from the perspective of the mythic past, the texts have paved the way for a counter-memory to establish a new social order.

[This is a revised and enlarged version of an invited lecture at a national conference organised by the Department of English, Reva University, Bengaluru on 3-4 February, 2017. This paper also uses some textual materials which I used during an invited talk at a seminar organised by the PG Department of English, Malda College, Malda,West Bengal on 23-24 June, 2017. I am indebted to my Ph.D scholar Shyamasri Maji for going through the draft and making some useful suggestions].

Notes

1. The reference is to my article "Fiction as Discourse: Rudrani Sharma's *Damitar Dastaves* and Mahasweta Devi's "Draupadi" where I have made a detailed comparison between the two texts. It will be published shortly by the Department of MIL of Gauhati University, Assam.
2. Nilima Devi, however, points out that 'gender' intervenes here. She informs, "Two male musicians [in her team] objected to my rendition, saying, 'But Rama is god; and he never meant to hurt Sita...why is this all about Rama's faults?' Before I could explain, the vocalist of our group — a quiet young woman — answered pointedly, 'But it is not about Rama...it is about Sita, that is why it is called From the Diary of Sita...remember?" (115).

References

Devi, Mahasweta. "Draupadi." *Mahasweta Devir Choto Golpo Sonkolon*. New Delhi: National Book Trust, 1993. 29-39.

Devi, Nilima. "The Diary of Sita: Nilima Devi and A.K. Ashby in Conversation." *In Search of Sita: Revisiting Mythology*. Malashri Lal and Namita Gokhale. New Delhi: Penguin, 2009. 112-117.

Divakaruni, Chitra Banerjee. "Author's Note" *The Palace of Illusions*. London: Picador, 2008. xiii-xv. "The epic poem Padmavat is fiction." *Scroll* Thursday 23 Nov., 2017. http:// scroll.in/bulletin/94. Accessed on 23 Nov. 2017.

Ganguly, Nibedita Halder. "Kuri Shobder Kolpobigjan." *SeraKolpobiswa 2016: Notun Diner Kolpobignan O Fantasir Sombhar*. Ed. Ranen Ghosh. *Kolkata: Protisruti*, 2017.8.

Kesavan, Mukul. "Rajput Redux." *The Telegraph* (Calcutta ed) xxxvi.135 (Thursday 23 November 2017): 16.

Kingston, Maxine Hong. *The Woman Warrior: Memories of Girlhood among Ghosts*. New York: Vintage International, 1989.

McDowell, John. 'From "Perspectives on "What is Myth?"' *Folklore Forum* 29.2 (1998): 75-89.

Pattanaik, Devdutt. *Myth=Mithya: Decoding Hindu Mythology*. Gurgaon: Penguin, 2006.

Plate, Liedeke. *Transforming Memories in Contemporary Women's Writings*. Palgrave, Mcmillan, 2011.

Rich, Adrienne. "When We Dead Awaken: Writing as Re-Vision Author(s)." *College English* 34.1: 18-29. JSTOR.

Sanders, Julie. *Adaptations and Appropriation*. London and New York: Routledge, 2006.

Sarma, Rudrani. *Damitar Dastaves*. Guwahati: Jyoti Prakashan, 2014.

5

Women's Movements in 19th Century and as it reflected in Bengali Women's Writings

Anindita Bandyopadhyay

From the beginning of the 19th century the Bengali Society began to experience a lot of change in its values. English education and European ideas began to spread especially in Calcutta and its neighbourhood. Rammohan Roy (1774-1833) the great Indian reformer came to Calcutta in the year 1814, in 1815 he established a society named 'Atmiya Sabha'. This is the first learned society of Bengal. The members of the society began to discuss a lot of unusual things. The conservative society reacted sharply. In the year 1817 the Hindu College was established to spread western learning, western science. In 1826, a young Eurasian H. L. V. Derozio recruited in the Hindu College as a teaching staff. He was a very popular teacher and impressed by his teaching, the students began to question practises prevalent in the then Bengal Society. The conservatives became shocked. Rammohan Roy and his followers adopted a moderate tone in this respect.

In the first half of the 19th century a cruel custom was prevalent in Bengal society. According to this peculiar custom when the husband dies, his wife seldom accompanies him in the funeral pile. The Christian Missionaries began to question the utility of this practice. William Carey, William Ward, Joshua Marshman preached against this inhuman custom. From the year 1817 Rammohan Roy took his pen to propagate the futility of this custom. In the year 1817 Rammohan published a tract (A Second Defence of the Monotheistical system of the Vaidas in reply to An Apology for the Present State of Hindoo Worship). So it he exposed the character of the Brahmans and wrote –

> It is however, remarkable that, although the learned Brahman and his bretheren frequently quote the name of the Vaidas, and other Shastras both in Writing and in verbal discussion, they pay little or no attention in practice to their precepts.........

In the following year Rammohan began his crusade, he published a book in Bengali against widow burning or Sati (1818). The Bengali press welcomed this publication. Gangakishore Bhattacharya reprinted it in his newspaper *Bengal Gejeti* (1818). The then English press such as *Calcutta Journal*, *Friend of India*, *Bengal Harkaru*, *Government Gazette* etc. appreciated the book. The conservative section of the society protested vehemently. Radhakanta Deb, Maharaja Kalikrishna, Bhabanicharan Banerjee became very furious. In their opinion this is an attempt to encroach their age-old custom.

At their initiative Kashinath Tarkapanchanan wrote a rejoinder *Bidhayak Nishedhaker Sambad (সম্বাদ নিষেধকের বিধায়ক)* (1819). Rammohan again took up his pen and answered all the queries of Mr. Tarkapanchanan. With the advancement of the time the movement against Sati became stronger. Rammohan was associated by his friend and the members of the Brahmasamaj namely Dwarakanath Tagore, Prasannakumar Thakur etc. Harihar Dutta, editor of an Urdu Journal and a close associate of Rammohan protested strongly against this inhuman custom. As a result of their untiring efforts the government passed a law in the year 1829 – women were allowed to live their full lives. The conservative section challenged this law in the Privy Council but they defeated. From this very juncture Bengali Society was sharply divided into two sections. Rammohan Roy became the leader of the liberals and the conservative part of the society gathered together under the leadership of Raja Radhakanta Deb.

From the thirties, the students of Derozio better known as Derozians or Young Bengal came to limelight. Their ideas were rather radical. They ridiculed Rammohan Roy as 'half-liberal'. In consequence of their attitude the Bengali Society was divided in three sectors. First – (1) The conservatives – who practised age-old customs and different rituals. (2) The Brahmasamajis better known as liberals. This group was represented by the followers of Rammohan Roy- such as Debendranath Tagore, Akshay Kr. Dutta, Dwarakanth Gangopadhyay, Durgamohan Das, Kesab Chandra Sen etc. (3) The Young Bengal group may be called radicals. They were represented by Ramgopal Ghosh, Radhanath Sikdar, Madhabendra Mallik, Rasik Krishna Mallik etc. The three groups preached their own ideas in their own newspapers and journals. Such as – the radical ideas were expressed through the papers *Enquirer*, *Jnananweshan*, *Bengal Spectator*, *Masik Patrika* etc. The Brahmasamajis expressed the view in the *Tatwabodhini Patrika*, *Dharmatatwa*, *Tatwakaumudi*, *National Paper*, *Brahma Public Opinion*, *Indian Messenger* and a few others. The conservatives attacted relentlessly the liberals and the radicals. In their journal *Samachar Chandrika*, *Durjan Daman Mahanavami*, *Hindudharma Chandraday* etc.

In the thirties, the Bengali woman was the most neglected part of the society. They had no right to education they could not inherit their ancestral property, they had to spend the whole life in the inner apartment of their house – *andarmahal*. They were not allowed to go outside. Early marriage was prevalent, widow marriage had no place in upper class Bengali Society. The polygamy also a curse. A slight change was visible from the forties. The Brahmasamajis and the Young Bengal expressed their views in favour of women's education as a result of which girls were allowed to learn some elementary things. Before them, a close associate of Rammohan, Prasanna Kumar Thakur first published a newspaper in English in 1831 as a Bengali. In his paper The Reformer, Prasanna Kumar strongly advocate in favour of education for women. In this context we have to say – the Christian Missionaries first established a female school in Chinsurah. Robert May is the pioneer in the field in the year 1818. Miss Cook tried her best to spread education for women among Hindu and Muslim girls. The Bible was compulsory in all these schools and the main aim was to convert them to Christianity. The first girls' school was established at the initiative of some middle class Bengali gentlemen in Barasat in 1847. Now it is known as Kalikrishna Girls' School.

In the year 1849, Mr. Drinkwater Bethune, with the support of some liberal Bengali gentleman, established a girls' school in Calcutta with twenty one (21) students. There was a great uproar in the society as usual. Mr. Bethune tried his best to upgrade the school and it became the first institution in Bengal Presidency to impart higher education to women. From this school Kadambini Basu passed the entrance examination in the year 1878.

From the sixties of the 19th century the Brahmasamajis questioned the society why girls should be confined to only elementary education? The conservative group reacted but at the initiative of Dwarakanath Ganguly and a few others, Hindu Mahila Vidyalaya (1873) and Banga Mahila Vidyalaya (1875) was established. The Banga Mahila Vidyalaya was amalgamated with Bethune School and from the year 1878 Bengali women were allowed to sit for the University exam. It is to be specially noted that from the fifties of the 19th century journal for women began to flourish. The *Bamabadhini Patrika* appeared in the year 1863 under the editorship of Umesh Chandra Dutta. Writings of the first generation of educated Bengali ladies, their opinion in favour of female education and widow remarriage were published in this journal. They condemned child marriage and polygamy also. We may mention a few lines from the writing of Mrs. Madhumati Gangopadhyay of Rarhipara, who wrote in *Bamabodhini Patrika* (December, 1864) –

> ... যে নহে অভিপ্রায় কখনই ইহা সর্ব্বমঙ্গলাকরের সেই সুখ বিশুদ্ধ জ্ঞানজনিত পুরুষেরাই করিবেন সম্ভোগ, সহ্য কষ্ট অতি নিবন্ধন অজ্ঞানতা জিয়ন্তে আমরা আর । করিব

They also wrote pamphlets and books in favour of female education. We may mention here the names of Bamasundari Devi, Kailasbasini Devi etc.

Not only they preached in favour of female education, they wrote a series of articles in the *Bamabodhini Patrika*, *Bangamahila* and *Abalabandhab* in favour of widow marriage and against the curse of polygamy.

It is well known that from the fifties of this century Iswarchandra Vidyasagar fought relentlessly in favour of widow marriage and against the curse of polygamy. He began his social reform movement by considering early marriage which was an evil practice in 19th century Bengal. As the girls got married in the premature age of 12/13. They remained illiterate and a source of different superstitions. In 1854, he published a pamphlet describing the miseries of Hindu widows. The conservative section of the Bengali society reacted strongly against this pamphlet. Not less than 25 books and pamphlets were written against it. Vidyasagar was a brilliant Sanskrit scholar and quoted different Hindu legislators in support of his argument. He based his arguments on those of mainly Parashara Samhita and quoted a passage from it -

> "। পতৌ পতিতে চ ক্লীবে প্রব্রজিতে মৃতে নষ্টে
> ।। বিধীয়তে পতিরণ্যো নারীণাং পঞ্চস্বাপৎসু"

A woman is entitled to marry in the following cases:

(a) After his husband's death

(b) If the husband is a lunatic

(c) If the husband becomes a sage or saint or

(d) If he is impotent.

After a few months Vidyasagar published his second book on widow marriage. In it he countered the arguments of his opposite group one by one. In the year 1855, he arranged for a mass petition to the government of India requesting them to legalise Hindu widow marriage. He also appealed to Indian government to declare the children of that married widow as legal descendants. From different quarters of India people also urged the government to pass a law legalising widow marriage. The conservative section of Indian society did not sit idle, they also appealed to government not to promulgate any such law. Not only from Bengal the inhabitant of Pune, Dharwar, Satara, Orissa, Bombay, Ahmedabad and Surat also appealed to the government not to pass any such law. For the untiring efforts of the great social reformer Iswarchandra Vidyasagar, the government finally passed a law legalising Hindu widow marriage. This is known as Act xv of 1856. The first legal marriage of a Hindu woman was held in Calcutta on 7th December 1856. The bride groom was an educated person named Srishchandra Vidyaratna. The bride was Kalimoni Devi aged about eleven.

The views of Vidyasagar was supported not only by the Bengali intellectuals but also by a large section of a Bengali womenfolk. Women now began to question the dictates of the agents of patriarchy. Be that in the domestic sphere or in the public articles, pamphlets and books on their own conditions.

In *Chittabilasini* ('চিত্তবিলাসিনী') (1856) the first published book by woman Krishnakamini reports the conversation between two women – Soudamini and Matangini on the issue of widow marriage. They appreciate the efforts of Vidyasagar whose contribution to the cause has been discussed earlier in the paper. The widow marriage act has been passed recently and in such a concept Soudamini is a bit sceptical about whether they will be fortunate enough to enjoy its benefit. Matangini is more emphatic and dismisses all such doubts. She asserts that since it is a law now, where is the doubt now? She further informs Soudamini 'for the last two years there is much controversy about this. Some God forsaken villains put hurdles to the enactment of the law. They have lost their faces now.'—

সৌদামিনী। সি কি বোন ই কি কতা ? আমরা হতভাগী, আমাদের কি আবার এমন গিভাগ্ হবে।

. . . .

মাতঙ্গিনী। আর কতা কি, আইন হয়ে গিয়েছে তার আবার কতা কি। .... আজ দু বচ্ছোর ধরে হলো ঐ ঘোঁট হচ্চে, কেবল গুলোকতক্ পোড়ারমুকো বাদে নেগে এদ্দিন হতে দিই নি, তা তাদের মুক এবার পুড়িয়ে দিয়েচে।

সৌদামিনী। হেঁ লো, এমন গুণমণি গুণের সাগর কে আছে যে আমাদের দুখের দুখী হয়ে একান্ড বল্লে।

They also praised the person was responsible for this, the person who is popularly known as 'The Ocean of Virtues' and 'The Ocean of Learning'—

। বিদ্যেসাগর নাম সাগরের গুণের সে নাকি শুনিচি। মাতঙ্গিনী

They were apprehensive that no parents would venture on their own to give their widow daughters in marriage to bride grooms because of the social pressure. Matangini is more forthright of the two and insists that widows must articulate their own desires. She reiterates, 'since it is a newly introduced law nobody would try to carry it into action on their own. After twenty or twenty five cases of implementation it would naturally come into vogue.'—

মাতঙ্গিনী। .... এখন যে নতুন নতুন, আগে কেউ হাত দিতে চাবে না, এর পর বিশ পঁচিশটে হয়ে হয়ে গেলেই আবার চলে যাবে।

Soudamini argues that widow marriage should not be considered as a bad practice because in its absence women tend to go wayward. She observes a lot of widows have been committing abominable acts surreptitiously. Some are violating their castenorms, some others are giving bad names to their family, some others, being unable to remain in the family are deserting it (family). 'Aha! If there were provision for the marriage of the widows, widows would not have to resort to such activities. Look my sister, how many sisters have aborted out of shame and social diatribes.'—

সৌদামিনী। কেন বোন ? এতো আর নিচু মন্দ কম্ম নয়, যে লোকে আগে ভাগে হাত দিতে চাবে না ? কত লোক লুকিয়ে চুরিয়ে কত কাণ্ড কচ্চে, কেউ জেতের মাতা খাচ্চে, কেউ কুলের মাতা খাচ্চে, আবার কেউ কেউ ঘরে না থাকতে পেরে বেরেও যাচ্ছে ; আহা ! রাঁড়ের বিয়ে যদি আগে দিঅব্ থাকতো তবে আর এসব কম্ম কেউ করত না,দেক দিকি কত বোন্ লোক লজ্জার ভয়ে, লোক নিন্দের ভয়ে,........... পেটের ছেলে যে প্রাণ চেয়েও বড়, তাও নষ্ট করচে। ....

মাতঙ্গিনী। কে জানে দিদি ? সে কালের পোড়ারমুকোরা, যে কি এক দেশাচার করে রেকে গিয়েছে, একালের পোড়ার বাঁদরেরাও সেই দেশাচার দেশাচার করিই মলো।

This suggests that women too are taken to be passive objects for the gratification of the male sexual desire are not really so. They too have their sexual desire which the widows could not ventilate in the claustrophobic domestic environment and for lack of provision of their re-marriage. We know in his book Vidyasagar made an appeal to humanity—

মানবগণ! তোমরা কাল কত আর, মোহনিদ্রায় হইয়া অভিভূত, থাকিবে করিয়া শয়ন প্রমোদশয্যায়! উন্মীলন জ্ঞানচক্ষু একবার দেখ করিয়া, ও ব্যাভিচারদোষের ভারতবর্ষ পুণ্যভূমি তোমাদের যাইতেছে হইয়া উচ্ছলিত স্রোতে ভ্রূণহত্যাপাপের............................ কর মনে তোমরা, হইলেই বিয়োগপতি, পাষাণময় শরীর স্ত্রীজাতির যায় হইয়া; না হয় বোধ বলিয়া দুঃখ আর দুঃখ; যন্ত্রণা আর যন্ত্রণা না হয় বোধ বলিয়া; । যায় হইয়া নির্মূল এককালে রিপুবর্গ দুর্জয়

Same reactions reflected in *Chittabilasini* as we see above.

It has to be remembered that a woman writer is speaking of widows' reactions to the newly introduced widow act. It suggests that *andarmahal* or the domestic space is really changing, that women themselves are critical of the older practices and responding to the changes very positively.

Bamasundari Devi is the first woman to have published a pamphlet – entitled '*Which Superstitions are to be Eradicated to Ensure for the Prosperity of the Country*?' (পার হইতে শ্রীবৃদ্ধি এদেশের শীঘ্র হইলে তিরোহিত কুসংস্কার কি কি?) (1861), which basically dwells on the irrational customs and prejudices women used to face in the 19th century. Four of the important areas she discussed are:

1. Women's education,
2. The social custom of *Kaulinya*,
3. Child widows and
4. Early marriage.

About the second issue she makes scathing comment. 'The abolition of the custom of *Kaulinya* will do immense good to the country. *Kulin* Brahmins can now marry as many times as he wish. Even a man more than eighty years old does not have any problem in this regard. A five-year-old girl is surrendered to a sixty years old groom. One hears that quite a good number of Brahmins have married 40/50/60/70/80 and even hundred times. Aha! The death of a polygamous husband caused the widowhood and intolerable sufferings of hundreds of his wives.'—

> ...... কৌলিন্য প্রথা এদেশ হইতে অন্তর্হিত হইলে এদেশের অশেষ মঙ্গল সংশোধন হইতে পারে, কুলীন ব্রাহ্মণেরা যত ইচ্ছা ততই বিবাহ করিতে পারেন। অশীতিপর বৃদ্ধ হইলেও তাঁহাদের বিবাহের ব্যাঘাত হয় না। .... পঞ্চম বর্ষীয়া বালাকে ৬০ বৎসরের পাত্রের হস্তে সমর্পণ করিতেছেন। শুনিতে পাওয়া যায় যে কত কত কুলীন ব্রাহ্মণেরা নাকি ৪০/৫০/৬০/৭০/৮০ এবং একশত পর্য্যন্ত বিবাহ করিয়া থাকেন। আহা! বহু বিবাহকারী একটি পুরুষের মৃত্যু হইলে কত কত স্ত্রী বৈধব্যদশায় পতিতা হইয়া কি এক অসহ্য যাতনা সহ্য করিতে থাকেন।

She welcomes the issue of the remarriage of young widows she points out that many of such helpless girls go through intolerable sufferings. Interestingly, she rhetorically refers to the unfulfilled sexual desires of the young girls. They are 'suffering from inexpressible and intolerable burning sensations, they are ceaselessly suffering mentally and crying silently, nobody gives them any palliative or medicine to cure this pain.'—

> বালা বিধবাগণের পুনরুদ্বাহ প্রথা প্রচলিত হইলে মঙ্গলোন্নতি হইতে পারে। আহা! ঐ সকল পতিহীনা দীনা ক্ষীণা অবলা বালা কি এক অনির্ব্বচনীয় অসহনীয় জ্বালা সহ্য করিতেছে, অনবরতই হৃদয় ব্যাথায় ব্যাথিত হইয়া মনে মনে রোদন করিতেছে, কেহই দয়া করিয়া তাহাদের এই ব্যাথা নিবারণের ঔষধ প্রদান করে না।

What is more interesting that she suggests that this suffering can be really stopped through proper means. But no initiative is however taken in this regard to alleviate this suffering obviously because there is a lack of sensibility and sympathy in the society. She points out that 'they do not get medicine even when there is medicine.'—

> তাহারা ঔষধ থাকিতেও ঔষধ পায় না।

She complains, 'The burning sensation continues ceaselessly, nobody feels pity and offers water to douse the fire, they do not get water even when there is water.'—

> অনবরতই মনের আগুনে জ্বলিতেছে, এই অগ্নি নিবারণার্থ কেহই কৃপা করিয়া বিন্দুমাত্র জল প্রদান করে না, তাহারা জল থাকিতেও জল পায় না।

She directs her attention to the early marriage. Physiological condition of young women who are married off.: 'If a young girl produces a child without attaining physiological maturity, the child does not become strong and vigorous.'—

> বাল্যবিবাহ প্রথা দূরীভূত হইলে দেশের শ্রীবৃদ্ধি হইতে পারে। হা ঈশ্বর ! অস্মদ্দেশীয় এই দোষাকর দেশাচারের ক্ষমতা কি উত্তর উত্তর বৃদ্ধিই হইবে ? ...... হায় ! কি পাপ ! ....
> আর শরীরের পূর্ণাবস্থা প্রাপ্ত না হইতে সন্তান উৎপাদন করিলে সে তাদৃশ বলবান বীর্য্যবান হয় না। ....

After Bamasundari we get an ancestor named Kailasbasini Devi. She was married at the age of 11, to Durgacharan Gupta. At that time she was totally illiterate. Then she learned Bengali alphabets from her husband and to read and write. At first, she had reservation because of some superstitions. She said in this context -

She also said—

> আমার স্বামী শ্রীযুক্ত বাবু দুর্গাচরণ গুপ্ত মহাশয় . . . ১৭৭১ শকের শ্রাবণ মাসে আমাকে বর্ণমালার প্রথম ভাগের উপদেশ দেন। আমি সেই অবধি গোপন ভাবে কিঞ্চিৎ কিঞ্চিৎ অধ্যয়ন করিতাম।

But after being educated she wrote her first book about the grief and adversity of Hindu female- *Hindu Mahilaganer Hinabastha* ('হীনাবস্থা মহিলাগণের হিন্দু') (1863). The book was published from Gupta Press, owner was her husband Sri Durgacharan Gupta. In this book she acknowledges the influence of Bamasundari Devi. She considers Bamasundari to be a pioneer who influenced her and many other women. She gave them vision and freed them from the shackles of passivity and inaction. Kailasbasini accepts her as an effective predecessor-

> আমি এ স্থলে শ্রীমতী বামাসুন্দরী দেবীকে ধন্যবাদ প্রদান করিতে বর্ণ ও বিদ্যা শ্রেষ্ঠ প্রযুক্ত প্রণাম করিতে বাধ্য হইলাম। বামাসুন্দরী আমাদের পথ প্রদর্শিকা ... তিনি এই বঙ্গদেশে আবির্ভূতা হইয়া আমাদিগের লোচন হইতে লজ্জাবরণ মোচন করিলেন... তাঁহার অনুকম্পা প্রাপ্ত না হইলে আমার এই হাঁড়ি বেড়ি ধরা হাত কখনই লেখনী ধারণ করিতে ইচ্ছুক হইত না।

And hopes that 'other sisters' will give expression to their inherent qualities—

যেমন আমি এতাবৎ কাল কেবল একজন অগ্রবর্ত্তিনীর অনুসন্ধান করিতেছিলাম এবং ঈশ্বরানুকম্পায় সেই প্রার্থনীয় অগ্রবর্ত্তিনী প্রাপ্ত হইয়া তাঁহার অনুগামিনী হইলাম, তদ্রূপ আমাদিগের মত অন্যান্য ভগিনীগণ আপন আপন গুণপনা প্রকাশ করিলে কৃতার্থ হই।

Kailasbasini Devi therefore, discovers a link between women of different generations. This kind of link in fact creates possibilities of female bonding and formation of a common platform. This is one of the earliest sign of creating a female lineage and female bonding in Colonial Bengal. Kailasbasini Devi, for instance, raises the following very important issues in her book '*Hindu Mahilaganer Hinabastha*' (Despicable Condition of Hindu Women):

1. Why are women not acceptable in society since their birth? Why is there discrimination between male child and female child?
2. Why are the girl child deprived of education, while the male child receives privileges in this respect? Why are girls made to waste her time by playing with dolls and engage in different social and religious rites in the domestic sphere?
3. Why should the girls be married off early in their lives? Early marriage makes them burdened with family and procreative responsibilities and renders them weak physically.
4. Why shouldn't be *Kaulinya* system abolished?

Kailasbasini Devi's husband was instrumental in educating her. This education made her conscious about the condition of women in Colonial Bengal. Her reflections on this problem are found in the different books written by her. Her book Hindu Women's Education is titled '*Hindu Abalakuler Bidyabhyas o Tahar Samunnati*' ('সমুন্নতি তাহার ও বিদ্যাভ্যাস অবলাকুলের হিন্দু') (1865). This is the first book written by a woman on women's education.

Kailasbasini wrote in this book that, in ancient time there was practice of education for the females, but afterwards this practice was abolished. She thought that, modern education system was not totally appropriate for female. So she suggested in her book to look through a new process of education.

An anonymous female author makes woman the protagonist of her novel '*Monottoma*' ('মনোত্তমা') (1868), which is the first novel by woman. Interestingly she turns the social world upside down by making the female protagonist a voracious reader who is willing to read out the books to her uneducated husband Nilabrata. Her husband is not only unwilling but is also angry with her. —

> রজনীযোগে মনোত্তমা দুই এক খানি মনোহর পুস্তক লইয়া পতিকে শ্রবণ করাইতে বসিতেন। নীলব্রত কোন কোন দিন তাহাতে বিরক্তি দর্শাইয়া হয়ত গৃহ হইতে বাহির হইয়া যাইতেন। কোন কোন দিন বা পত্নীকে তিরস্কার করিয়া অন্য গৃহে যাইয়া ক্রোধভরে নিদ্রা যাইতেন ভাবিতেন। যে, এই। হইয়াছে কুকর্ম্মই কি করিয়া পাণিগ্রহণ কামিনীটার দুঃশীলা

He mocks her habits and gossips about it with his friends. The wife is strong-wilt and encounters her husband directly. The reversal of the social order in the novel tilts in favour of women. This is a reversal of the power structure. This is something which is not palatable to her husband and other men folk for that matter. This representation of the reverse world is the result of a creative agency exercised by a female author.

The reflection of consciousness also seen in the plays of 19th century, written by women. A play titled *Santapini* ('সন্তাপিনী') by an anonymous woman. In this drama Bisweswar (one character) talks about Kamalekamini's (another character) early marriage. Bisweswar babu introduces 'Kamalekamini' as one whose marriage was performed immediately after her birth with a male baby who was also just born and who later died.' Hence the baby girl became a widow at (that moment) her destiny was determined at that very moment. The evil marriage custom between Baidik caste was like this.—

> আপনারা বোধহয় শুনেছেন বৈদিকের বিবাহ কতদূর কভয়ান,তাহাদের পরিণয় কার্য্য প্রায় পেটে পেটেই সমাধা হয়। কমলেকামিনীর আঁতুড়ে যে বালকটির সহিত বিবাহ হয়েছিল সেটীও আঁতুড়ে,উহাদের আঁতুড়েই পরিণয় হয়েছিল, পরে আঁতুড়ে রোগে সেই বালকটীর মৃত্যু হয়।

Kaminisundari Devi in her play *Usha* advocates in favour of the equal status the girl child should enjoy in the family space. Through the dialogue between two characters called 'Konchu' and 'Montri'(Minister) she speaks of the unequal social position of the girl child in the prevalent social conditions and drives home the point that the family would be dysfunctional without the existence of women.—

> কঞ্চু। ...... আমার বোধহয়, তিনি কন্যা বলে মনে মনে অশ্রদ্ধা করেন।
> মন্ত্রী। -- সে কি কথা, সন্তানের প্রতি কি কারু অশ্রদ্ধা হয়?
> কঞ্চু। -- হবে না আর কেন, এইরূপ ত প্রায় দেখা যায়।
> মন্ত্রী। -- ছি ছি তাও কি কত্তে আছে, কন্যা পুত্র না হলে কি সংসার চলত?

In the case of the death of the husband wives were usually blamed as '. Usha, the main character in *Usha*, too is blamed when her husband dies. The members of her family, particularly her father put pressure on her to sacrifices her life as *Sati*. But interestingly her companion (Chitra and maid servant) discourages her and want to divert her attention to the rituals going on in the temple. The indication is that she should be devoted to the worship of God more intensely now. What is striking is that this female companions are unconventional in attitude. It is evident that she refuses to internalize the patriarchal norms and in fact goes against the conventions. This is a clear indication of a perceptible change in women's consciousness.—

> ঊষা। পিতা প্রাণনাথের প্রাণ বধ করেছেন তাঁর সেই মৃতদেহের নিকট আমাকে লয়ে চল আমি সহমরণে যাব।
> পরিচারিকা। বালাই ও আবার কি কথা।
> চিত্র। তুমি সাধ্বি, তোমার পতির কি বিনাশ আছে, শুনেছ তো সাবিত্রীর পতিকে শমন স্পর্শ কত্তে পারেন নাই।

Sukumari Dutta wrote Apurbasati ('অপূর্বসতী') which presents an unusual situation. The protagonist Nalini, a prostitute by profession is also a daughter of a prostitute. (Nalini's mother is 'enlightened' enough to educate her daughter.) She must have envisaged education of women as a means of their emancipation. Nalini herself has received the light of education, prays for an educated husband and even writes poems which are full of youthful vigour. Nalini is frustrated at the general mindset of the patriarchy and vents her frustrations in the following words–

> সামান্য অজ্ঞ লোকে বিবেচনা করে, যে স্ত্রীলোকের বিদ্যাশিক্ষার কিছুমাত্র আবশ্যকতা নাই। কিন্তু হায়! জগৎপিতা কি তাঁহাদিগকে এত নীচ উপাদানে সৃজন করিয়াছেন যে তাহারা পুরুষ হইয়া স্ত্রীশিক্ষার অপূর্ব্ব মহিমা স্পষ্ট দেখিয়াও দেখিতে পান না?

The above quotation points out that semi-educated people usually consider women's education to fully unnecessary or irrelevant. She laments that the conservative society perceive women to be made of inferior materials and the conservative people refused to discover the utility of women's education.

Nalini falls in love with Chandraketu because he is educated. Her mother also supports her in this regard. The playwright probably wants to convey the message that women, when educated develops agency and can take decisions on their own. Nalini has developed his own personality because she is equipped with education and was not afraid to contest the teasing and lewd comments made by notorious men. She is able to defend herself and is courageous enough to confront such men with proper weapons. She is looked down upon by these people because of her profession which is prostitution.—

নলিনী । (সক্রোধে) পামর ! তোরা চাস কি ? সহজে কি তোরা আমাকে পরিত্যাগ করবি না ? আয় রে রাক্ষসেরা আয়, তোদের আর নিস্তার নাই । হয় এই অস্ত্র (কাটারি) দ্বারা আত্মহত্যা করব না হয় তোদের খুন করব । জানিস না, উৎপীড়িত হলে পক্ষীরাও আত্মরক্ষার চেষ্টা করে ।

In the drama *Santapini* (1876) we have seen Santapini, the protagonist character left the family after her husband married again. This is a protest against the practice of polygamy. She prefers death to living with her *Satins* (co-wife). She tells her husband that the death is preferable to living with co-wives.—

......................জিজ্ঞাসায় ২ বহু কষ্টে এখানে এসে দেখি আপনি বিবাহ করেছেন, আমাকে যদি শত শত বার সমুদ্রে ফেলিতেন তাহাও অধিনীর সুখ, কিন্তু একটি বিবাহ অসহ্য, এই জন্য পুনর্ব্বার বনবাসিনী হইলাম ।

Here the author (anonymous lady) said courageously in this drama—

স্ত্রীলোকের রসপত্নী অপেক্ষা কষ্ট আর জগতে নেই ।

Women also protested against their confinement. A section of Brahma leaders such as Annadacharan Khastagir, Durgamohon Das, Dwarakanath Gangopadhyay, Keshab Chandra Sen and many others expressed their opinion in favour of liberty of women. The conservatives and the followers of Debendranath Tagore were against this move. They tried their best to keep their indoor members under confinement. This issue became stronger day by day as a result of which Brahmasamaj was divided into two groups – (1) headed by Debendranath known as Adi Brahmasamaj and the (2) Bharatbarshiya Brahmasamaj under the leadership of Keshab Chandra Sen. This event took place in the 1866. The Bengali ladies also expressed their opinion in the context of the liberty of women. We come across an astonishing letter from one Mayasundari. The lady wrote a long letter to the editor of the *Bangamahila* (Shraban 1282 Bangabda). The title of their letter is – 'Narijanma ki Adharma!' (" অধর্ম্ম কি নারীজন্ম!") We quote a portion of that which acts as a trend letter from *Bangamahila* –

। করিয়াছি জন্মগ্রহণ দেশে এই হইয়া নারী কুক্ষণেই কি আমরা... নাই হুকুম দেখিবার কিছু স্ত্রীলোকের, পুল উপর গঙ্গার কলিকাতায় হইল নির্ম্মাণ, করিল প্রশংসা তাহার কত লকে; শোনাই আমাদের কিন্তু হইল সার, । না পারিলাম করিতে ভঞ্জন বিপদ চক্ষুকর্ণের নওদি এক যদি আমরা...... না করিতে সার্থক জন্ম দেখিয়া দৃশ্য অদ্‌ভুত জগতের পারিলাম, । সুখ অল্পই জীবনে আমাদের তবে

A radical change took place from the seventies of the 19th century. The Bengali began to travel abroad with their wives, daughters and relatives. We may mention the name of Rajkumari Banerjee, wife of Shashipada Banerjee. They also began to travel at their own risk. References may be made to the well-known episodes of Jnanadanandini Devi, Kadambini Ganguly, Nirmala Som etc. They also began to write their travel narratives. In this context we may mention the name of Krishnabhabini Das. She went to England with her husband, spent some years there. In the year 1885, came out her unique publication *England-e Bangamahila ('বঙ্গমহিলা ইংলন্ডে')*. In it she made a comparative study of Bengali women with her counterpart in England –

সাধিত উপকার সব যে দ্বারা কুমারীদের দেশে প্রভৃতি ইংল্যন্ড ইউরোপের কাজ সব সেই অনায়াসে পাইলে শিক্ষা বিধবারা দেশের আমাদের ,হয় । পারিবেন করিতে

She appealed to the members of her own sex to break the chain, come out and enjoy the sunshine. A well-known Bengali writer Prasannamayee Devi travelled in different parts of India and in the year 1891 came out her well-known work *Aryabarte Bangamahila* – In it she narrated her experience in Etwa, Agra, Mathura, Brindavan, Delhi etc. After a few years Hemlata Sarkar, daughter of Shibnath Shastri wrote her experience in Nepal. She was followed by Hariprabha Takeda narrated her experience in Japan.

The talent of Bengali women also began to flourish in various literary activities. They wrote poetry, essays, novels, dramas and also began to publish their own life sketch. The name of Rasasundari Dasi is well-known. Her autobiography *Amar Jiban* (*জীবন আমার*) was published in 1876 – the first autobiography by a Bengali woman. She was followed by Kailasbasini Devi, Nistarini Devi, Prasannamayee Devi etc. Rasasundari wrote in her autobiography –

না জানি কিছুই লেখাপড়া আমি । লেখা হস্তের নিজ আমার বইখানি এই মহাশয়েরা পাঠক ।, কর না অবহেলা নযে তোমরা, করিও ঘৃণা দেখিয়া বাহুল্য লেখা অধিক । না, । করিবা হয় সফল পরিশ্রম যাহাতে

In the beginning of the 19th century Bengali women were nowhere in the social scenario. But by the series of social reform movements particularly about the female portion, a vital change came in our society. The Bengali ladies received the blessings of education, and began to question the existing social system. They were well supported by the reformers of the then period. As a result in the last quarter of the century they were well educated, earned their livelihood, maintained their families, expressed their opinions in different issues (as for example – they supported the vernacular press act, they petitioned to Lord Ripon to pass the Ilbert bill, shed their tears in the death of Pandit Iswar Chandra Vidyasagar). As told before they also began to express their thoughts and became the part and parcel of the society. In the year 1823 Rammohan Roy wrote a pamphlet in favour of female inheritance of ancestral property. The Bengali Society did not bother about the views of Rammohan. But at the end of the century the ladies themselves asked the society why they should be deprived from their ancestral property! A well-known pamphlet was written by a Bengali lady entitled – 'Stri Dhan'. We should not forget to mention the name of Mrs. Indunibhushan Devi who published a book named 'Ain ! Ain !! Ain !!!'('আইন! আইন!! আইন!!!') (1891). In it she expressed her views vigorously in favour of the age of consent bill. Thus, we can see the reflection of the movement in the contemporary writings of Bengali women. We can observe their growing consciousness about society, about their self also. Think about the miserable condition of the Bengali women in the beginning of the 19th century and we compare it with the condition in the later part of the century, the gulf of difference is visible. They were allowed to live of their full lives. Their right to remarry, their right to education and their right to be treated as a human being were established. A long journey indeed!

Books

Bandyopadhyay, Anindita [Ed]. *Kailasbasini Devi Racanasangraha,* Bangiya Sahitya Parishad, Kolkata, 2011.

Biswas, Adris. [Ed]. *Janaika Hindoo Kulakamini – Manottoma,* Ananda Publishers, Kolkata, 2011.

Das, Krisnabhabini. Englandey Bangamahila, Banerjee Press, Calcutta, 1885.

Dasi, Kaminisundari. Usha, Title page missing, Calcutta, 1871.

Dutta, Sukumari. *Apurba Sati.* Printed by Nutan Bharat Jantra, Calcutta, 1875.

Ghosh, Baridbaran. [Ed] *Rasasundari Dasi – Amar Jiban,* NBT, New Delhi. 2011.

Janaika Hindoo Mahila – Santapini, Printed by Smith & Co., Bagbajar, Calcutta, 1876.

Roy, Raja Rammohan - *A Second Defence of the Monotheistical system of the Vaidas in reply to An Apology for the Present State of Hindoo Worship*, Printed for The Tuttabodhiney Sabha at The Tuttabodhiney Press, Calcutta, 1844.

Samanta, Dr. Basanta Kr. [Ed] *Bangamahila Racita Pratham Duti Mudrita Grantha*, Sahityalok, Kolkata, 1994.

Journals

Abalabandhab

Bangamahila

Bamabodhini

Sadharani

6

Decoding the Ideal Woman in Rituparno Ghosh's *Unishey April*

Dr. Amitayu Chakraborty

Introduction

The auteur, Rituparno Ghosh, created a niche for himself in Indian cinema with his thought-provoking, women-centric films. Many of his cinematic endeavours deal with gender dynamics that prevail in contemporary Bengali middle-class society. Written, scripted and directed by Ghosh, *Unishey April* (April Nineteenth) (1994) explores the tumultuous relationship between a celebrated dancer, Sarojini, and her daughter, Aditi/Mithu, on a nineteenth April, the day on which Sarojini's husband, Manish, died eighteen years ago. The tussle between the mother who allegedly has no time for her family because of her vocation and profession (that is dancing) and the daughter who seeks refuge in her deceased father's memory lies at the heart of the film. I shall try to study how the film addresses the issue of a woman's function in familial, domestic space in order to argue that Aditi has a longing for a "traditional" mother and this longing is predicated upon the age-old patriarchal archetypes of ideal womanhood. My aim is to unearth the filmmaker's capitulation to certain patriarchal discourses, even as he sets out to expose and critique them in the context of a woman's function in the domestic, familial space. The discussion is divided in two sections followed by concluding remarks. The first section is devoted to the explication of the problematic while the second formulates the key arguments of my critique. The discussion gains its relevance for two reasons: first, because of the dearth of critical works on Rituparno Ghosh's films in general and on *Unishey April* in particular; second, because it rereads the film in a new light by arguing that the women-centric filmmaker unwittingly bolsters gender normativity in the film.

Section One: Arriving at the Problematic

The opening scene depicting the rituals of mourning at Dr. Manish Sen's residence in Kolkata on the very next day of his demise, prepares us for the introduction of Sarojini and her plight. The distinctions between the "public" and the "domestic," and Sarojini's absence in the "domestic" or "home" are ingeniously underscored through the minor anonymous characters (supposedly, relatives of Manish) by the filmmaker. We encounter some fragments of conversations among the relatives and learn that Aditi, the eight-year-old child, was clever enough to call Bela, the loyal and caring maidservant of the Manish-Sarojini household, when Manish was struggling for survival after the heart attack (Ghosh 00:00:00-00:01:45). Two women, the senior one (Female Relative 2) appearing to be a master of household duties and the junior (Female Relative 1) behaving like an apprentice to her (their conversation is punctuated by their ease at "domestic" affairs like arranging tea for the guests at the funeral), sneer at Sarojini's absence in the ongoing funeral:

Female Relative 1:	[While wiping the washed tea cups with a cloth] Will the body of Manish be kept like this?
Female Relative 2:	[While preparing the tea tray for the guests] Wait! [With a sarcastic sneer] Let Sarojini return!
Female Relative 1:	[With a sarcastic chortle] She is in Chennai now.
Female Relative 2:	[With mild annoyance] I don't know whether she is in Chennai or Mumbai! Nothing can be done before her return. [In a matter-of-fact tone] Pass me the sugar container.
Female Relative 1:	Has she been informed about Manish's demise?
Female Relative 2:	[With sarcasm] What's the difference! We know what she feels for her husband.
Female Relative 1:	She may not have any affection or feeling for Manish; but she must be having a sense of duty toward her husband.
Female Relative 2:	[Sneering] Forget about her sense of duty. If she had any sense of duty toward her family, she would have taken care of her young daughter.
Female Relative 1:	[After a pause of recollection] Have you seen the latest edition of *Illustrated Weekly*? [With a

smile and gesture mocking Sarojini's dance] Sarojini's photo is on the cover page!

Female Relative 2: [Contemptuously] Fine! Then she should have pursued only dancing. Why on earth did she plan to have a family? (Ghosh 00:01:46-00:02:46)[1]

It is evident that Sarojini's career in dance and her absence in Kolkata—when all the relatives do the mourning—becomes an index of her sheer negligence toward *sansar* (familial and household duties) in general and Manish and Aditi in particular. On the other hand, Ghosh indicates that Sarojini is not an ordinary dancer, but a famous one who has recently appeared on the cover page of *Illustrated Weekly*. Since she has a family to look after, Sarojini's identity as a notable dancer becomes a mark of deviance for the two female relatives (who are, as it were, in pursuit of the ideal *grihini*, the lady of the house). Worth mention is the fact that at the end of the scene, Ghosh skillfully undermines the views of the two characters:

Female Relative 1: [Like an apprentice] Aunty, is it not the norm to discard everything edible from the kitchen before the death rite?

Female Relative 2: [Taking a pause to ponder upon the problem] That is for the cooked food …there's nothing wrong in having tea. (Ghosh 00:02:34-00: 02: 46)

In this way, the scene ends with the sarcastic stance of the filmmaker who seems to mock at the hollowness of the two relatives scrutinising Sarojini's demeanour. In the beginning, thus Ghosh critiques women's complicity in promotion of patriarchal discourses within the familial, domestic space: two women who deem Sarojini's dancing career to be contemptuous must have internalised the patriarchal ideological construct (the ideal woman) that promotes the archetype of domestic/homely wife/mother. Ghosh is critical of their pseudo-knowledge and their judgments over Sarojini's position in the domestic space. By showing how they unapologetically bend norms at their convenience, he subtly problematises their confident disapproval of Sarojini. This is how Ghosh seems to formulate his critique of patriarchal constructs that undermine or subjugate women of Sarojini's kind, women who seek to balance between work (artistic vocation) and family (domestic, familial duties).

Moreover, the critique is extended by the auteur as he dexterously exposes the inner contradictions in the chauvinist gender politics within the context of familial space. The scene that follows portrays another anonymous relative, a middle-aged man scrutinising the rough draft of Manish's obituary to be published in his personal column in a newspaper. His primary concern is whether the epithet "famous dancer" should be placed before Sarojini's name: he says with a sigh, "'famous dancer' doesn't look nice here!" (Ghosh 00:03:10-00:03:35). As it can be inferred, his concern is the possibility that the epithet may glorify Sarojini, and in so doing, undermine Manish. Besides, he has issues with Sarojini's natal surname; to him, Sen, her marital last name, should be used instead of her natal name, Gupta. Here, we may note that the decision to retain the natal name after marriage is apparently a prerogative of the woman concerned. However, in India, often women are influenced to shed their natal names so much so that "petty bureaucratic set-ups, especially State passport officials, pressurize women to change their names to match their husbands" (Menon 34-35). The relative's anxiety in Sarojini's nomenclature is thus political. In order to comprehend this politics of nomenclature, we may note that surnames register a colonial hangover: the British law in India demanded "caste names" to be used as "surnames" (32-33). The introduction of surnames then was a colonial interpolation and hence the assumption that women should take/incorporate their husbands' names reeks of a caste-ridden, gendered colonial hangover. It might then be said that the concern of Manish's relative about Sarojini's surname is engen-dered by the patriarchal ideology which imposes a condition on women—that they should continue to bear a colonial "legacy" in order to have a "proper" identity. Worth mention is Ghosh's ingenuity in exposing the vulnerability of the patriarchal ideology behind the relative's anxiety in Sarojini's nomenclature. On the one hand, the male relative dealing with Manish's obituary is anxious about Sarojini's putatively towering fame and name; on the other hand, he cannot resist the chance of employing Sarojini's celebrity status (that is more recognisable for her natal surname) to increase the noticeability of Manish's obituary in the newspaper—his assistant, the actual writer of the obituary, cleverly points this out: "Would it be recognisable if we use 'Sen?'" (Ghosh 00:03:10-00:03:35). Ghosh's stance is critical because the scene enables us to reread the otherwise innocuous familial space in a gender-sensitive light, thereby exposing the vulnerability of the apparently powerful patriarchal ideology.

The problematic that I shall try to address in my critique of the film is that although in the outset (more than once), the auteur exudes an awareness of the gendered domestic space, and distances his representational politics from his characters' complicity in perpetuation of patriarchal dominance, the film concludes with a naïve bolstering of patriarchal discourses. I shall argue that Aditi's reconciliation with Sarojini is predicated upon a patriarchal ideology, and that is why the film's conclusion defeats its purpose: it aspires to critique the lopsided social equation between men and women but ends up strengthening patriarchal constructs. Ironically, Ghosh's nuanced, gender-sensitive representation of women's function in the familial, domestic space visible in the first part of the film as well as in the selection of the theme, is jeopardised by the way in which Sarojini (the pivot of Ghosh's gender politics) gets venerated in Aditi's mind at the end.

Section Two: The Critique

The film unfolds the conflict between Aditi and Sarojini in terms of woman's function in the domestic space, the space from which Sarojini has allegedly been away. For Aditi, Bela/Boya, the in-house maidservant, is the "ideal mother" and the reason behind this is that Aditi perceives her as diametrically opposite of Sarojini. Aditi/Mithu's Boya stays with and looks after Mithu; whereas Sarojini has to stay away from home for her dance performances. In Sarojini, "we meet the 'bad' mother who is portrayed as unfeeling and absent from her daughter's life" (MacDonald, 13). That is why it is convenient for Aditi to think that her loving father has been wronged by Sarojini. It would have been better had Sarojini been an "ordinary" housewife instead of such a famous dancer; and by winning the prestigious Sahitya Akademi award on the death anniversary of Manish, Sarojini has done another disservice to Manish as well as Aditi. Aditi's "complete interpellation in patriarchal discourses" impels her to deem Sarojini's award-winning success as an act of violation of the codes of motherhood/ wifehood (Datta et al, 226). Anger and frustration lead the depressed Aditi to a suicide attempt which is aborted by Sarojini's dramatic return from her journey to receive the award (due to cancellation of her flight)—symbolically representing the return of the "unhomely" mother to the familial, domestic space. The climax enables the mother and daughter to get a chance to spend time together and the moment "brings about a catharsis reconciling the two estranged individuals" (227). As I shall argue, this reconciliation smacks of Ghosh's naïve bolstering of patriarchal discourses.

Aditi's first admiration for Sarojini emerges out of her knowledge that the latter used to cook after marriage and took great interest in new cooking recipes:

Aditi : What's this?

Sarojini : It's my cookbook! When I got married, I used to jot down recipes from various sources.

Aditi :	You used to cook after marriage...let me see…! (Ghosh 01:31:33- 01:31:50).

As Bela is absent and there are no ready-to-eat items in the house, the estranged mother and daughter team up to cook. Sarojini advises Aditi to follow a shortcut recipe to cook a healthy and palatable meal for the night. It can be inferred that her approach to cooking is more pragmatic than Aditi's. She used to cook for her family and friends when she was young; with the increasing number of her professional commitments she started depending upon Bela for day-to-day cooking. However, in Aditi's mind, cooking is inextricably linked to a married woman's care and love for her family. As she reckons, Sarojini's early interest in cooking waned due to her pursuit of dance. In her justification for having a career in dance, Sarojini informs Aditi that her dance has produced the necessary financial support for the family, especially for Aditi's education (01:46:40-01:48:32). When this proves of little use against Manish's towering image of the "wronged husband" of a "bad wife" in Aditi's mind, she tries to defamiliarise Manish: Aditi has to unlearn the glorified image of her loving father. Sarojini makes Aditi aware of the fragile male ego of Manish that was always susceptible to Sarojini's fame and fortune. She also informs Aditi about how she once renounced her career in dance to appease Manish; but Manish did not change.

Sarojini :	An artist cannot put up with an ordinary individual. I learnt the lesson through my life!
Aditi :	[Sneering] Everyone adjusts in marriage, mother!
Sarojini:	Who told you that I haven't? When I knew that my fame had been giving him complex, I left dance…! By that time you had come to our lives. I thought, what's the big deal in being an ordinary homemaker!
Aditi:	[With exasperation] So why didn't you continue to be a homemaker?
Sarojini:	I did! I didn't see a stage for three years! I neither practised at home nor did any stage shows. Nothing! But your father couldn't take that as well! (01:46:40-01:48:32)[2]

However, Aditi continues to grieve saying she craved for her mother's love throughout her childhood. As we see, the index of Aditi's sorrow boils down to the fact that Sarojini, unlike other mothers, neither cooked food nor baked cakes for Aditi (during her childhood) on birthdays: "Boya used to console me by saying 'Next birthday, your mother will cook for you'" (02:00:00-02:00:30). I reckon that in order to understand Aditi's conceptualisation of cooking as well as Sarojini, we can look at the intersection between gender and cooking that is underpinned by patriarchal discourses.

It can be argued that women's interest in cooking is political as the societal equation between men and women vis-à-vis cooking is thoroughly gendered. In particular, "the key features of…[the] institution [of marriage] is the sexual division of labour" (Menon, 11). Women are responsible for "the reproduction of labour power," which "goes into making people capable of working day after day" (11). Hence they have to cook, clean, rear and organise things at home. This association is naturalised through patriarchal ideology.

However, when "'women's work' is professionalised there is practically a monopoly on it by men" (12). At that time, cooking is no more a mere "domestic work"; professional men become highly paid chefs at expensive hotels and restaurants. Interestingly, this gendered division of labour can be traced back to nineteenth-century colonial Bengal where "at home cooking was considered a feminine task, [but] when [it was] translated into being a profession it became a male job" (Ray, 62). However, the distinction between the "feminine task" and "male job—" was infused with the gender discourse that while the hired man cooks for monetary gain, the married woman, the lady of the house or *grihini*, cooks out of her love and care for the family (Ray, 63; Goody, 193). Thus, cooking as a "feminine task" was prioritised over that as a "male job". Many nineteenth-century periodicals like *Bamabodhini Patrika* and *Antahpur* are testimonials of this intersection between gender and cooking, and of the ways in which cooking was reified as a virtue of the *grihini* in the domestic, familial space: it was a widespread belief that "[the] ideal modern *grihini* (mistress of the household) was one who was skilled in the new ways of cooking as well as the old," and "the real zing in a recipe came from the love and nurturing care of the *grihini*, which professional cooks were unable to provide" (Sengupta, 92-93). Concurrently, cookbooks emerged as "a new cultural artifact" which was employed by the native patriarchy (constituted by the bhadralok, the modern Bengali middle-class man and the *bhadramahila*, the female counterpart) "to advise a newly-wed woman in the culinary arts and to reassure the young wife that skills in the kitchen would ensure a happy married life" (90-91).

Prioritisation of women's cooking over men's in colonial Bengali middle-class household was integral to the larger practice of reification of women's physical labour in the same domain (Ray, 64-65). This reification was a way in which the native middle-class patriarchy tried to sanctify the "home," the imaginary, as a feminine domain which was to be insulated from the colonial onslaught: "The discourse on women's cooking enabled a happy imaginary and an escape into an imagined past, whereby the more agreeable aspects of life could be placed alongside the losses that they had suffered under colonial rule" (66). When the masculine "ground [was] surrendered to the colonial power" the feminine home became "the original site on which the hegemonic project of nationalism was launched" (Chatterjee, 147-148). The hegemonic nationalism resisted colonial bondage by creating another ideological bondage, a culturally normative identity of woman of the new nation, the image of the "new woman" (nabina) who would embody the "essential" elements of the "native culture" by being markedly different from the "Western woman" (6-9). Women themselves were instrumental in propagation of this patriarchal archetype (Bannerji, 174; Sengupta, 92).

Coming to Ghosh's treatment of cooking, it can be argued that Aditi's veneration for Sarojini is predicated upon the patriarchal archetype of ideal woman prevalent in the colonial, middle-class Bengali families. Sarojini fulfils one of the main criteria for being a loving and caring wife when she brings out her old cookery book. She has to prove to her daughter that she, like an ideal wife, once renounced her vocation as well as profession for the sake of her family in general and husband in particular. Sarojini qualifies to be a suitable mother when she seems to fulfil the criterion for an ideal wife providing food and care for her family out of love. She earns her daughter's admiration because she proves to have the "labour of love." Neither her professional identity nor her dancing skill matters; to be vindicated, she needs to be a good cook, or at least a woman who takes interest in cooking, a mother who cooks out of love. Besides, when Aditi is struck by Sarojini's interest in cooking, the latter seems to be concerned with the cookbook not out of "love" or "care," but out of necessity: Bela's absence, lack of ready-to-eat foodstuff and of time demand a shortcut recipe for sustenance (Ghosh 01:31:33-01:31:50). However, for Aditi, the fact that Sarojini prepared a cookbook to please Manish over-shadows the question of necessity.

On the other hand, Aditi never clearly admires Sarojini's dance or her dedication towards her profession. One may argue that the fact that Aditi uses the word "beautiful" as a sign of her admiration for Sarojini is indicative of the former's appreciation for the latter's vocation: "When you were going for the photo session wearing the traditional costume, I thought how beautiful my mother is!" (Ghosh 02:06:15-02:06:27). I argue that this is not a mere sign of admiration for her mother as a dancer; what she admires is a beautiful woman appearing to be a dancer. The time which Aditi talks about was before the photo session of Sarojini. At that time, in the authentic costume, Sarojini appeared to be extremely beautiful to her thereby fulfilling another important criterion for the ideal womanhood: to be beautiful. Beauty has conventionally been one of the prerequisite for being an ideal woman: "As women released themselves from the feminine mystique of domesticity, the beauty myth took over its lost ground, expanding as it waned to carry on its work of social control" (Wolf, 10). Beauty becomes a politically charged ideological construct, when it comes to women's identity: "Where modern women are growing, moving, and expressing their individuality, as the myth has it, 'beauty' is by definition inert, timeless, and generic" (17). Aditi's conceptualisation of an ideal mother here overlaps with her conceptualisation of an ideal woman. She is proud to have a beautiful woman as her mother. While Sarojini's identity as a nationally acclaimed classical dancer foregrounds her subjecthood, Aditi's veneration for her "beautiful" mother objectifies Sarojini relegating her into a world which is "inert, timeless and generic." The image of Sarojini in Aditi's mind thus undermines the former. Sarojini's dancing skill, as we know from earlier conversations between the mother and daughter, has been employed by her not only for artistic self-expression but also for financial necessity; but it is displaced by Aditi, and this displacement is attuned with the previous glossing over the necessity-factor involving Sarojini's cooking. While Sarojini takes cooking as a work necessary for sustenance, Aditi views cooking as an act of "motherly" love and affection. That is why she considers Sarojini's lack of time to cook as a sign of her waning care and love for her family. She unwittingly ignores the obvious fact that Sarojini stopped cooking because of her professional commitments. Thus, Aditi considers Sarojini's profession as a deterrent to domestic virtues. She displaces Sarojini's cooking, she dislocates Sarojini's skill in dance, but wonders at the appearance and beauty of her mother bedecked with finery. In so doing, Aditi betrays her own complicity in perpetuating the patriarchal archetype of ideal woman—esteemed because she cooks out of love and is praiseworthy for her beauty. Sarojini is only admired by Aditi as a good-looking dancer (not as a professional dancer); as a woman who took interest in cooking to appease her husband and family (not as an individual who can cook). Moreover, Ghosh never foregrounds Sarojini's dancing performances—at most, Sarojini is seen teaching classical dance to her young students at home (Ghosh 00:08:35-00:09:20). Like Aditi, the auteur seems to focus on Sarojini's appearance as a dancer, the glamour quotient of her stardom: she is seen either jejunely desiring to showcase her enlarged portrait in the living room (when Manish is detesting the same); adjusting her earrings in traditional costume before the photo session (when Aditi is crying after being jilted in love); or carefully scrutinising and tuning her make-up in her boudoir (when the depressed Aditi is receiving sleeping pills for suicide) (Ghosh 01:54:03-01:55:50, 00:43:10-00:44:20, 01:03:00-01:04:50). Sarojini the dancer is never particularly visible in the film; all we see is Sarojini the star who is initially insensitive to or ignorant of her family's wellbeing. Therefore, when Aditi praises Sarojini's beauty, she confirms to the auteur's appraisal of Sarojini. Thus, the reconciliation between Aditi and Sarojini smacks of the auteur's capitulation to gender normativity. The representational politics of Ghosh, in this way, jeopardises Sarojini's subjecthood relegating her to an inert, generic state.

Conclusion

In the first part of Section One, I have analysed two moments in *Unishey April* in which the auteur's representational politics seems to be distanced from the characters' affirmation of gender hierarchy and gendered domestic and familial space. Then I have located the problematic that although in the outset (more than once), the auteur exudes a critical awareness of gender dynamics which prevails in the domestic and familial space, the film concludes with a naïve bolstering of patriarchal ideology. In Section Two, I have argued that Aditi's conceptualisation of her mother conforms to the patriarchal archetype of "ideal woman". Although the happy reconciliation between Sarojini and Aditi comes at the right time (saving Aditi's life) and probably pacifies them for good, it is fraught with the filmmaker's compliance with gender normativity. By drawing upon nineteenth-century discourses on *grihini* and cooking prevalent in Bengali middle-class households, and considering the preponderance of Sarojini's stardom and beauty in the film, we can reckon with the ways in which Aditi's conceptualisation of Sarojini affirms the normative gender construct that the ideal woman infuses cooking with her labour of love and is praiseworthy more for her external beauty than her vocation or profession. Sarojini, the "bad mother," is apparently vindicated in Aditi's mind; but this vindication can be read as veneration evoked in Aditi's mind by the patriarchal archetype of ideal womanhood. Aditi displaces Sarojini's interest in cooking as well as the latter's skill in dance. In so doing, she unwittingly robs Sarojini of her subjecthood. More importantly, Ghosh's vision of Sarojini is akin to Aditi's conceptualisation of her mother. Failing to have the necessary critical distance from Aditi's gendered perception, the auteur undermines Sarojini's agency, her subjecthood. It is therefore ironical that Sarojini, who seems to be the pivot of Ghosh's gender politics from the outset, becomes a victim of his myopic gender-sensitivity. The film thus aspires to subvert the patriarchal discourses that gain prominence in contemporary Bengali middle-class domestic, familial space, but naïvely bolsters gender normativity.

Notes

1. The dialogues quoted from the film are translated from Bengali to English by me.
2. Ghosh punctuates Sarojini's account with flashbacks consisting of feuds between Sarojini and Manish to authenticate her narration.

References

Bannerji, Himani. "Textile Prison: Discourse on Shame (lajja) in the Attire of the Gentlewoman (*bhadramahila*) in Colonial Bengal." *The Canadian Journal of Sociology* 19.2 (1994): 169-93. JSTOR. Web. 22 Jan. 2018.

Chatterjee, Partha. *Nation and Its Fragments: Colonial and Postcolonial Histories*. New Jersey: Princeton UP, 1993. Print.

Datta, Sangeeta et al. "The World of Rituparno Ghosh: Texts, Contexts and Transgressions." *South Asian History and Culture* 6.2 (2015): 223-37. Routledge. Web. 2 Dec. 2016.

Ghosh, Rituparno, dir. "Unishey April." *Angel Digital*, 2015. Youtube. Web. 20 Dec. 2016.

Goody, Jack. *Cooking, Cuisine, and Class: A Study in Comparative Sociology.* Cambridge: Cambridge UP, 1982. Print.

Macdonald, Alison. 'Real' and 'Imagined' Women: A Feminist Reading of Rituparno Ghosh's Films." *UCL*, Dept. of Anthropology (2009): 1-22. UCL. Web. 28 Mar. 2012.

Menon, Nivedita. *Seeing Like a Feminist*. New Delhi: Zubaan & Penguin Books, 2012. Print.

Ray, Utsa. "Aestheticizing Labour: An Affective Discourse of Cooking in Colonial Bengal." *South Asian History and Culture 1.1* (2010): 60-70. Routledge. Web. 30 May 2014.

Sengupta, Jayanta. "Nation on a Platter: The Culture and Politics of Food and Cuisine in Colonial Bengal." *Modern Asian Studies*, 44(1): 81-98. JSTOR. Web. 19 Jan. 2018.

Wolf, Naomi. *The Beauty Myth: How Images of Beauty are Used Against Women.* New York: Harper Collins, 2002. Print.

7

Theatre as Forum for Women's Rights Activism in India: The Case of Tendulkar's *Silence! The Court is in Session* (1968) and Jana Natya Manch's *Aurat* (1979)

Debayan Deb Barman

I

Among the art forms, theatre has proved to be the medium of mass approach, a direct medium of interaction between the audience and the performers. Moreover, being a composite art form it has used the contribution of other art forms like music, art, song and dance, acrobatics, martial arts, mime and many more to carry across the message to the people. No doubt that it has served as a vehicle of agitation and propaganda (agit-prop), especially in the twentieth century in which the rise of ideologically loaded leftist political theatre has bestowed a political/activist function to theatre which was not available in the nineteenth century naturalistic theatre. Again, the increasing tendency of experimentation with form and space, often using 'found spaces' and non-formal spaces like parks, street-corners, fields, courtyards, garage space, studio space, market areas, trains, community blocks and many more has taken the message and content of such theatre to the people's doorsteps. It is worth recalling here what Bertolt Brecht proposes in the theatre of the scientific age:

> Once the content becomes, technically speaking, an independent component, to which text, music and setting 'adopt attitudes'; once illusion is sacrificed to free discussion, and once the spectator, instead of being enabled to have an experience, is forced as it were to cast his vote; then a change has been launched which goes far beyond formal

matters and begins for the first time to affect the theatre's social function. ("The Modern Theatre is the Epic Theatre," *Modern Theories of Drama* ? 229).

Both Artaudian experimental theatre (theatre of cruelty) and leftist political theatre following Brecht have worked towards making theatre a vehicle of political message and agitation.

II

Twentieth century has also seen a slow but sure growth in the consciousness of nation states and international bodies as well as social activists and organisations about the rights and empowerment of women. Though there is a long way to go, at least a start has been made in the direction of women's empowerment. Women's rights movements in the West and Europe, the rise of Feminisms have contributed in this area. The United Nations Organisation has come forward from time to time to facilitate and encourage nations to take steps for women's empowerment. The year 1975 was declared by the UN as the 'International Year for Women', and 1975-85 was declared as the 'UN Decade for Women. The year 2001 was declared as 'International Year of Women Empowerment'.

In case of India, legal provisions have been made from time to time for the safeguard of women's rights. After Independence, the Constitution has guaranteed equal rights to every citizen of the nation, both men and women. Many special Acts and Amendments were made from time to time to ensure women's empowerment and participation in the polity. The 73rd and 74th Amendments of the Constitution have made possible the reservation of seats for women in Gram Panchayats and Municipal bodies. Similarly, Article 15 (1) and (3); Article 15 (1); Article 15 (3);Article 39 (d); Article 51-A (e) etc. have been useful judicial interventions. Acts like the Dowry Prohibition Act 1961, The Immoral Traffic (Suppression) Act (SITA) (1956), The Protection of Women from Domestic Violence Act 2005, The Sexual Harassment of Women at Workplace (Prevention, Prohibition and Redressal) Act, 2013, The Special Marriage Act, 1954, The Marriage Laws (Amendment) Bill, 2010, The Maternity Benefit Act, 1961 (Amended in 1995), The Medical Termination of Pregnancy (MTP) Act, show a growing concern to address the practical problems and situations faced by the women.

In the field of Law, the Indian Penal Code (IPC) has evolved with newer sections since Independence to address issues related to women.

Crucially, following the 1990 National Commission for Women Act, the Government of India has set up the National Commission for Women in January 1992 to pursue all matters pertaining to women.

Though the above mentioned efforts have been taken in legislative and judicial terms, there is a long way to go for the goal of women's rights and empowerment to be fully achieved. The deeply embedded structures of gender discrimination in the patriarchal society are a social juggernaut hard to crack. The patriarchal norms that subjugate, oppress, exploit, discriminate and marginalise the women (belonging to different social strata) have to be defeated before any emancipation can happen. There is need to educate through awareness programmes not only the women but more importantly the men to neutralise the patriarchal forces. The Government at the local and national levels do conventional *'sarkari'* (Government) awareness programmes; there are the NGOs and SHGs who also work in this field. In this regard, 'theatre' can be effective as a agit-prop weapon for awareness about women's issues. Theatre, with its political intent as discussed above, can and has proved to be an effective weapon for spreading the awareness about women's rights and empowerment. It can work in tandem with NGOs and Government bodies at the local and national level by taking the information and issues relevant to women, even right up to their doorsteps, especially in the case of street theatre: the kind of theatre done by Jana Natya Manch, Samudaya, Buland Natya Manch, Nishant, (erstwhile) Theatre Union. Many women playwrights/ directors have made significant contribution to the field of modern Indian theatre, focusing on women's issues. Usha Ganguli's Rangakarmee has mounted important plays like *Rudaali*, based on the eponymous story by writer/activist Mahasweta Devi, and *Hum Mukhtara*, based on Mukhtaran Mai, a Pakistani woman who was gang raped as a result of clan rivalry. Saoli Mitra has done thought-provoking feminist readings of the epic *Mahabharata* in *Nathbati Anathbat* and *Katha Amrita Samaan*. Some other important names would include Maya Krishna Rao, Anuradha Kapur and Rati Bartholomew of erstwhile Theatre Union who did important street plays like *Om Swaha* (on dowry deaths) and *Dafa No. 180* (on the rape law). Other important women in modern Indian theatre are Deena Mehta whose *Brides are not For Burning* (1993) won the first prize in worldwide competition sponsored by BBC in 1979, Manjula Padmanabhan's *Lights Out* is a study of social attitude towards a rape victim Amal Allana staged a thought provoking presentation of the life of Nati Binodini, the famed Bengali actress of nineteenth century. The play is based on *Aamar Katha and Aamar Abhinetri Jeebon*, autobiographies of Binodini. The life of the nineteenth century courtesan

Umrao Jan Ada had been portrayed by Mohammad Hadi Ruswa in a novel in Urdu in 1905, which was adapted as *Umrao* (in 1993) by Geetanjali Shree. It was directed by Anuradha Kapur and produced by Vivadi for the stage. Tripurari Sharma's *Bahu* (Daughter-in-Law) (1979) and Polie Sengupta' re-interpreting marginalised characters/narratives in *Thus Spake Shoorpanakha, so Said Shakuni* (2001) (for an elaborate discussion of above playwrights see "Aesthetics of Indian Feminist Theatre" by Anita Singh in *Rupkatha Journal,* 1.2).

III

Now, if we come to the issue of gender as Judith Butler has explained in her study *Gender Trouble: Feminism and the Subversion of Identity* (1990) we know that gender is a social construct, moving independently from biological determinism. The patriarchal 'gaze' sees the woman/female in a particular way that is deeply embedded in the 'collective unconscious' (to use Jung's concept) of the society. All 'phallogocentric' (to use Derrida's term) literature, art and performance genres employ this male 'gaze' when it discusses/explains/defines/imagines a woman. Sometimes this works very subtly, as in the case of the Fair and Lovely advertisements. (see Dia Da Costa's essay 'Mirrors of Value?') The patriarchal society wants women to behave in a particular stereotyped way. What feminist literature, art, performance genres and feminist re-readings and deconstructions of texts do in such a scenario is to create a body of expression that subverts, challenges, and counters the dominant 'phallogocentric' narrative and exposes the male 'gaze'. This is exactly what Vijay Tendulkar is doing in his phenomenal play *Shantata! Court Chalu Ahe* (Silence the Court is in Session) and Jana Natya Manch is doing in *Aurat*. Here are two examples of theatre in post-1947 India where conscious counter-narratives are being constructed which is providing a forum for the female voice and at the same time exposing/unmasking the patriarchal attitudes.

IV

In *Shantata! Court Chalu Ahe* (Silence the Court is in Session) (1968), Tendulkar has used comic sequences which apparently seem innocent and casual until we are driven into the disturbing arena of 'theatre of cruelty'. G. P. Deshpande observes:

> With *Shantata* a new phase begins. In that play (along with *Sakharam Binder*, *Gidhade* (Vultures), *Ghashiram Kotwal*, and *Kanyadaan*), Tendulkar appeared in a destructive mood. One finds these plays powerful

but rather black, some might even say nihilistic. Their power was undeniable. But so was their nihilism. In this phase we see Tendulkar moving towards a position that treated violence and cruelty as primordial. A potential rebel has now turned into a nihilistic metaphysician (Deshpande, 19-20).

The focus is on the middle class and it's deeply embedded patriarchal structures. The intention is to take the target audience (the middle class) and expose their masks. But the play makes ample use of all the usual patriarchal narratives directed to suppress the voice of the woman, represented chiefly by Miss Leela Benare, a school teacher. The 'court' is a farcical court, a false court/mock court replete with phallogocentric discourses mouthed by the judge Kashikar, the lawyer Sukhatme and the prejudiced notions about the female in other characters like Ponkshe or Karnik. A double irony works in the character of Mrs. Kashikar, herself a victim, dominated and without a voice of her own in front of her husband. Unfortunately, though a woman, Mrs. Kashikar is very much playing by the rules of patriarchy and instead of rising in protest, collaborating in the mental harassment/psychological torture of Benare. Tendulkar's expose of middle class hypocrisy is of classic proportions in this play. However, educated and modern we may become, however independent a character like Benare may try to be, she is severely discriminated against by a society which is not ready to accept her as a single mother. Benare, who is pregnant with the child of Professor Damle, is facing trial in the mock court. Tendulkar uses play-within-a-play format, with the trial of Benare being a pass-time, a camouflage used by the other characters to victimize and psychologically torture by interrogating her personal life. But typically the arbitrator of the crime (of sexually exploiting Benare and later backing off from the responsibility of marriage), Damle is absent and outside the ambit of this 'patriarchal' trial. We know about the social evil of female infanticide in India. But Benare, pregnant with child, wants to give birth to it but the patriarchal society or any male acquaintance of hers won't take responsibility. So we see Benare trying desperately to 'fit in' the norms of the patriarchal society by wanting to marry someone so that the child gets social acceptance. And when she fails, she tries to commit suicide which this very society accuses to be tantamount to indirect infanticide. But ironically, the verdict/solution of the mock court is abortion of the child which the patriarchal society brands as a signifier of 'sin': "...no memento of your sin should remain for future generations. Therefore this court hereby sentences that you shall live. But the child in your womb shall be destroyed." (Silence! 76) As I have said, the play uses play-within-a-play structure. This stratagem by Tendulkar works brilliantly in shocking the middle class audience at any theatre hall out of its complacency when it faces the unmasking of its class on stage. They are not purged out of any emotion as Aristotelian 'mimetic' theatre would do. Instead they are left to feel guilty and the prick of conscience. Here we see theatre performing the function of "conscientisation", something Badal Sircar does with his theatre. (see Anjum Katyal, *Badal Sircar: Towards a Theatre of Conscience*).

In the play, the innocent character of Samant also unknowingly becomes an accomplice with the other members of the amateur theatre group in accusing and torturing Benare, when he enters the witness box and gives witness against Benare (though he was relaying an episode from a novel), thus legitimising the dominant patriarchal narrative. What is remarkable and prevents the play from becoming utterly bleak is Benare's soliloquy where the voice/ narrative of the woman is generated. Here the play is performing an activist role of feminist theatre.

V

Jana Natya Manch has contributed greatly in the field of especially leftist political theatre. No surprise, they have also been attached to various women's organisations and movements on whose behest they have created and mounted plays addressing different issues that plague women in India. They have however, concentrated mostly on working class women. The repertoire of women centric plays of Jana Natya Manch include plays like *Aurat* (Woman), *Police Charitram* (Police Nature), *Woh Bol Uthi* (She Spoke Up), and *Yeh Bhi Hinsa Hai* (This too is Violence).

Aurat (1979), the first play to focus on women's issues, was co-authored by Safdar Hashmi and Rakesh Saxena. In the play, the depiction is of women in various situations where they are victimised or are conditioned by the gender discrimination of the patriarchal society. It was first performed at the North Indian Women's Conference on March 25, 1979. It begins with a poem by Marzieh Ahmadi Oskooii, martyred under the Shah of Iran in 1973. As the poem ends the woman actor is raised up by the co-actors as she raises up the red flag symbolising revolution. With minimum props like the flag, or a police cap, stylised gestures, sharp pointed dialogue and casual black kurtas they create classic street theatre, performed in open air and outdoors mostly, at what we may call 'found spaces', but usually in working class areas. Being street theatre, the play works through the montage of multiple short scenes depicting lives of multiple women. The problems of economic discrimination, eve teasing, domestic violence and gender discrimination are shown through the sub-stories. What is interesting is that since its launch the play has, most often, used one single female lead (mostly Moloyasree Hashmi) playing all the female roles. At first it was a strategic decision since Moloyasree was the only female actor in the group. But over the years, it has been proved that the use of a single female lead instead of multiple ones adds an extra edge to the performance, as the similar plight of women from various age groups and socio-economic standing is better underlined. The first performance was at Rup Nagar, a middle class area of northern Delhi. It was done in an underconstruction building. Banners were hung from the brick wall and the audience, consisting mostly of women sat in a round on mattresses within which the play was acted. The character of a drunken abusive husband was played by Deepak Gulati, factory owner was played by Sripal and the multiple women characters were played by Moloyasree Hashmi. *Aurat* has been a phenomenal success not only for Jana Natya Manch but many other activist groups throughout the country over the years, both in Hindi and in several other Indian languages. It was also performed in Pakistan, Nepal and Bangladesh. Another significant thing was that it brought to the forefront the woman labourer, joining hands with the labour union which is shown to be a body that works for the safeguard of the work of this woman. However, highlighting the plight of women from different strata and situations, *Aurat* broadens its scope. As Kanika Batra has rightly pointed out: "*Aurat* primarily dramatises women's lives within the broad framework of class relations; it also succeeds in highlighting other seemingly nonclass sites of oppression, specifically the family and the state." ("*Aurat* and its Afterlife") Sudhanva Deshpande, actor-director of Jana Natya Manch in a reminiscence of Safdar Hashmi recounts how Habib Tanvir had described *Aurat* as a "poetic abstraction realistically encapsulating sharply etched out vignettes of a woman's life." ("Remembering Safdar Hashmi...") Deshpande further remarks how: "Along with plays like Jyoti Mhapsekar's *Mulgi Zhali Ho* (Marathi) and Theatre Union's *Om Swaha* (Hindi), *Aurat* gave voice to the feminist upsurge of the late 1970s and early 1980s." ("Remembering Safdar Hashmi..."). So, *Aurat* becomes an agit-prop which highlights the need for direct political action and revolution and performs the function of activist political theatre. Jana Natya Manch, through their repertoire of women centric and other street plays has been a powerful wing for feminist movements as well as proletarian issues.

In conclusion, we can say that post-Independence Indian theatre, in many instances has shown the will and determination to act as a platform for projecting the demands for women's rights and actions. In doing so theatre is not only restricted to an aesthetic role, but a political and didactic role. And it is forging alliances with women's organisations, NGOs and activists in working towards empowering women and facilitating their emancipation. In the twentieth century's growing awareness towards rights and empowerment of women for a holistic development of the human civilisation, theatre is also doing its bit.

References

Batra, Kanika. "Aurat and its Afterlife". *Feminist Visions and Queer Futures in Postcolonial Drama: Community, Kinship, and Citizenship*. London: Routledge, 2011. Print.

Brandt, George W. Ed. *Modern Theories of Drama: A Selection of Writings on Drama and Theatre 1850-1990*. Oxford: OUP, 1998. Print.

Butler, Judith. *Gender Trouble: Feminism and the Subversion of Identity*. London: Routledge, 1990. Print.

Costa, Dia Da. "Mirrors of Value? Advertising and Political Theatre in the Hegemonic Construction of Women in India." *Theatre of the Streets: The Jana Natya Manch Experience*, ed. Sudhanva Deshpande. New Delhi: Janam, 2007. Print.

Deshpande, G. P. "Remembering Tendulkar." *Economic and Political Weekly* 43.22 (May 31-June 6, 2008): 19-20. Web. 18 Feb. 2012. Deshpande Singh, Anita. "Aesthetics of Indian Feminist Theatre." *Rupkatha Journal* 1.2 (Autumn 2009): 150-170. Web 3 Feb 2017.

Deshpande, Sudhanva. "Remembering Safdar Hashmi" (03 Jan 2017): n.p. https:/ / scroll.in/magazine. Web 29 Jan 2018.

Tendulkar, Vijay. *Silence! The Court is in Session*. New Delhi: OUP, 1978. Print.

Katyal, Anjum. *Badal Sircar: Towards a Theatre of Conscience*. New Delhi: Sage, 2015. Print.

Section - III
Women's Movements

8

Claims for Equal Justice and Universalistic Hopes

Rakesh Chandra

In this short paper, I try to engage with the questions of multiculturalism and standpoint epistemology with reference to women's gendered identity and claims for equal justice and I show a few problems as they appear in such frameworks. Like many others, I often have to deal with the charge on philosophy for being overly abstract *apriori* and masculinist. I briefly try to understand and make a case for such apriorism and cultivated benign blindness to contingencies.

While I may agree that strategically a soft, polite invitation could be extended to neo-liberal cultures, yet this epistemic restraint cannot be followed too far and for too long; also we have to be wary of granting legitimacy to all life worlds too easily as they often go counter to rights of individuals.

I argue that culture identities which are sources of humiliation are often used as weapons of subversion but there may still be scope for some people to understand histories of oppression through such marks of identity bond to struggle on the platform of such identity, but they may claim to be recognised with or without these identities in their future with hope of minimal universalism. The moral choice must still be open.

"Chal buleya chal utthey jayiye jinne saare anney
Na koi saadi jaat pechane na koi saanu manne."

Susan Opin in her essay 'Is multiculturalism bad for women?' argued that majority of world cultures are patriarchal and the 'liberal' policies that protect minorities typically entrench gender hierarchies and individual rights to equality must be normatively prior to group rights to cultural determination. Opin's universalism has predictably been dubbed as privileging western liberal priorities of cultural forms. Interestingly, this 'descriptive' account is supposed to be preferable to abstract definition of autonomy usually found in liberal theory in terms of sovereignty, self-authorship and revisability. Scholars like Charles Taylor have often supported equal value of cultures (*Multiculturalism and the Politics of Recognition*; A Gutmann (ed.) Princeton Printing University Press; 1992), but how does this not become a patronising romantic ethnocentricism through what he calls an imaginative engagement with the other without a minimal universalism is not clear.

In *Strange Multiplicity* (Cambridge, Cambridge University Press, 1996), James Tully interestingly offers an account of participatory intercultural; deliberation for recognition which could include women's serialised location in culture. He adheres to three insights:

(a) that language is aspectual in Wittgensteinian sense that meaning and value vary according to forms of life,

(b) understanding is achieved in dialogue and

(c) that disputes should be regulated by flexible conventions rather than comprehensive principles (p.111).

It is interesting to note that when a more upfront list of human capabilities is put forward by Nussbaum over Amartya Sen, she is accused of combining Aristotelian idealism, political liberalism and Kantian ethics which eradicate the possibility of women making their own 'cultural choices' which to some seem harmful 'adaptive differences'. Pushed to accommodate non-liberal religions and cultural diversity, Nussbaum in *Sex and Social Justice* (1999; Oxford University Press, 1149) outlines three indicators or conditions to guide judgment on the issue:

1. Lack of false information,
2. Lack of reflections and
3. Lack of options.

It may be pointed that this would not satisfy the multiculturalists, as they would worry about what is to constitute falsity of information, how reflection is a hegemonic construction and how the idea of options is in-itself in need of clarifications that are cultural, historical and social. Are we aspirationally encouraged to such a universalism or do we accept non-dynamic ossification of incommensurable pluralities which have permissive oppression in the name of a strange liberality?

Multiculturalism apologists like those worrying about religious pluralism have a range of questions to address. The pluralistic position envisaged is a position where all considerations of truth, value and dialogue have been internalised or is there some scope for what they call fusion of horizons? When Davidson points that pluralism is true, is unsayable and if sayable is false. How do we respond? How are ontological and epistemological claims of cultures and religions to be seen? Is the perspectival view consonant with their self-perception or unacceptably revisionary?

It is perhaps wise and strategic to encourage respectful discussion among different believers but what are the implications of equal difference and how do we ensure equal value? How is moral certainty of sources to be squared with critical thought? In his often used work, *Rethinking Multiculturalism* (2000; Bosingslok Macmillan) Bhiku Parekh argues that multicultural education inspires practical, not merely theoretical familiarity with the fact of both thick and thin diversity. In an earlier paper, he had argued that, after all, the purpose of liberal education could not be to encourage future citizens to adapt an unrealistic view from nowhere, but to make available a cluster of 'mini' Archimedian standpoints from which they explore the strength and weaknesses of inherited perspectives.

William Damon in his "To not fade away; Restoring civic identity among the youngs" (2001, D. Ravitch & J.P. Vitterati (eds.) *Making Good Citizens*, New Haven, Yale University Press, pp. 122-41) argues that constructive criticism is an essential requirement for civic education but this capacity...must build on a sympathetic understanding of what is being criticised. Parekh however calls attention to the fact that education is not only concerned with making good citizens but integrated human beings.

It would perhaps be in order to consider what to make of these observations. Much of the criticism of modernity and enlightenment is to be associated with a certain cultural times and not just a set of ideas.

Descartes' *A Discourse on Method* is fairly upfront claim about doing reasoning in science. He is aware of the distance of scientific opinion from truth through the reading of history of science and his travels made him remark that all those opinions which are decidedly repugnant to ours are not on that account barbarians and savages but on the contrary, that many of these nations make an equally good if not better use of their reason than we do. He is aware of differences brought out by upbringing in different countries and our changing sense of fashion. No one's opinion can be given preference and so he chooses his own reason to conduct his life. He questions logic's contribution to something new, algebra's over abstraction and science's combination of the correct with the incorrect. He then moves to create some simple rules to cultivate his mind. Interestingly, he has a belief that all things, to the knowledge of which man is competent are mutually connected and nothing is so far removed from us as to be beyond our reach and so hidden as we cannot discover it. He chooses to reform his own opinions basing them on his own foundation stripping temporarily all accustomed opinions slowly and circumspect he advances.

This father of modern philosophy is often understood as a father in a very Freudian sense where all those who follow begin with parricide. But is he an advocate of the splendid isolated ego with no regard to cultural constructions and contingencies? Is he the champion of the objectively master male reasoner?

As we all recall the certainty of the belief in the existence of 'I' is credited to it being known with clarity and distinctness, while the validity of the principle that clarity and distinctness guarantee truth is based on the veracity of God.

Interestingly, the attempt is to get away from the contingencies of culture but it is not clear that after the 'I' is established, the cultural nature is to be discounted? Almost all beliefs about the world are restored with the belief in the veracity of God. The doubt was only methodological. What is finally obtained may well be the thickly accultured 'being' in time.

The medieval authority of church on all ethical conduct weighed heavy and we find an attempted escape in what Kant so famously said 'put all beliefs deliberately to the test of reason'. But neither Kant, nor Descartes give up on divine authority, interestingly in Descartes and Leibnitz the laws of logic and reason get their credibility from God unlike Aristotle. However, to some God in Logic may be ad hoc and arbitrary, but God in social practice is claustrophobic. On that account, Descartes can plead not guilty perhaps.

Cartesian ego as splendidly isolated is a strange construction. To accuse him of modernist discreet separate knowledge from the knower is also perhaps a devise to create a counter position. He is perhaps one of the most connectivist as is the other nationalist Spinoza. His opposition to emotion is also not clearly drawn, he would perhaps celebrate it as God's bounty. The suspicion is of uncritical opinion and the hope is for certainty. Is this mechanism and wallowing in opinion feminine/feminist seems distressing?

Liberal educators are often being questioned for their pre-conceptions on what is to be classified as harmful in educational sphere. Can we portray diversity of faith in classrooms? 1987-Mozart vs. Hawkins case involving "born again" Christian parents in Tennessee provided an interesting discussion. But Mozart and Vicki Frost, among others complained that Holt readers include positive depictions of different world views which did not privilege the literal interpretations of the Bible and which notably contained images of women who had been recognised for achievements outside the home. They argued that exposure to their children of such material including a boy making a toast for a girl isolated their constitutional right to freedom of religion. Alan Bloom, at the same time, had become popular with an attack on secular education in *The Closing of the American Mind* (?) which failed to inculcate passion for truth and encouraged soul destroying materialism.

Should multiculturalist apologetics allow for home school, faith schools what is the compromise? Even mild skepticism is often seen as a threat to strong religion commitment. Is tolerance to have limits? How to decide its reasonableness? America's first amendment is supposed to create a divided life of shared political identities and divergent ethical conviction. But this is difficult. How are we to introduce ethical diversity wither it is promoting or denigrating any one? How do we accomplish this epistemological restraint?

Monica Mookherjee in her *Women's Rights as Multicultural Claims* (Edinburgh University Press, 2009) that women worldwide campaign for change and yet the local and context-specific character of their claims appears increasingly more salient than their universal commitment to freedom and equality that historically underwrite feminism. She responds through what she calls 'a flexible theory of rights' where she uses Iris Young's account of 'gender as seriality' ("Gender as Seriality: Thinking about women as a social collective" *Signs* 19:3, pp. 713-38, 1994). Women rarely share any concrete interest. They are a self-alienated series as a collective bound together not by common experiences, but in terms of the loose relation that their actions have to material structures such as normative heterosexuality, the rule-bound body and sexual division of labour. She emphasises on meditation wherein the meaning of human values is always conveyed through citizens' diverse conceptions of good and argues for women's 'political autonomy'. Her claim is that all persons have interest in reflecting on their religious and cultural mandates, as well as in cultivating the civic virtues of reasonableness and tolerance that would enable them to participate as citizens of the wider multicultural society. So she defends a form of liberal education which recognises gender equality as well as social justice. She engages with several specifics with examples of Shah Bano, Sati, veiling in French schools and finally seems to provide a strategic answer to handle the cultural gender tension through civic reciprocity or else many would be denied even opportunity to participate in the dialogue.

Three questions could perhaps be raised here of different orders. The first is of a practical kind: how do we engage with the gender question where it is related to other more entrenched and volatile identities. It may be wise to step gently – most programmes in India to promote education call attention to Islamic conference about learning being so valuable that you may even go to China. They also use a certain reading of IQRA, IQRA, IQRA. Polis drops are also administered by Pundits and Maulvis in advertisements. This is strategy. There is also further argument: let the question come from within. This is also strategy. Personal and global experiences may be granted to demonstrate that it has worked but perhaps there are many instances where it has not and may risk a legitimation of orthodoxies.

The second is of a philosophical kind. How are ontological and epistemological beliefs related to questions of public morality? There are many who believe that our ethical and moral concerns are completely non-metaphysical, while some agree that they are contingently related to any one metaphysical set of beliefs. But how does it play out? My religious belief may make it necessary for me to save other with TRUTH and when offered a perspectival account, I may reject it as not my self-understanding. You need to recognise my self-understanding of absolute correctness of my metaphysical as well as ethical beliefs in order to respect me. I am not to be accommodated – I have the TRUTH. Peshkin's study of Baptist Academy reveals that Evangelical Christians students typically form 'Personally Crafted Patchworks' of meaning of religious beliefs. This may be true of many, Hindus, Muslims and Jews for the observer but will this be the deciding feature of their terms of reference for recognition? When in disagreement will there be non cultural/human/moral/civic constitutional considerations? Philosophers accused of reductive abstractions may plead not guilty of insensitivity. Many could claim that what they are arguing for can be viewed in a twofold way. They are well aware of the diverse ways of culture but they are privileging a minimal sense of human dignity impeopled by patriarchal heterosexual normativity. They may well agree that strategically it may be necessary to be polite to oppressive systems which incarcerate both men and women in adaptive preferences but this restraint of elignate cannot be treated as an epistemic or metaphysical restraint. The foundational philosophers will find it impossible to reconcile gender justice with much of multicultural claim, while the pragmatic may also worry about the fact, has it worked? Many other questions can be raised about essentialism?

Both religion and gender seem on the one hand to be social constructions but in very important way form part of our essences. Hindus would consider their birth in a religion, caste and sex to be part of a cosmic Karmic order. Even in a Krippkean sense, here is a case of necessity of origin being born of the parents one is born of. What role should this essentially play in the ethical domain of mutual recognition? Being woman, being dalit, being black are natural/cultural essential?

Some philosophers accused of abstraction and apriorism could argue that their aspiration is to create humanity free from the burden of both nature and culture and their emphasis on reason seemed to them to be perhaps the only way to lead. They know particularities but they hope for a minimal universalism of the Beatle's imagination and Martin Luther's dream.

The third question is perhaps metaphilosophical or perhaps not. Are the demands of multiculturalism and stand points demands to replace the hopes of a philosophical reflective universal culture with a post-philosophic culture of accommodation, overlapping, consensus of liberal and non-liberal values, conversation of postmodern bourgeoisie liberals. We stop talking about truth, reality, knowledge, right, wrong, good and virtuous to be capacious enough to accommodate multiple cultures. Curiously, those whom we generously and fashionably wish to accommodate might not be so willing to accommodate, might not be so willing to give up their notions of Truth, Good and God. The multicultural view is strangely a view from nowhere. Those involved with gender struggles may stager their pace, prioritise their issues but could they give up on the universal hopes and should they give up the philosophic apriorism altogether is not clear.

One of the very popular approaches to feminist research and inquiry has been the standpoint epistemology. Sandra Harding in her famous *The Science Question in Feminism* (1986) distinguished between feminist empiricism Feminist standpoint and feminist postmodernism. The first assumes that social trios of socialism can be corrected by rational scientific knowledge. Feminist standpoint asserts that scientific rational knowledge is produced in ways which are gendered inherently. Women's viewpoints are to be preferred as they are the 'other' and will bring more inclusively and critically coherent understanding of truth than that of the oppressor.

Feminist postmodernism accepts validity of knowledge created by certain oppressed groups but does not privilege any viewpoint being critical of any totalising.

The standpoint view argues that feminists or women have distinctive outlook because their experiences are different from others who occupy other positions in society. Alessandra Tanesini (1999, *An Introduction to Feminist Epistemologies*) happily seems to conflate all women as feminists and all feminists as women as she explains the importance of standpoint in feminism. She explains "This feminist or womanly perspective, furthermore, is not merely different from, say a masculinist perspective; it is also a privileged perspective." (p.138)

Scholars with feminist's persuasion have called attention to how gender power and knowledge are treated by philosophers and how through they may not be treated as creators of inequality they often justify and perpetuate unjust inequalities.

Knowledge is a veritable battlefield and some much celebrated superstars of the recent discourses claim that modern scientific discourse subjugated, crushed and muted traditional, native knowledge of tribes, women and the powerless. Many have criticised philosophic apriorism not just as a play of distancing to get an overview but actually a convenient way of allowing status quo in complicity. Sexist remarks of philosophers with rare exceptions of Russell and Mill are often quoted as testimony to the suspicion of essential male centeredness of philosophy. Luce Irigaray believes that nationality has been symbolised as male and excluded the feminine. Plato in some works subtly separates different natural capabilities and aptitudes. Socrates is supposed to have described philosophers as men of exemplary courage and disparaged women as weeping and waiting. Aristotle too is said to justify women's suppression as they like slaves have absence of leisure and back of authority over reasoned speech. In metaphysics of morals for Kant slaves of merchants, minors and women do not qualify as active citizens.

Interestingly, Harding and others accuse Newton and logic of formal semantics as masculine. She calls attention to the most hackneyed example "All men are rational. Socrates is a man; Socrates is rational" as an illustration.

Some argue P is male and not p is female and formal logic is created by defensive male who can only recognise negation and not difference. Scientific neutrality and objectivity are in fact misogynist. This may appear to be strange anthromorphising of logical symbols and a confounding essentialisation of women and their ways of thinking.

Feminist standpoint theory according to Tanesini finds its ancestor in the Marxian notion of the standpoint of the proletariat. According to Marx, the positions occupied in society by different classes gives them different perspectives on social reality and the standpoint of the working class is less distorted than those appeared by other perspectives and standpoints. Nancy Hartstock starting from the Marxist tenets that material conditions of person's everyday life inform the understanding of society, develops her feminist standpoint (1983). She chooses 'sexual' to gendered to remind us that there are some biological bodily content to human existence. Hilary Pose (*Love, Power and Knowledge Towards a feminist transformation of the Sciences*, Cambridge Polity Press, 1994) calls attention to women's work concerning reproduction as laborer of love where not just the hand and brain but the heart is also unified. This is her opposition to de-personalised character of traditional science.

Interestingly, while some readers have pointed out that idealist thinkers like Plato and Sankara have created two world ontologies and justified social stratification and hierarchies of caste and class in this world stand point epistemologists contest the very notion of objectivity which creates a charm between appearance and reality. Curiously, Tanesini thinks that Locke's distinction between objective features of reality which he calls primary qualities and subjective features or secondary qualities is based upon a false visual metaphor of representation. Many may contest this as a bad careless reading of Locke and certainly to conclude that his theory exposed that accurate representation can be achieved only by screening out any possible influence of the subject on the content of the representation is a mistake of Berkelian origins in reading Locke.

Tanesini like many others holds that we cannot ever step outside ourselves, we can never achieve a new from nowhere. What we can achieve instead is perspectival knowledge which is sometimes only indirectly conceded to immediate practical concerns. One may recall that Kant had attempted to identify the general features of our experience which were not part of the object but not subjective in an individual sense. There is no knowledge of thing in itself but there are objective conditions of all experience. These features of knowledge are however too general and do not include specificities of experience. What is it to be Malti, a battered housemaid racing 3 boys on the ride of a railway track predicting them and being related by others and them is not captured in this epistemology. How does she see the so called acts of kindness of her masters?

How does she deal with her licentious neighbour, who sleeps with the Havaldar and light man to ensure comfort and safety. How does she see reality? Does she have an alternate feminist womanly standpoint? Can she develop a feminist critical perspective? Traditional epistemology and metaphysical discussion often leave us cold in these areas but not necessarily the ethical theories. The Kantian principle of 'treating every person as not only a means to an end but an end in himself' as well as Aristotelian capability theory have been very well used by many feminists for their struggles and inspirational goals. Well standpoint idea help in case of epistemology? Donna Harraway (1988, "Situated knowledge: The Science Question in Feminist and Privilege of Partial Perspective", *Feminist Studies* 14 (3). 1988. 575-99) claims that situated knowledge requires that the object of knowledge be pictured as an action and agent, not as a screen on ground as resource never finally a slave to the master that closes off the dialectic in his unique agency and his authorship of objective knowledge (p. 592).

Tanesini thinks that trying to gain practical mastery over environment is not always a form of domination. She thus separates herself from over-romanticisation of a passive acquiring female existence in nature.

There is an interesting discussion often on the relation between subject and object. Object is the dominated and the oppressed. Keller (1985, *Reflections on Gender and Science*, New Haven: Yale University Press) calls for an interaction between emotional and cognitive experience and seeks a subjective experience in the form of love which enables a sense of oneness with the object.

Now, many may argue that differentiation is not necessarily domination and if we are to listen to feminist psychologist like Nancy Chadrow, they opine that an overly permeable ego boundary of women is pathological. There is no reason to blur the boundary between the self and the other to experience relatedness. In fact, many could argue that ignoring other person's independence is often the source of oppression. Patriarchy and Paternalism both infantilise women and disregard their autonomy.

Keller's idea of love may remind one of Sartre's analysis of the essential tragic nature of love it objectifies as one gives away oneself as a subject to be objectified in either case- there are no two left to be in mutual reciprocal relation. Many other critiques of objectivity based on the romantic idea of fusion have the same problem.

It may be true that objectivity has been traditionally associated with an unemotional way of reasoning which is often considered masculine.

This has been associated with the subject/ object split in the Cartesian enlightenment tradition. I am unsure of both the scholarly accuracy or the philosophical plausibility of this reading as suggestion. Some scholars suggest that objectivity in science should not be identified with 'a view from nowhere' but must be taken as an approximation arrived at through inter subjective criticism.

Now, the notion of reality as constructed does not completely cancel out the idea of objectivity. The pragmatist theory has enough philosophical heritage to demonstrate this. That there is an ethical dimension to knowledge is supposed to be forgotten by those who argue for 'a true from nowhere'. This may however not be true. It may be that the contingencies of opinions and especially the suspiciously dominant oppressive ones are being awarded by this aspirational true form nowhere. Scientists from Galileo to rationalists like Dobhalker in Pune have been killed by emotional ideological perspective lists in power.

Helen Longino H. ('Feminism and Philosophy of Science' Journal of Social Philosophy. 1990. 21. pp.150-9) argues that community of researches should try to neutralise influence of political values on the results of research: objectivity is a matter of Maximal minimisation of the subjective. Harding also speaks of objectivity as an indispensable notion of epistemology since it accounts for the necessary gap between how we want the world to be and how it is. Do all values have the same harmful effects in medieval Europe may share notes on the issue.

How do we examine scientific localism of researchers and how do we order our preference. Harding argues that objectivity is increased if we take the locations of the marginalised people as starting points of scientific inquiry. This romance requires factual as well as logical corroboration by mean spiritedness and expansiveness are not class qualities in fact the power in privilege greater the causal justification.

It is well to recognise that knowing in a social context specially knows people. But knowing other people may not necessarily require detachment but perhaps emotional attachment. So do we abandon objectively. Larraine Code (*What Can She Know? Feminist Theory and Construction of Knowledge*, Ithaca Carnell University Press. 1991.) charmingly speaks of objective constraints the minimal constraints that derive from the reality of the world and of cognitive agency constitute a residual set of objective limits on adequate responsible inquiry. Knowledge may not be purely objective but it does not follow that reality is socially constructed and there is a power in trying to discover how things are.

Knowledge as engagement and interaction is a much forward true but does it necessarily constrain universalistic paper of boundaryless communication. Many philosophers and philosophies have fairly modest self understanding of their task. Many seek abstraction to find scope for inclusive dialogue. Hegemonic discourses of cultural specifications have always and well always the problematic. Early classes of logic try to explain difference between logical relation and informal accusations about being a liar as not relevant to the argument. Women as essentially emotional prostitutes as loose women without honour are ideas rejected in logical argumentation but strangely contextualism is brought out in some thick epistemic notions Kripke, Platinga and even Putnam seemed to entertain the question it priori for whom? This vocabulary confuses historically embedded concepts.

This is not to say that the terms and concepts cannot be peopled with new meanings however if we are to be sympathetic to the multiple stand point and multicultural apologists we will have to explain how do we accommodate the exclusivist? It may also be worthwhile to examine whether false inclusivism it itself strongly revisionary recommending to all 'situations' that they are after all situations and this perhaps can be said only from a non situated point.

How do we then examine dalit and feminist voices? To say that all women voices are feminist and all dalit voices are subversive would be problematic. Do they represent stand points in epistemology is a question requiring much serious thought. Liberal feminist voices may be universalistic as may be the dalit voices seeking inclusion.

Identities are plural and one may decide to use one particular identity for her struggle or fight for many. Denial of identities is certain kind of useless blindness but identities are to be understood as categories to understand historical oppression as well as sources of forging bonds of solidarity. But aspirationally will all those who have been humiliated for certain identities, will they wish to be recognised with or without those identities cannot be predecided. Many still have universalistic hopes:

uleya chal utthey jayiye jinne saare anney
saadi jaat pechane na koi saanu manne."

9

Vanguardship of Women in Vedanta Movement – Lanjigarh, Odisha

Urmimala Das

Present days Indian Women's Movement can be categorised under three heads- the autonomous women's groups, the left, the bourgeois liberal and NGOs led activities which rejects mass politics as a means to bring about gains for women (Karat, B.: 2005)[1]. As the discussion and understanding regarding structures which impact on women's status grew within the movement, so did the realisation that the movement was fundamentally political in the broader sense. It became possible to discuss straight political issues as part of women's movements. Being "political" did necessarily get equated with being a member of any political party but it did require not taking position on what are considered political issues (Karat:2005)[2].

Annually, the lives and livelihoods of nearly ten million people across the globe are affected by forced displacement due to infrastructure projects such as dams, mines, factories and roads and emerging research shows that this number is likely to increase, rather than decrease. The last two decades have witnessed an immense surge of literature on the process forced displacement and its far-reaching social, economic and cultural impacts (cf. Thukral 1992[3]; Fernandes and Thukral 1989[4]; Cernea and McDowell 2000[5]; McDowell 1997[6],Parsuraman 1999[7]; Morse et al 1992[8]; Dreze et al 1997[9]). Despite this vast documentation, national and international debates have been highly ungendered. The project-affected communities have tended to be portrayed in a rather homogenous and undifferentiated way by researchers, activists and state actors. The massive changes in the division of labour, in negotiations within communities and households, in property rights and in access to and control over resources clearly affect men and women differently, requiring an analysis through the lens of gender. The malaise of gender-blindness is also found in policy related guidelines concerning resettlement where the settler or oustee is unproblematically assumed to be male. However, beyond the general recognition that women might suffer more than men in the course of the displacement process, there has rarely been a systematic analysis of the gendered dimensions of forced displacement processes and resettlement programmes, barring a few exceptions. Also in standard works on displacement and resettlement references to gender have a rather add-on character (e.g. Cernea, 1997 and 2000; McDowell, 1997)[10].

The Bauxite mining project is one of the world's most controversial projects, not least because of the potential displacement of tribal people. Since the 2005, Lanjigarh has been the site of tremendous resistance and the protest movement has influenced anti-mining struggles in Odisha. Communities living in south-west Odisha in eastern India – already one of the poorest areas of the country – are at threat from the expansion of an alumina refinery and plans for a new bauxite mining project. The people living next to the refinery have already suffered violations of their human rights to water and health, including a healthy environment, because of

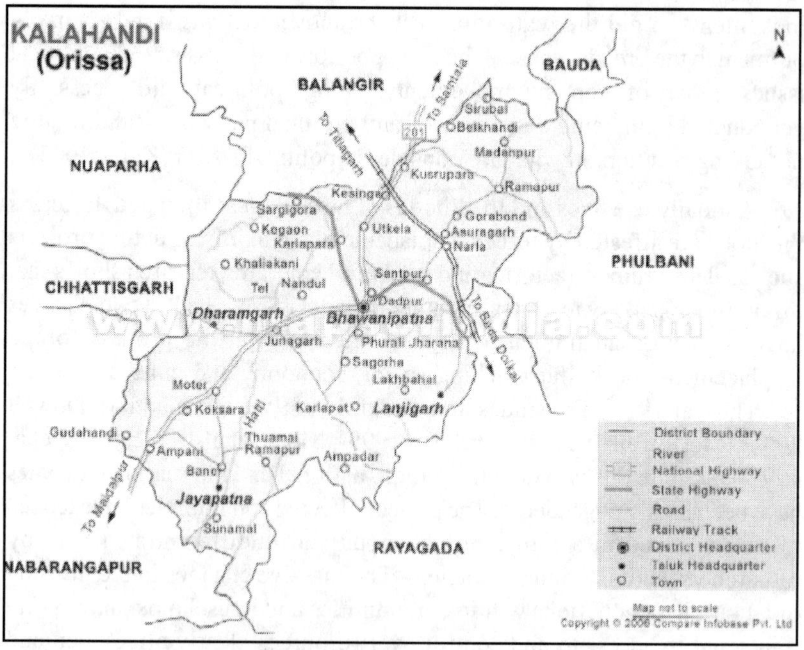

Map-1. Lanjigarh and Original Villages.

pollution and poor management of waste produced by the refinery. The mining project would be located on the traditional lands of the Dongria Kondh, an Indigenous community, which is considered endangered. They now live under the fear of losing their way of life and their sacred hills, as well as having their rights to water, food, livelihoods and cultural identity undermined.

The Bauxite mining project would cover 700 hectares of land on top of the north-western part of the Niyamgiri Hills and involve excavation of a large section of the hill to a depth of about 30 meters. The hills are home to the Dongria Kondh, an 8,000-strong Adivasi community spread over 90 villages in and around the hills. The Dongria Kondh consider the Niyamgiri hills as sacred and do not cut trees or practice cultivation on top of the hill as they worship Niyam Raja Penu, who they believe lives on top of the Niyamgiri hills. Their identity is closely tied to the Niyamgiri hills, which they believe are essential to their culture, traditions, and physical and economic survival.[11]

Movement Against Vedanta Project, Lanjigarh

The protest movement began much before the signing of a memorandum of understanding between the Government of Orissa and Sterlite Industries (India) Ltd, a subsidiary of Vedanta Resources plc, for establishing a bauxite mine on the plateau atop Niyamgiri, as well as an associated alumina refinery plant at the foot of the mountain, near the town of Lanjigarh. This was followed by an official agreement signed on the 5th of October 2004 between the Orissa Mining Corporation (OMC) and Sterlite Industries for the purpose of mining of bauxite reserves at Lanjigarh. The company plans to mine over 1 million tonnes of bauxite a year from reserves within Niyamgiri mountain. Official studies have suggested that this is likely to lead to massive deforestation on the slopes, the destruction of protected local ecosystems rich in biodiversity, and the disruption of key water sources that supply springs and streams on the surrounding. In addition to the proposed mine, Vedanta has already constructed a huge alumina refinery plant near the town of Lanjigarh, and is now digging 'ponds' to hold the toxic waste that the factory will produce. This plant and associated perimeter wall and feeder road has been the source of major conflict with local villagers, who claim that homes and farms have been bulldozed without due consultation or compensation. In response to these developments, villagers from the surrounding area have been organising in ever greater numbers to protest against the company and are gaining support locally, nationally and internationally.

As reported by a respondent, Vedanta Company came to Lanjigarh in 2002 much prior to signing of MOU. Village people were not aware about entry of Vedanta project in Lanjigarh area. They were just listening about Vedanta that it may excavate a bauxite in Niyamagiri Mountain and the project was going to start in the area of Basantapada, Kinari, Jagannathpur villages of Lanjigarh. People didn't cooporate with the company for its installation.

Company people were sent to attract simple tribal people of the area in favour of installation. At the beginning Mr. Sailendra Singh a company man came to the village of Lanjigarh area and tried to convince people about the forthcoming Vedanta project. But People didn't cooporate with the officers of the company. The company people somehow managed to convince elected representatives (Samiti sabhya and sarapancha) of these villages in support of Vedanta project.

The company with an ill intention arranged a party to allure the villagers in the area. The simple people did not understand evil intension behind it and enjoyed the feast happily. Next day the company people demarcated the spot for Vedanta project at the proposed area which were in and around their villages. People protested the sudden entry of company through demarcation. All the villages protested against this and did not allow the company people to mark demarcation in their villages. People's protest movement started from the next day where women participated in large number. The movement started from Jagannathpur, Rangapali, Narayanpur, Badapada, Kinari, Kendubadi, Basantapada, Kenduguda, Chhatrapur, Sindhibali, Bandhaguda, Belamba, Kasibadi, Lanjigarh, Kortdawar villages in the first phase.

In the meantime the company proposed to grab agricultural land and houses of the villagers in phased manner. Very shortly the company started the first pillar of refinery construction. People protested against the company and gave memorandum to RDC office and in district collector office. The state government through its police force suppressed the rebel to give protection to the company activities. In the struggle, the police had beaten and injured the head of women protesters named Jamuna Majhi (Chhatrapur), Musa Majhi (Kendupadar) as reported by the respondent. These people raised their voices against company under the leadership of Shri Bhakta Charana Das, a notable member of Indian National Congress party. In the beginning, the government did neither consult the villagers nor call the grama sabha before starting the company.

In 2003, the company intruders dragged the people of the Khortduwar, Kinari, Barabhat, and Bandhaguda villages forcefully from their houses. The men and women protested against the forceful displacement. In this struggle, villagers of Lanjigarh had given memorandum with fourteen fold demands[16] and important of those were as follows:

1. Immediately scrap the MOU signed by the Government of Odisha and Vedanta Sterlite for the latter's mining and refinery projects in Niyamgiri.
2. Immediately shut down the refinery at Lanjigarh and award the local people who have suffered due to the coming-up of the plant and its activities with adequate compensation, in terms of land, money, and all civic amenities.
3. Immediately put in place effective and measurable systems of health services in and around Niyamgiri—a constitutional duty the state has so far criminally abdicated from. This is an unconditional duty of the state, and not of any corporation in exchange of people's livelihoods and cultures.
4. Revoke all the clearances already given to Vedanta/ Sterlite for its project in Niyamgiri.
5. Stop any processes to clear the pending clearances.
6. Declare Niyamgiri a permanent 'no-mining zone'.
7. Drop all legal/criminal cases registered against people of the area for voicing their dissent.
8. Investigate cases on attacks against people by the company goons and the police.
9. Allow people of the Niyamgiri area to exercise their rights to choice, livelihoods, and lifestyles.
10. Revoke all kinds of forest diversions made so far to make way for mining in Niyamgiri violating the rights of people under PESA and the Forest Rights Act, 2006.

Company didn't listen to the demand and on the other hand, they sent the men and women to jail on false cases of theft and murder. Women who underwent imprisonment in 2003 were Gorama Harijan (Kendupadar), Mandara Harijna (Kendupadar), Mukta Dalapati (Kendupadar), Dipa Harijana (Chhatra Pur), Lataka Majhi (Chhatra Pur), Mukta Jhadia (Kendupadar). The name men were imprisonment in 2003 are as follows Paramananda Gouda (Jagannath Pur), Pramada Majhi (Jagannath Pur), Daka Majhi (Basanta Pada), Praffula Majhi (Basanta Pada), Pramada Nayak

(Basanta Pada), Narayan Nahak (Kendu Padar), Dandashi Majhi (Basanta Pada).These people were released after six month of imprisonment in the year 2004. When they came out of the jail, the company made a plan with village leaders who were supporting the project and people who came out of the jail were sent to Puri to make them free from untouchable and to make them eligible to mix with the other villagers of the area. This was a plan by company to demoralise the people regarding untouchable's myth of being imprisoned. This plan was carefully strategised to ensure their absence. The expenses for all those were borne by the company for a fifteen days Puri trip of the imprisoned men and women in 2004. In the absence of the male persons of their family, company people pursued the females and forcibly took the thumb impression and signature and encroached the land of simple tribal. When the male persons of the families came back, found that their agricultural land were taken away by the company.

Despite the corporate forces trying to destroy their struggle, Niyamgiri people's movement is alive. In 2004 on May 17th, in the 45 degree heat of summer, landless oustees organised a rail and road blockade demanding adequate compensation. They cut big trees and blocked the only incoming road to the factory, creating a long line of heavy trucks unable to enter the plant to collect Alumina. At the same time around 100 women and men sat on the railway that runs into the factory, planning to stay until their demands were met. They heard speeches from the movement's leaders on the politics of corporations and the importance of making global connections to strengthen their local struggle. They shouted slogans which recalled the 1855 killing of adivasis (tribals) led by Rendo Majhi, who revolted against British imperialism in Odisha.

On May 16, 2006, a huge meeting was held in Lanjigarh where 10,000 mostly indigenous people from the affected districts of Rayagada and Kalahandi unanimously opposed the construction of the refinery. The women's network was particularly strong. On March 1, 2007 local women gathered under the banner of the Adim Adhikar Surakshya Manch near Bijapur to voice their concerns. The meeting was witnessed by British journalist Stuart Freedman who wrote: "Frail looking tribal women take the microphone in turn and address the overwhelmingly female audience of perhaps several thousand squatting cross-legged under the midday sun. Some have walked 25 kms just to be here. The women's shrill, weak voices cause the microphone to squeal and pitch but the messages were clear". The Dongria protested against Vedanta locally, nationally and internationally. They held roadblocks, formed a human chain around the Mountain of Law and even set a Vedanta jeep alight when it was driven onto the mountain's sacred plateau. But as long as the refinery sits at the foot of their hills, they do not feel their mountain is safe and will not give up their fight.

The company was aware that the project would spark protests, but it did not apprehend its strength initially. The resistance against the project continued to intensify the movement against Vedanta in Lanjigarh. Movement was gaining support from residents of nearby urban areas and has enlisted the support of local, national and international lawyers and activists. Community representatives and campaigners supporting their case came together as Sachetan Nagarik Manch (SNM), chaired by local lawyer Sidharth Nayak. SNM and other local activists had confronted Vedanta furiously and were demanding that the company to cease its activities in Niyamgiri. Protests under the banner of Niyamgiri Suraksha Samiti, an organisation of one thousand tribal people of the area has been on to protect the forest, land and water of the area, giving the slogan, 'Vedanta Hatao' (Remove Vedanta). Another organisation known as the Green Kalahandi was also active in the area.

People's protest against the project

On 5th October 2009, more than 3000 adivasis, dalits, and others, gathered in Muniguda town at the foothills of the Niyamgiri Mountains in Odisha, blocking the highway for several hours. Amidst heavy police deployment and Vedanta's goons, rebels were thundering with slogans what they have been asserting for more than five years by now, "We will not let Niyamgiri – our lifeline and sacred mountain – be mined, come what may".

This was only one of the many expressions of the people to resist Vedanta's refinery at Lanjigarh and bauxite mining on Niyamgiri. They have been militantly resisting the destruction of their forests, the fragmentation of their community, the decimation of their culture and religious beliefs, the loss of their livelihoods. On 27 January 2009, over 10,000 men, women, and children formed a 17-kilometre-long human chain around the Niyamgiri Mountains, holding placards that said: "Niyamgiri is Dongria land! Vedanta cannot come here without our permission. We say NO!"[12]

Hundreds of tribal women and men from the Niyamgiri Mountain and Lanjigarh staged a protest against Vedanta's mining and refinery project that will ruin the sacred Niyamgiri Mountain along with its water sources, rich cultural values and religious beliefs of thousands of Dongrias and the Dalits living there for millennia. The protestors drew a line on the way where Vedanta was forcefully building the mining road, giving a strong message that the company would not be allowed beyond that line. This protest was part of the Global Campaign against Vedanta carried out all across the country and other parts of the world. The activists demanded immediate closure of the refinery and scrapping up of mining permission given to Vedanta's subsidiary Sterlite Industries India Ltd. This protest went to peak at such a time when the Vedanta Resources plc. was gearing towards its annual share holders meeting in London next week.

In 2004, the houses of the 132 families of Kinari, Khortduwar, Bandhaguda, Baraghata were demolished by the company in the first phase. In the second phase again 20 houses of Kinari, Khortduwar, Bandhaguda, Baraghata villages were demolished. In total 152 families were taken to Vedantanagari, R&R colony of Vedanta company. The Vedantanagari is

Women's Protest on Railway Track

situated within one kilometer from the company near Jagannathpur and Basanta-pada villages. There were no facilities of toilet, water and electricity in the colony at the beginning. After a year these facilities were provided in the colony on demand.

Apart from this housing colony, compensation for agricultural land was not given to half of the fully displaced people. All these families of Vedanta Nagar R&R colony had some sort of agricultural land on which they were depending for their livelihood. All of these people were promised to be given a job at least to one member per family in the company. But only seventy percentage had received some manual job like peon, coollies etc. Company did not allow them to collect minor forest products from jungle and land which is considered as common property resources of the area. They were given houses to stay in place of their own houses which were demolished by the company.

The people who have lost their agricultural land due to Vedanta Alumina Project after displacement are from the Kinari, Kothduwar, Bandha Guda, Barabhatta. 400 households were affected by the project but their houses were not demolished. Before displacement all had some short of landed property in their families in the name of male members and after displacement all have become landless. While looking to the data of homestead land position in the families of respondent before displacement; we mark all respondent had a home and homestead land in their families where as 17 percentage of male had lost their houses, 20 percentage of female lost their houses after displacement.

Number of schools were also affected due to the project. Classes were unable to be conducted due to the high sound coming from the refinery. Students found it difficult to listen in the class. Even people who are bound to stay near the refinery are facing the same situation. Most of the families who are having agricultural land still nearer face precarious situation.Since the plant has started operating, emission of toxic elements into air and water by the refinery is badly polluting the water and air. The springs and fountains that have been an integral part of the tribal have gone toxic causing skin, kidney and cardiac ailments to the tribal. Not only adult members, even small babies are suffering from bronchial asthma, lungs problems, scabies and other skin ailments caused due to the pollution of air and contamination of water. Many have died also due to various water borne diseases. People and animals are dying, the number of cases of tuberculosis has shot up due to dust and smoke from the refinery and the presence of the red mud pond.

The Polluted Water Due to the Plant

Impoverishment of Displaced Women

India's decision to reject a London miner's request to mine bauxite on tribal landmarks a major victory for human rights in the country. For too long, tribal communities have been pushed off their land in the name of development and industrialisation, their attempts to defend their lands brushed aside or brutally suppressed. The Dongria Kondh's determination to protect Niyamgiri hills from the mining heavyweight Vedanta Resources has paid off, despite the state government's complicity in the $2bn project. Like many tribal communities worldwide, the Dongria have a strong connection to their land. They have expert knowledge of local forests, plants and wildlife – families grow more than 100 crops and gather food from the forests including mangoes, mushrooms and honey. The 8,000-strong community has been campaigning against the mining project for almost more than a decade amid alleged intimidation by paramilitary police and local goons.

Police and company people united together and harassed tribal women even who were found in and around the Vedanta project area, and refinery etc. Unnecessarily police had man handled women, dragged, pushed forcibly in to Vedanta vehicles and taken to court (Bhabanipatna). Police also forcibly took one to two years old small children to jail along with their mothers. These women were not aware even why they are being taken to jail and court. The police and lawyers have been bought by the company.

There was no-one to listen to the cries of the poor. When the police had taken women in the Vedanta vehicle to jail, they within two days, that took a whole month and three days. The police and company was trying to scare and intimidate them, so that they can break their will, voice and struggle.

As the Dongria leader, Lodu Sikaka, put it: "We'll lose our self-esteem if they take away our hills and forests. Other Adivasis [India's tribal peoples] who have lost their homes are dying of desperation; they are being destroyed. Earlier they used to till their land but now they are only drinking without working. They have become a kind of beggars."[13] The proposed Vedanta mining project threatens to undermine the traditional land rights and religious beliefs of the Dongria Kondh. It also poses serious risks to their rights to water, food, work an adequate standard of living and their cultural rights.

The streams which originate from the top of the Hills are the only source of water for communities who live on top of the Hills and a major source for others who live lower down the hill (some of these villages have tube wells), in a region that receives limited rainfall through many months of the year and is often subject to drought conditions. Any negative impacts on the streams, through pollution or disruption of water re-charging capacity and drainage patterns or any other effects on the quantity and quality of water could have disastrous consequences for the communities, most of whom are completely dependent on this water in order to continue to live on the hills.

Recent Development

According to the Supreme Court-appointed CEC, the protected Niyamgiri hills constitute the "origin of Vamsadhara river and other rivulets" and there is a likelihood of "adverse effect of mining on bio-diversity and availability of water for the local people." In addition, the CEC noted that the mining project could result in soil erosion, affecting the flora and fauna in the entire region and this should be studied in-depth by reputed institutions.[14]

According to Supreme Court order of 18th April of 2014 ,Government of Odisha had selected seven villages of Rayagada and five villages of Kalahandi districts to hold Gram sabha between 18th July to 19th August where people would decide whether bauxite mining in Niyamgiri be permitted to Vedanta.

More than 400 Dongria Kondh from other villages in Niyamgiri and around 100 outsiders including International NGOs like Actionaid, Survival International, Amnesty International, local NGO representatives, and local and national media persons observed this Gram Sabha. Tribal activist Kumuti Majhi of Niyamgiri Surakhya Samity, Indu Netam from Chhattishgarh, Bidulata Huika of Odisha Adivasi Manch, Lingaraj from Farmer's Movement, Environmentalist Prafulla Samantara, Lingaraj Azad, Bhala Sadangi of Lok Sangram Manch witnessed the meeting on the hill top that said clear no to mining in Niyamgiri. The serene Niyamgiri hills, a chain of 4,500-ft high mountains, is spread across 20 km in Kalahandi and Rayagada districts and inhabited by about 2,000 Dongria Kondhs. All of them in the gram sabha meetings of village Khambesi on Aug13, Lakhapadar on Aug 8, Lamba on August 1, Ijurupa on 30 July, Phuldumer on 29 July, Batudi on July 27, Palberi on 25 July, Kunakhadu on 24 July, Tadijhola on 23 July, Kesarpadi on July 22, Serkapadi on July 18 said no to the Vedanta project with an overwhelming majority.[15]

Religion, Culture Livelihood and Common Property Resources

The forest slopes of the Niyamgiri hills and the many streams that flow through them provide the means of living for Dongria Kondh and Kutia Kondh, Scheduled Tribes that are notified by the government as 'Primitive Tribal Groups' and thus eligible for special protection.

While the Kutia Kondh inhabit at the foothills, the Dongria Kondh live in the upper reaches of the Niyamgiri hills which is their only habitat. In the polytheistic animist worldview of the Kondh, the hilltops and their associated forests are regarded as supreme deities. The highest hill peak, which is under the proposed mining lease area, is the home of their most revered god, Niyam Raja, 'the giver of law'. They worship the mountains (dongar from which the Dongria Kondh derive their name) along with the earth (dharini). These male and female principles come together to grant the Kondh prosperity, fertility and health. As Narendra Majhi, a Kutia Kondh from Similibhata village, said, 'We worship Niyam Raja and Dharini Penu that is why we don't fall ill'. Sikoka Lodo, a Dongria Kondh from Lakpadar village said, 'as long as the mountain is alive, we will not die'. Dongria Kondh art and craft reflect the importance of the mountains to their community—their triangular shapes recur in the designs painted on the walls of the village shrine as well as in the colourful shawls that they wear. All the Dongria and Kutia Kondh villagers that the Committee conversed with emphasised the connection between their culture and the forest ecology of the Niyamgiri hills. Their belief in the sacredness of the hills is rooted in a strong dependence on the natural resources that the mountains provide. Their customary practices in the area include agriculture, grazing and the collection of minor forest produce (MFP). The Kutia Kondh in Similibhata village and Kendubardi use the foothills to cultivate cereals such as mandia (ragi, finger millet), kosla (foxtail millet), kango and kedjana, pulses such as kandlo (tuvar, pigeon pea), biri (urad, black Gram), kulath (horse Gram) and jhudungo, as well as oil seeds like castor and linseed (alsi). Their cows and buffaloes spend six months grazing in the forest. They listed some of the items that they collect from the forest ,different kinds of edible tubers (bhatkand, pitakand, mundikand); mahua flowers, siali (Bauhinia) leaves and jhunu (aromatic resin from the sal tree) for sale; and bamboo and wood (for implements and fuel) for their own use. Different parts of the PML are identified by specific local names depending on the nature of the vegetation. The grassland edge area of the PML is locally known as Aonlabhata for the large number of amla (Emblicaofficinalis) trees found on the plateau which the Kondh harvest for medicinal use and for sale. With small land holdings that average 1-2 acres, the Kutia Kondh of Similibhata depend heavily on the forest for their livelihoods. Since the forest resource satisfy the bulk of their material needs, only four households out of 50 supplement their income with wage labour. The tiny community of Dongria Kondh, who live in the upland areas of the Niyamgiri hills, depend on the hills even more intensely. Their distinctive cultural identity is intrinsically linked to the Niyamgiri hills where they have crafted a diverse and intricate agro-forestry system that uses mountain slopes and streams to great advantage. Dongria Kondh cultivate patches of land cleared from the forest that are rotated to maintain soil fertility. Since their population is very small, they regard land as plentiful and leave most of it forested. Besides the crops mentioned above, the Dongria Kondh also cultivate bajra (pearl millet) and beans such as kating (lobhia, cow pea) and sem (broad bean, Lablab purpureus). However, the skill that they are renowned for is horticulture: pineapple, banana, orange, lime, mango, jackfruit, turmeric and ginger. This produce grown on forest plots fetch them a handsome income throughout the year. In addition, they collect a variety of forest produce: all the ones mentioned above as well as edible mushrooms and honey (both these items are important sources of nutrition in the Kondha diet as well as marketable commodities that fetch them a good income), edible leaves (koliari, betkaand kodikucha) and tubers, grasses for making brooms, and herbs for medicinal use. They also rear chicken, pigs, goats and buffaloes.

Special mention must be made to the livestock that the Dongria Kondh rear, especially the buffaloes that have particular cultural importance for them. Livestock is not reared for milk but for draught and meat. Buffaloes are highly valued for ritual purposes—religious and wedding-related festivities involve the sacrifice of buffaloes. Their biggest festival, Meria, is celebrated every three years in the month of Magh (January-February). During this festival, buffaloes are offered to Niyam Raja and their blood is allowed to seep into the earth. Buffalo meat is eaten fresh and dried for later use. Payments of bride-price also usually include one or two buffaloes. The maintenance of buffaloes is a challenge, because pasturage is scarce on the hill slopes where the villages are located. Hence villagers' customary rights to graze livestock in the forest is crucial for their livelihood economy. When the Committee visited the grassy plateau that forms the PML area, we found a herd of fifty buffaloes grazing. Since they were unaccompanied by any person, the village they belonged to could not be ascertained. Traces of old campfires at the edge of the plateau indicated that the area is used extensively and regularly by cattle and their herders. Given that the PML has excellent grass growth, this large number of buffaloes on the site was not surprising. In discussions with villagers in the neighbouring villages of Rengopali, Bandhaguda and Kendupardi, the Committee was repeatedly informed that their cattle graze on the PML for substantial lengths of time, ranging from four months to eight months each year, as part of their customary rights.

The Dongria Kondh from Kurli, Khambesi and Lakpadar villages to whom we spoke appeared to be substantially better off than the Kutia Kondh of Similibhata and Kendubardi villages. Their crops, animals and forest produce not only provide them with enough food for self-consumption (mandia and kosla are their staples), but also fetch them substantial returns from the market. One indication of this economic well-being is the bride-price recently paid in the Dongria Kondh village of Lakpadar. Besides a jhaula payment of Rs. 8000 to the bride's village for a community feast, the bride's family was given a maulapayment of Rs. 50,000 in cash, two buffaloes, 20 kg of rice, 10 kg of ragi, salt, chillies and two canisters of mahua liquor. Despite the scale of such outlay, no funds were borrowed from moneylenders. This self-sufficiency is a testimony to the prosperity of the upland hill economy. This entire sum was raised by the sale of agricultural and forest produce. Notably, no one in the village has ever worked for wages. The Dongria Kondh we met were proud of their economic independence and freedom from want. Over and over again, they attributed their well-being and contentment to the Niyamgiri hills and their bounty.[16]

Displacement is a process of alienation which is created by separating men and women from their source of livelihood. This is a process of fragmenting and separating living beings. Marxist feminist and Marx himself have rightly discovered the theory of alienation as a state of mind when we experience life as meaningless and self worthlessness, it is only based on illusions about ourselves and our conditions. The process of displacement from peoples perspective is unjust.

Four basic kinds of alienations in Marxian sense are created as visible in the case of workers, labourers, poor and middle class peasants. Firstly, they were alienated from the product of their labour in terms of paddy crops, fishing, beetle vine, forest products and the very source of livelihood i.e., 'dangar', 'padar' (hilly slope lands), water bodies and all other common property resources (CPR). Secondly, they are alienated from themselves because in the process of displacement and post-displacement period, work becomes unpleasant and full of drudgery; as their own fields and work as owner, share cropper's work within community is snatched away by the alliance of corporate sector and state. After being displaced they are sent to a new place where they fail to cultivate on barren lands without irrigation facilities and so on so forth. Their own skill based work usually are not available in the new settlement area.

Women are more or less nesting by nature. So when their nest is blown away by bulldozers, they feel fish out of water in comparison to men, without a house and four walls of any type mud or pucca, its different for women and girls to stay and spend a night without a roof where as men can spend many nights without roof and walls. It is not only the health insecurity; but physical psychological and sexual problem arises as women are always taken and considered as sex category and thus, they are used as commodity. In addition to unpleasant shelter-lessness, the problem of work engagement easily near their household and within household economy is not available after displacement. Whatever the work available to men and women, those source of earning field usually given very far from the settlement area; which made the women difficult to manage both ends meet. The available work of contractual labourer, agricultural labourer or contract works which used to be very much disgusting and full of drudgery. Under these circumstances naturally women feel alienated from their work itself.

Every year about ten million people across the globe are forcibly displaced due to infrastructure projects such as dams, mines and roads. The majority of displaced people are from poor and marginalised communities and among them, women are particularly vulnerable. As recent research conducted by the Institute of Development Studies on gender and forced displacement indicates, several male biases underline the design and implementation of resettlement and rehabilitation policies and programmes. For instance, compensation is usually directed to men, and women are rarely involved in decision-making and implementation processes of resettlement schemes. Thus, resettlement programmes often make worse gender inequalities among displaced people.

The path-breaking Impoverishment Risks and Reconstruction (IRR) model, developed by World Bank sociologist Michael Cernea, has been vital in showing how displacement risks, when ignored, evolve into processes of physical, social and economic exclusion, which results in a broad range of impoverishment risks. The IRR model refers to the risks encountered by sub-groups within a community (such as the landless and women) who suffer specific losses that might not be predicted by policy-makers and planners (Meheta, L: 2006)[17]. Consequently, they suffer a more severe impact. Indeed, as research among displaced women and men of the Vedanta project in Odisha shows, women largely have rights and control over resources in customary law or informal arrangements. For example, in the forest villages women earned an independent source of income from the sale of minor forest produce. But the resettlement programme neither grasped this loss nor compensated them for it. As a result, women's economic dependence on men increased upon resettlement.

The IRR model, by explicitly proposing eight risks, spells out how impoverishment occurs through displacement. More importantly, it highlights measures that need to be taken to diminish risks and reconstruct livelihoods. The model intends to redress the inequities of forced displacement and achieve resettlement based on the principle of equity. But the research findings suggest it does not go far enough in teasing out the dynamics of social differentiation among resettled populations, especially with respect to the reconstruction phase. For example, it is argued that the risk of landlessness can be eliminated through land-based relocation schemes. But the elimination of risks for one group may increase the vulnerability and risks of another group. The resettlement package in Odisha correctly widows major sons (over 18 years of age) with five acres of land. But major daughters receive nothing and married women face growing insecurity. Conflicts over land have also intensified, given the struggle for survival due to the poor quality of the land endowed and the absence of the forest and other common property resources to meet basic subsistence needs. Thus, while sons may welcome being considered beneficiaries of the compensation package, many women bear greater risk.

Protest against displacement in Odisha specifically against Vedanta project had many issues starting from the snatching of their source of livelihood, shelter, health, fodder, water and all sort of common property resources. Spell of Marxist feminist consciousness can be located among rebel women of different classes. Of course the displaced women and men were partly from the middle class category who had hardly participated or taken leadership in their movements. Purposefully lower and middle class women whose means of sustenance and subsistence were depending on their tiny household economy and common property resources, mostly they joined in the struggle. Class formation and class struggles were much conspicuous and special .Class consciousness was very much present among rebel men and women. They knew their class interest and targeted their class enemy as company people and state machinery, the struggle is still on.

References

1. Karat, B., 2005. "Three Essays Collective", *Survival and Emancipation-Notes from Indian Women's Struggles,* Gurgaon, India. p. 7.
2. Karat, B., *ibid.* p. 15.
3. Thukral, E. G. (ed). 1992. *Big Dams, Displaced People. Rivers of Sorrow. Rivers of Change.* Sage, New Delhi.
4. Fernandes, W, and Thukral, E G. (eds) 1989. *Development Displacement and Rehabilitation,* Indian Social Institute, New Delhi.
5. Cernea, M. and McDowell, C. (eds.) 2000. *Risks and Reconstruction: Experiences of Resettlers and Refugees.* The World Bank: Washington D.C.
6. McDowell, C. 1997. *Understanding Impoverishment. The Consequences of Development- Induced-Displacement.* Oxford: Berghahn.
7. Parasuraman, S. 1999. "The Development Dilemma." *Displacement in India.* Basingstoke: Macmillan in associated with ISS, the Hague.

   Morse, B. et al. 1992. Sardar Sarovar. Report of the Independent Team. Ottawa: Research Futures International.
8. Dreze, J., Samson M. and S. Singh (eds.). 1997. *The Dam and the Nation. Displacement and Resettlement in the Narmada Valley.* Delhi: Oxford University Press.
9. Cernea, M. 1997, 'The Risks and Reconstruction Model for Resettling Displaced Populations'. *World Development.* 25: 10. pp. 1569-1587.
10. Cernea, M. and McDowell, C. (eds.) 2000. *Risks and Reconstruction: Experiences of Resettlers and Refugees.* The World Bank: Washington D.C.
11. *Amnesty International,* 2010. "Don't mine us out of existence; Bauxite mine and refinery devastate lives in India", Amnesty International Publications 2010, p. 17.

12. http://landmovements.wordpress.com/, 04.11.2009. 'Wildlife SEZ Forest Mines: Struggles for Land in India', Land Movements in India, P-12.
13. 01.2014, 03.15 PM. "India's rejection of Vedanta's bauxite mine is a victory for tribal rights", Pub-Theguadian, P-1, http://www. theguardian. com/ global-development/ poverty- matters/ 2014 /jan/14/ india- rejection-vedanta- mine-victory-tribal-rights.
14. 09.2005, "Report in IA No.1324 regarding the Alumina Refinery plant being set up by M/s Vedanta Alumina Limited at Lanjigarh in Kalahandi District Orissa", Central Empowered Committee appointed by Supreme Court, pp. 1-54.
15. Patnaik, Santosh 19.08.2013. "12th gram sabha too votes against Vedanta mining" Pub-*The Hindu*, P-1, http://www.thehindu.com/news/national/12th-gram-sabha-too-votes-against-vedanta-mining/article5039304.ece.
16. August 16, 2010, Ministry of Environment and Forest, "Report of the four member committee for investigation into the proposal submitted by the Orissa mining company for bauxite mining in Niyamgiri", Published by Ministry of Environment and Forest, Government of India, New Delhi, p. 29.
17. Mehta, .Lyla (2006),Ssr (Dfid) Final Research Report, Gender, Displacement And Resistance: Drawing Lessons From The Narmada Experience, (R7578). Institute of Development Studies,University of Sussex, pp. 1-45.

Further Reading

1. Mzumdar,V., Agnihotri, I : July 1995, *Economic and Political Weekly*, pp. 1869-1888.
2. 26.07.2009, "Protests against Vedanta's mining of Niyamgiri", Pub-EPG Odisha, p. 2.
3. Niyamgiri. http://landmovements.wordpress.com/NOV4posted by jansaty-agraha.
4. Bera, S, 2013, "Niyamgiri answers", Pub-Odisha concerns, p. 2.
5. Mahapatra, B, 10.05.2010, "In the name of development: Rights and livelihood sources of tribals sacrificed for Vedanta Alumina", Pub-VOICE OF PEOPLE, VOICE OF NATION, p. 5.
6. 19.07.2013, 'Badapanda: displaced women and children imprisoned for a month by Vedanta and police', Pub-Foil Vedanta, pp. 1-5.
7. August 16, 2010, Ministry of Environment and Forest, "Report of the four member committee for investigation into the proposal submitted by the Orissa mining company for bauxite mining in Niyamgiri", Published by Ministry of Environment and Forest, Government of India, New Delhi, p. 29.

10

Mainstreaming of Women in Kolkata Police

Tumpa Mukherjee

Policing is one of the world's most masculinised occupations dominated not only by men, but also by male values. The institution of police has been heavily influenced by army corps or militia, adopting a military model for its training, uniform, promotional structure, formal work culture and informal cultural ethos. Culturally ascribed and stereotyped masculine traits such as boldness, risk-taking, aggression, competitiveness, assertiveness, commanding voice, assertion of autonomy, and authoritative expertise are regarded as quintessential attributes to be successful in this profession. The 'cult of womanhood' emphasising the role of women as wives, mothers, nurturing families, and submissiveness dominates the imagination and consciousness of women, generation after generation, as a result of gendered socialisation. The masculine attributes are antithetical to the feminine qualities women acquire due to cultural, ideological and psychological gender conditioning. But women have entered the institution of police considered to be a male bastion. The present paper traces the socio-historical growth and expansion of women in Kolkata Police. The paper discusses the problems women in police confront at their workplace. Jennifer Brown, after an indepth study of the evolution and growth of women police in the western world (the U.S.A. and the U.K.), has identified a sequence of stages through which women in the police have gone through with the ultimate goal of total integration with mainstream police culture and structure. This chapter examines such a model of gender mainstreaming in the context of Kolkata Police. The paper suggests an alternative model taking into account the social structure and cultural values of contemporary Indian society.

The below mentioned table (Table 1.0) presents the initial strength of women police in various states in India:

Table 1.0: Initial strength of women police in various states of India

State	*Year*	*Women sub-inspector*	*Women assistant sub-inspector*	*Head Constables*	*Constables*
Erstwhile State of Hyderabad	1952	1		6	12
Andhra Pradesh	1959	1		6	32
Assam	1967		2	-	13
Bihar	1952			3	27
Chandigarh	1977				10
Delhi	1948	1		2	18
Haryana	1966		1	2	25
Himachal Pradesh	1966				2
Gujarat	1948 * 1949		1		9
Jammu and Kashmir	1965	1	2	3	27
Karnataka (Mysore State)	1960*	1		18	123
Kerala (Old Travancore state)	1939	Not Available		1	12
Madhya Pradesh	1953@				
Manipur	1961	1	1	1	6
Meghalaya	1973	Not Available		2	4
Nagaland	1968	5	6		
Orissa	1961	7	7		16
Punjab	1948 1949				35
Rajasthan	1955			2	12
Tamil Nadu	1973	Not Available		1	20
West Bengal	Mid 1960				
Calcutta	1949	9	23		

Source: Statistics provided by S. K. Ghosh.

Indian Police Journal 15, 2, 1968.

Indian Police Journal 3, 1969.

Indian Police Journal 16, 2, 1969, office of D.G.P., Madhya Pradesh Bhopal.

There have been a few research on women in police in India by Amarjit Mahajan,[2] Shamim Aleem,[3] Om Raj Singh Vishnoi.[4] Most of these researches are descriptive in nature. Mangai Natarajan's cross-sectional research on women police in India especially Tamil Nadu offers a valuable alternative to the western model of integration of women in police. She has advocated the unique experiment of all-women units in Tamil Nadu which has helped in enhancing the professionalism of women officers in

Tamil Nadu.[5] Ranu Sinha's research is a comparative study of women police in India and USA.[6] But no in-depth socio-historical research on women in Kolkata Police have been conducted to the best of the knowledge of the present author. The article aims to fill up this lacuna.

For the present article methodological triangulation method has been followed. Both primary and secondary data have been collected. By using purposive sampling (a form of non-probability sampling), 200 women police personnel at the middle managerial level and subordinate ranks deployed in the Kolkata Police were interviewed with a semi-structured questionnaire from the year 2006 to 2016. They belonged to the middle echelon of the society. Around 92.5 percent are Hindus whereas Muslim and Christian comprises of 5 and 2 percent respectively. Less than 30 percent are in the age group of 41 to 50 years, around 35 percent are in the age group of 31 to 40 years. Around 44 percent of these women police personnel were graduates; 23 percent have passed higher secondary examinations; less than 12 percent have passed secondary level examination. Majority (around 81 per cent) of women police personnel are married, 12 percent are single, unmarried whereas less than 2 percent are separated / divorced. For the historical evolution of women in Kolkata Police, archival records and manuscripts available in the West Bengal State Archives, Writer's Building; and the Kolkata Police Museum, both located at Kolkata have been consulted.

The entry and expansion of women in the Kolkata Police may be divided into the following stages:

1949-1980

1980-1989

1990-2000.

2000-2017

While the years 1949-1980 represents a time period where the initial recruitment of women in Kolkata Police took place; the years 1980-1989 represents expansion at the middle and subordinate ranks; from 1990s mainstreaming of women in the Kolkata Police took place. During the decade 1990 to 2000 'formalisation' of women in Kolkata Police took place. From 2000 to the present times (2017) traces the impact of socio-political and legal changes on women in Kolkata Police.

1949-1989: Formal entry of women into the Calcutta Police[7]

In 1948, the Ministry of Relief and Rehabilitation, Government of India, New Delhi, requested the provincial government to make use of women officers to enquire about the parda-nashin ladies who desired to travel from India to Pakistan. The underlying assumption behind the recruitment of women police personnel was to prevent refugee women in distress to having to come into contact with men outside the family. In Indian society women symbolises the *'izzat'* (honour) of the community. The honour of the community is supposed to be vested in women and the task of maintenance of this honour is bestowed upon her. A woman's identity is presumed to be based on her sexuality, hence the regulation of women's sexuality and retainment of her sexual purity is the prime virtue and aim of the individual and as well as the society. The chastity of a woman is revered. It is widely believed that if a woman comes in contact with an outsider and an alien male person, it will pollute her purity and render her impur. Thus, a drive for inducting women in the Calcutta Police was launched at that time. A copy of a letter from Shri P. K. Basu, JP., deputy commissioner of police, Special Branch, to L. A. D`Costa, Esq., B. E. M., Asstt. Secy. to the Government of West Bengal, Home (Political Department) states, 'I would suggest that the Special Branch be given the service of a lady officer with the status of a Sub-Inspector to make enquiries about Parda Nashin ladies preliminary to the issue of No Objection Certificates'.[8] A letter (dated 14 June 1949) by the assistant secretary to the secretary to the Government of India, Ministry of Relief and Rehabilitation, New Delhi, states that 'with reference to your letter no 13939/48 N*I dated 6.1.49 on the above subject I am directed to say that the services of a lady Sub-Inspectress will be made available for the Special Branch from the existing staff on requisition and that no extra expenditure will be required on this account'.[9] A women's section of Calcutta Police was set up on 1st June 1949.[10] Nine women sub-inspectors and twenty-three assistant sub-inspectors were recruited for the Calcutta Police, for the first time in the year 1949, marking the formal entry of women into the Calcutta Police.[11] They received residential training at 8 Theatre Road. Mrs. Edward (the superintendent's wife) was the matron-in-charge during the training period. Married women were given a day-off on Saturday. They had to return to the barracks by Sunday evening. Except rifle training, the indoor and outdoor training for men and women police personnel remained identical.[12] On 12th June 1949, women police were out on public duty for the first time during elections.[13] The sixth company consisting of women police officers (under the command of Mr. Williams, assistant commissioner of security control) for the first time participated at the Annual Police Parade on 19 September 1949 at the Police Training School.[14] Initially, they were kept as reserve at Lalbazar, the Calcutta Police Headquarters. To control refugee demonstrations in the streets of Kolkata or any other law-and-order problems where women agitators were involved, women police were assigned duty.[15] They mostly performed non-field administrative and clerical duties. The sphere of work remained restricted to women and children only. Only when required women police were used for frisking women offenders. The official rate of crime committed by women as well as crime committed against women was negligible. As a result, no effort was made by the policy planners to recruit women police in large numbers. Only when required, they were taken to the police station where they had to record the statement of women victims. But on a regular basis they were never posted at the police stations. Meena Chowdhury (name changed) one of the sub-inspectors recruited in 1949 reminisces, 'I worked in the criminal record section recording the history of criminals, in traffic department plotting traffic incidents, but I never got an opportunity to work in police stations'.

Inside the Kolkata Police Museum, there is a photograph of the then Chief Minister Shri P.C. Sen, receiving salute from the women police contingent in the early sixties. The women police contingent was wearing sari.[16] Their uniform was the sari symbolising the caring role performed by them. At that time women police personnel were stationed at the police headquarters (in Lalbazar). In the late 1940s or even in the 1950s, men police personnel were used for searching houses.[17]

In 1960s, for the first time, a few women sub-inspectors were promoted to the rank of inspector, but were to remain posted at the headquarters only.[18] As inspectors, women officers received postings to the crime record section of the detective department and press and law section of the Calcutta Police. During the turbulent times of the Naxal movement in Kolkata, women police personnel mostly performed non-field desk duties. During the Naxal movement severe political atrocities were inflicted upon the workers of the movement. A large number of women were put behind bars. Police atrocities on those in jail began to cross all limits.[19] During the Naxalite movement the methods of torture varied. Naxalite men were forcibly stripped and then beaten, being burnt with cigarettes in their private parts, passing electric shock through their reproductive organs and pushing iron rod through anus. Women seem to be more vulnerable as their bodies were being continuously marked with sexually coded inscriptions of violence.[20] However, no women police was deployed to deal with women involved with the Naxal movement.[21] One possible reason may be that women police were few in number. Perhaps the police administration then had doubts whether women could perform coercive tasks, as women police personnel till then performed only protective roles. In 1975, a few women sub-inspectors and assistant sub-inspectors were recruited. But they never received postings at the police stations.

Mainstreaming of women in the Kolkata Police[22]

(a) 1990-2000: 'Formalisation' of women in police

Till the late 1970s / early 1980s, it was men police who would perform the normal police duties of interrogation, investigation, making arrests and working in the police stations. Women had a token presence in the Calcutta Police till the mid-1980s. The concept of utilising women officers in normal police work and treating them at par with men had not developed till then. The new women's movement[23] in late 1970s and early 1980s and human rights activities helped to create awareness in society. The trend started changing from the late 1980s / early 1990s. New legal provisions were introduced (such as the Criminal Law Amendment of 1983) and it became mandatory to recruit and deploy women police when arrest orders were issued for women accused or offenders.

This decade witnessed formalisation and systematic entry of women into the Calcutta Police. The year 1982 was a landmark year for women in the Calcutta Police. Kanika Banerjee, a sub-inspector of police, special branch, received the police medal for meritorious service along with few male officers on the occasion of Republic Day.[24] In April 1982, for the first time one of the five posts of inspector of police was upgraded to the post of assistant commissioner of police in the women police wing of Calcutta Police.[25] Mira Sarkar became the first assistant commissioner of police in the women police wing of the Calcutta Police.[26] On 1 March 1986, the temporary posts of sub-inspector were converted into permanent ones.[27] In September 1986, fifty permanent posts of women police constables were sanctioned and for the first time in the year 1986, women constables were recruited into the Calcutta Police.[28] In order to control the increasing rate of crime committed against women, the state government on 2 December 1987 considered the question of setting up for each Police Division in Calcutta, an Advisory Committee for assisting in the investigation and prevention of crime against women. The function of the committee was to periodically assess the state of crime against women in the area, to find out the progress of investigation of major cases relating to women by the police and to suggest measures to the local authorities for prevention of crime against women in the light of the particular needs of the area.[29] In the year 1988, the detective department of the Calcutta Police launched the women's grievance cell, which deals with cases related to atrocities committed upon women within the jurisdiction of the Calcutta Police. The work of the officer-in-charge of the women's grievance cell ranges from the investigation of cases (of violence against women) to counselling.

For the first time, a woman IPS officer, Mamta Anurag was posted as the deputy commissioner II (special branch) in the Calcutta Police on 8 March 1990.[30] Henceforth, women IPS officers have been posted in the Kolkata Police. From 21 August 1990, a formal uniform of trousers and shirt was introduced for women in the Calcutta Police.[31] The order by the commissioner of police states: women police personnel, deployed on law and order and other outdoor duties shall perform the duties in working uniform comprising of white slacks, white bush shirts/white shirts, belt, black shoes and helmet. They will also carry half lathi. The Assistant Commissioner, Women Police, will however, wear khaki uniform, brown belt and brown shoes.[32]

For a brief period in the early 1990s, women police personnel were assigned duty of controlling traffic in the streets of Kolkata. But some women complained that they were harassed by the passerby. As a result, this practice of deploying women for traffic duty was stopped.

(b) 2000-2017 : Socio-Legal changes and steps adopted for the increase in recruitment of women in the Kolkata Police

In present times, the capabilities of women police personnel are being 'tested' by the police department by assigning duties where women had not previously received postings. This phase may be regarded as the 'experimental phase'. They are being assigned field postings and are posted at police stations. In 2001, Deboshree Chatterjee became the first woman in the Calcutta Police to be appointed the additional officer-in-charge of the Hare Street police station. In 2010, she became the first woman to be posted as the officer-in-charge of the North Port police station.[33] Damayanti Sen, IPS, became the first woman IPS officer to receive field postings as the deputy commissioner of north and northern suburban division and central division in Kolkata Police. She became the first woman in the history of the Kolkata Police to be appointed deputy commissioner of the detective department of the Kolkata Police. For a considerable period of time she served as joint commissioner (crime) of the Kolkata Police.[34]

In the period 2007-16, numbers of incidents have taken place in Kolkata, as well as in different places of India, which have brought the workings of the police force under intense public scrutiny. In the year 2007, Rizwanur

Rehman, a young man belonging to a middle-class Muslim family in Kolkata fell in love with Priyanka Todi, daughter of a rich, influential Hindu businessman. They got legally married under the Special Marriage Act on 18th August 2007 and decided to lead a conjugal life from 31st August 2007. However, due to differences in religion and socio-economic status between the two families the bride's family refused to accept this relationship and the marriage. The bride's family utilised their police connection at the Lalbazar, KPHQ, to harass and separate the couple. In India, Supreme Court guidelines clearly states that government officials should protect and safeguard couples who have inter-religious marriage. But unfortunately the law-enforcement officials deliberately took the side of the rich businessman. They flouted the apex court guidelines and went beyond their jurisdiction to threaten, harass, mentally torture and separate the couple. Priyanka was informed of her father's sickness and was forced to separate on 8th September 2007 in the presence of police. According to media reports, her family took her to Tirupati in South India. On 21st September 2007, Rizwanur Rehman's dead body was found along the rail track near the Patipukur area of South Kolkata. Prasun Mukherjee, the then commissioner of police, Kolkata Police, at a press conference defined this act as a suicide even before the post-mortem report came out. This brazen remark of a senior police officer while justifying the action of his force, showed that the police had favoured an influential industrialists.[35]

On 8th June 2012, a homemaker was raped in a shuttle car, she boarded from the Exide crossing in south Kolkata. The driver shifted to the back seat, exploited her unfamiliarity with the city roads and for almost three-and-a half-hours raped her in a vehicle, which roamed freely without facing a police check at any point.[36] In April 2012, a twenty-seven year old victim, had gone to the Kalighat police station to lodge a complaint against her husband and in-laws. But she was turned away repeatedly. The police personnel refused to acknowledge that she was in trouble. The sub-inspector, R.N. Guha, asked her several times to 'patch up' with her in-laws. Instead of registering an F.I.R., a general diary was registered. The additional officer-in-charge Kalyan Datta, allegedly mocked her with comments of a sexual nature during subsequent visits to the police station.[37] In February 2012, a thirty-seven year old Anglo-Indian woman, was raped inside a moving car while she was returning home from a pub near the Park Street. But when she went to register complaint at the Park Street police station the police officer asked the victim awkward questions that 'hurt her modesty'. The local police station delayed medical / forensic examination. A male officer accompanied the victim for the medical tests and collected the medical reports two days later. They spent more time looking for inconsistencies in the victim's complaint than concentrating on the probe.[38]

On 31 October 2012, Aminul Islam had taken a sixteen year old rape victim to Karaya Police Station to lodge a complaint against Sahazada Baux. Sub-inspector Vinod Kumar and Nasim Khan started threatening them and even called up Sahazada to keep him 'updated'. Till few years ago, Sahazada was a motor mechanic, but currently he owns fifteen apartments in Kolkata. He is supposed to be one of the key figures in the illegal construction business in Karaya Police Station area in the heart of south Kolkata. According to police sources, the three accused officers were part of his network unleashing terror in that area. Sahazada had allegedly raped the teen aged girl at Boat Club after luring her on a false pretext. After that he terrorised her with threats of an acid attack, and continued to rape the girl at home, in absence of his wife. He also threatened to kill everyone in her family if she dared open her mouth. But when the girl felt ill, she confided in her grandmother, who turned to Aminul since everyone in the locality knew him to be an upright and helpful person. Aminul advised her to file an first information report (henceforth F.I.R.) and promised to accompany her to the police station. According to the victim girl, the police registered the case with much reluctance on 31 October 2012, only because Aminul insisted. However, the same night, Karaya police station accepted a complaint of theft from Sahazada's wife Nilofer Begum and promptly started a case under Section 397 IPC against Aminul. This became an instrument for the three policemen to harass Aminul. The case against Aminul dramatically changed into robbery (384 IPC) after Nilofer changed her version on 3rd November 2012. She claimed Aminul and his associates had broken into their home in Palm Avenue and robbed her jewellery. Meanwhile, Sahazada and his associates started putting immense pressure on Aminul and the rape victim's family to withdraw the case. According to the victim's family Sahazada even attacked them several times. Aminul repeatedly went to the police station demanding the arrest of Sahazada. Every time he was told that Sahazada was 'absconding'. Finally, on 3rd December 2012, Aminul set himself ablaze out of sheer frustration, hoping his death will draw the attention of the higher-ups in the Kolkata Police. He left a suicide note blaming Sahazada and three policemen for his death. On 4th December 2012, Sahazada was held for rape. After the death of Aminul, the victim's mother filed a complaint that her daughter was sexually abused by Sahazada for nearly a decade.[39]

A French student was chased and molested in a posh south Kolkata area. A Korean student was molested in a bus. A techie had to jump off a running train to escape molestation. A couple accused police officers posted at the Karaya police station of inaction after a gang molested a woman. One person was arrested but the three others returned to torment the couple on New Year's Eve. They molested her again and threatened to rape her unless she withdrew the FIR. When the couple went to Karaya police station, the officers allegedly said they were too busy with New Year's Eve security. However, only after Lalbazar HQ intervened that the FIR has been registered.[40] These incidents have once again highlighted the inherent male chauvinism of the police force. These incidents created a public furor and reinforced the significance of women police, because it was supposedly perceived that women police personnel would sensitively deal with women, whether as an accused or as a victim. The insensitive attitude of a few male police officers towards women victim also necessitated the deployment of women police for field and other related policing duties.

On 16th December 2012, a paramedical student accompanied by her male friend was brutally gang raped in a moving bus in Delhi. The incident caused a huge public furore in India. The Government of India in a bid to control this unprecedented anger among people appointed a committee headed by late Justice J.S.Verma to review the existing laws on offence against women and drafted a blueprint on safety and security of women. The Criminal Law (Amendment) Act, 2013 was enacted. Acid attack, stalking etc were included within the purview of punishable offence under Indian Penal Code. The new legal provisions especially in case of sexual offences, trafficking of women and children has made it mandatory to record the statement of women victims and abused by a women police officer. All these socio-legal changes necessitated increase in the recruitment of women in police.

After TMC government came to power in the state in 2011, one post of deputy commissioner (women police) has been created in Kolkata Police. Smt. Parbati Pal was posted as the first deputy commissioner (women police) in Kolkata Police. She served in that post from 20th November 2012 to 31st May 2014. On 6th August 2014, Smt. Deboshree Chatterjee became the second woman to be promoted as the deputy commissioner (women police).[41] In recent times, there has been an increase in the recruitment of women in the Kolkata Police.

Table 1.1: Total staff strength of Kolkata Police in 2008

Rank	*Total Police Force*	*Women*	*Percentage of Women Police to Men*
Commissioner of Police	1	NIL	NIL
Special Commissioner of Police	1	NIL	NIL
Additional Commissioner of Police	3	NIL	NIL
Special Additional Commissioner of Police	4	NIL	NIL
Joint Commissioner of Police	1	NIL	NIL
Deputy Commissioner of police (Head Quarter)	1	NIL	NIL
Deputy Commissioner	26	1	3.84
Assistant Commissioner	105	1	.95
Inspector	489	12	2.45
Sub-inspector	1747	92	5.26
Sergeant	954	NIL	NIL
Assistant Sub-Inspector	4030	42	1.04
Constable	18,172	288	1.58
Total	25,534	436	1.7

Source: Office of the Deputy Commissioner of Police, Head Quarter, Kolkata Police, 2008.

In the Kolkata Police, women police comprise only 1.7 percent of the force in 2008. Less than 3 percent women were inspectors whereas 5.26 percent women were sub-inspectors. Only 1.58 percent women were constables.[42]

Table 1.2 : Total staff strength of senior officers in Kolkata Police as on 26.03.2016 and 26.03.2017

Rank	*26th March 2016*		*26th May 2017*	
	Number of Men	*Number of Women*	*Number of Men*	*Number of Women*
Commissioner of Police	1	Nil	1	Nil
Special Commissioner of Police	1	Nil	1	Nil
Additional Commissioner of Police	3	Nil	4	Nil
Special Additional & Joint Commissioner of Police	5	Nil	2	Nil
Joint Commissioner of Police	4	Nil	6	Nil
Deputy Commissioner of Police	20	2 (10 %)	21	3 (14.2%)

Source: Calculated from the Kolkata Police website- www.kolkatapolice.gov.in/ Show Contact.aspx. last accessed 27th March 2017.

According to Table 1.2, there are no women officers in senior ranks of special commissioner, additional commissioner, joint commissioner in Kolkata Police. From the above table it can be concluded there are no women officers in decision making level. Less than 15 percent women police are in the rank of deputy commissioner deployed for field work as on 26th May 2017.

Table 1.3: Sanctioned, present and vacancy of women police in Kolkata Police as on 01.03.2014

Sl. No.	*Rank*	*Sanctioned Strength*	*Present Strength*	*Vacancy*
1.	Deputy Commissioner of Police (Women)	01	01	-
2.	Assistant Commissioner of Police (Women)	4	4	-
3.	Inspectress of Police	18	18	-
4.	Sub-Inspectress	143	109	34
5.	Assistant Sub-Inspectress	131	131	-
6.	Constables	910	411	499
	Total	1207	674	533

Source: Office of the Deputy Commissioner of Police (Women), Kolkata Police.

The total sanctioned strength of Kolkata Police force is 34,463 including that of 1212 women police as on 1st December 2015. The percentage of women in Kolkata Police is 3.51 percent. The total sanctioned strength of women police in different police station is 355. An average of 5 percent (approximately) women police is posted in each police station under Kolkata Police.[43] By and large, their work involves dealing mostly with women criminals and victims as well as women political agitators. Kolkata Police faces shortage of women police personnel. According to Table 1.3 a staggering 533 vacancies are available for women police personnel in Kolkata Police. With less than 5 percent of the total police strength of Kolkata Police constituting of women, it is claimed that the absence of adequate women personnel on several occasions jeopardised operations on the street.

To deal with the increasing law-and-order problem, women have been deployed in the Rapid Action Force (RAF) unit of the Kolkata Police.[44] There is no sanctioned post for women in Kolkata Armed Police. The sanctioned strength of women police in Special Task Force and Rapid Action Force is 5 i.e. 2.5 percent (approximately) and 30 i.e. 10 percent (approximately) respectively.[45] Women personnel have been deployed at the Rapid City Patrol (henceforth RCP) which is stationed at night to respond to any woman related crimes. They are seen patrolling the city on different locations throughout the day and also at night. The RCP works in two shifts. At night, there is an additional constable while during the day there is one sub-inspector and one constable along with a male driver.[46] However, how far this RCP is effective in curbing crime especially crime against women has not yet come to light. Though women personnel are kept on standby at police stations, the organisation is seriously thinking of inducting few women police personnel on police kiosks to help out women in distress.[47] The Kolkata Police has revived a proposal to raise their first all-woman battalion. The proposed battalion will be part of the Kolkata Armed Police.[48] But at present (March, 2017) no woman battalion is present in Kolkata Police. No women police in subordinate ranks are posted in armed police. The older generation of women police personnel, by and large, started their career with less educational qualifications, but acquired experience after working in Kolkata Police for years. A considerable section of such older generation of women police personnel believe that women in police should be deployed keeping in mind their biological differences from men and their priority towards their domestic commitments. Because of larger societal gendered roles along with the prevalence of patriarchal institutions of marriage and family, these women police personnel are doing a job rather than pursuing a career. 'Domestication' of women gets extended at their workplace. Patriarchy, gender and subordinate rank structure intersects denying such women agency at the workplace. The younger generation of women is educated and has received better professional training. A section of this young generation of women police officers at the middle managerial level, in the age group of 25 to 30 years, mostly unmarried, mostly graduates are ready to accept challenges and do not expect any kind of concessions or favours from their male colleagues. Feminists have debated on sameness verses difference. The concept of 'sameness' is influenced by Liberal Feminists, whereas Cultural and Third World Feminists essentialises the 'difference'. It may be pointed out that gender equality in police implies optimum utilisation of the skills and potentialities of the officers. It can be concluded that a trend towards equalising the nature of work / skills such as investigation and law and order duties; minimum eight hours work for both men and women officers is noticed in this phase. The training of women officers is also at par with the male officers in the Kolkata Police during this phase.

While interviewing women police personnel in the Public Relation Bureau (henceforth PRB) section of the Kolkata Police, it was found that they mostly perform law and order or bandobust duty (in police parlance) or are engaged in the clerical work of the police organisation. For law-and-order duties it is mandatory to wear the police uniform. Inside the PRB (when they are not deployed for the bandobust duty), at times women police personnel remain in civil uniform. The hierarchy between women sub-inspectors and inspectors is not very distinct. Women sub-inspectors address senior women inspectors as 'didi' and not 'madam' or by rank (as followed in the police organisation). In few instances, women sub-inspectors do not formally'salute' the officer-in-charge, PRB (a woman inspector) while entering her room. It is a convention in the police force to salute senior officials. Thus, it can be said that an informal culture prevails among women police personnel within the formal culture of the police organisation in the Kolkata Police. They spend most of their time talking with their colleagues and discussing mundane activities of their household at the PRB unit. The level of awareness of women police in subordinate ranks (such as assistant sub-inspectors and constables) related to career opportunities available in the police (such as applying for United Nations assignments and other training related issues) is very limited. In general women constables are as neglected as their male counterparts. The infrastructural facilities available at workplace, transport facilities, exposure to in-service training for both male and female constables is minimal. The social distance takes the form of physical segregation. A physical segregation exists between constables and senior women officers of the rank of sub-inspector and assistant sub-inspector. In 2008, this physical segregation got manifested in the allotment of a separate small room for constables near the staircase at the ground floor of the main building, at Lalbazar. The room was very small, congested and devoid of light. The interaction pattern was also different. The senior women officers address women constables by name or as 'chhottomeye' (here 'chhotto' symbolises a lowest rank within the police hierarchy). The condition of women police personnel at the public relation bureau inside Lalbazar is appalling. Earlier women police personnel of the rank of sub-inspector and assistant sub-inspector would sit in a large room located at the ground floor of the main building. But that room has been converted into a cyber laboratory. Now (July, 2014) the public relation bureau section has been shifted to an adjacent building. At the entrance of the public relation bureau section there is a male urinal. It is extremely embarrassing for a woman to enter from that path. In a room, without proper ventilation, women police of all ranks ranging from constable to sub-inspector, home guard, civic volunteers, under the joint commissioner of police (headquarter) sit together. Though the room has ceiling fans but the air does not percolate proportionally. Since it is located near the male urinal, there is a perennial bad smell. Women sub-inspectors, assistant sub-inspectors, sit on chairs, whereas constables mostly sit on benches in demarcated spaces inside the room. Old files have been dumped up inside the room. Adjacent to this room, there is a congested rectangular shaped room where home guards and civic volunteers (known as green police) sit on benches. A wooden partition separates officer-in-charge, public relation bureau section from the rest of the subordinate officers. One of the women police constables informed the present author that they have to bring drinking water in bottles from shops outside the Lalbazar, official headquarter of Kolkata Police. Women police personnel are required to perform night duties, hence have to stay back at night at the public relation bureau unit, however there are no rest rooms or changing rooms inside public relation bureau.[49] The assistant commissioner (women police) however sits in a separate room in a separate building at Lalbazar. The facilities available for male and female officers are far improved than their subordinate ranks.

A brief study of the evolution of women in the Kolkata Police reveals not only have they suffered discrimination in postings but also their progress is very slow as compared to other states in India. In states such as Tamil Nadu, women entered the police force in the year 1973, three decades later as compared to the Kolkata Police. Yet, they have progressed at a steady pace and has 12.42 percent women in police, the highest among the states in India.[50] The state of Tamil Nadu has the highest number of the AWPUs. An All Women Battalion and All Women Commando have also been established in Tamil Nadu. Initially, they dealt with women and children, but slowly they were integrated into more general police duties such as traffic operations. Currently, depending on their skills, women are deployed in four different sections-general police stations, AWPUs, woman's battalion and as woman commandos.[51] The improvement of the status of women in the police force in Tamil Nadu is due to its policy-planners, primarily to its late chief minister, Ms. Jayalalitha, as well as a few individual male and female officers who took the initiative in upgrading women police personnel through rigorous training. But there has been political apathy in policy-making regarding the recruitment and improvement of women in Kolkata Police as compared to other states in India especially Tamil Nadu.

Future plans of women in Kolkata Police

In recent times, there has been an increase in the rate of crime committed against women in West Bengal. The crime rate under crimes against women was reported as 56.3 in 2014. West Bengal has a crime rate of 85.4 percent. West Bengal accounting for nearly 7.5 percent of the country's women population, has accounted for 11.3 percent of total cases of crimes.[52] In a bid to curb the rise in crime against women, the present government in West Bengal has decided to take a few innovative steps, which include increasing the recruitment of women in the police force. In the Kolkata Police, the government intends to recruit 2,600 women or 10 percent of the existing strength of the Kolkata Police.[53] It is hoped that political patronage will help improve the position of women police in West Bengal, as has happened in Tamil Nadu.

Jennifer Brown suggest from her recent comparison of women police in European countries that women officers are gradually becoming more integrated into the police force by passing through six distinct stages which she characterises as 'entry', 'separated restricted development', 'integration', 'take-off', 'reforms', and 'tip-over'. The sequence of steps of integration of women in police as emphasised by Brown in her western model of integration is not applicable in the case of the Kolkata Police. In Kolkata Police, women have made an 'entry' into the police force. Women were assigned a 'separated restricted sphere of work'. They were assigned a 'peripheral' and 'specialist' role of dealing with women and children. The 'take-off' has taken place as seen in an increase in the recruitment of women in Kolkata Police. But the 'tip-over' from being a small minority of officers to a more equal representation has not yet been reached. At present women police personnel in Kolkata Police are passing through an 'experimental phase' where they are allotted a few challenging assignments such as for the T20 World Cup tournament in 2016, for the first time deputy commissioner (women police) was assigned to maintain surveillance and law and order at the prestigious club house section of the Eden Gardens. The Club House is a high security zone. So performing duty at that zone itself is very challenging.[54] Eight women police stations under the jurisdiction of Kolkata Police have been made operational. Senior women inspectors are been appointed as the officer-in-charge of these women police stations. Such women inspectors and their team of women police personnel are engaged in all policing activities where women are the perpetrators as well as victims of crime. However, no concrete effort by the policy planners to systematically 'reform', improve and upgrade the quality of women in the Kolkata Police have taken place. Majority of women police personnel at the subordinate level in Kolkata Police are not yet ready for total integration in the police force unless the infrastructural facilities improves at workplace, though in recent times few women have been given challenging field assignments and have accepted it. On the part of the police organisation, it is necessary to realistically prepare the ground for women police to emerge by modernising their training and improving their working conditions. There is also a need to improve the infrastructural facilities of the police organisation. The policy of the present state government indicates that they prefer women police in subordinate ranks (from inspectors to constables) to implement the 'gendered policing' model. Gendered Policing model implies policing by women for women. With increasing crime against women in the city, they cannot just be a force that would transform the image of women in society but will also be an avenue that is more approachable and receptive, helping victims of rape and other crimes related to women.[55] It is not possible to predict the time required for the integration of women in Kolkata Police though it can be concluded that a trend towards integration, though slow, has already started in the Kolkata Police.

References

1. Welter, Barbara. "The Cult of True Womanhood 1820-1860" in *Divinity Communications : The American Woman in the 19th Century,* edited by Barbara Welter, Ohio University Press, Atheno, 1976, pp. 21-41.
2. Mahajan, Amarjit. *Indian Police Women. A Sociological Study of a New Role,* Deep and Deep Publications, New Delhi, 1986.
3. Aleem, Shamim. *Women Police and Social Change*, Ashish Publication, New Delhi, 1991. Women in Indian Police, Sterling, New Delhi, 1991.
4. Vishnoi, Om Raj Singh, *Women Police in India*, Aravali Books International, New Delhi, 2002.
5. Natarajan, Mangai. *Women Police in a Changing Society. Backdoor to Equality,* Ashgate, England, 2008.
6. Sinha, Ranu. *Breaking Barriers. Women in Police Services in India and United States,* Ganga Publishing House, New Delhi, 2000.
7. When the former Commissioner of Police, Kolkata Police, was interviewed on 22 April 2010 he said in 2003-04 Calcutta Police was renamed Kolkata Police. Whereas another senior police officer in Kolkata Police, when interviewed on 18th May 2012 said that on 21st January 2001 Calcutta Police was renamed Kolkata Police. I have not been able to find out which is the case.
8. Government of West Bengal, Home Department, Police Branch. File No. P14 M-14/49.
9. Government of West Bengal, Home Department, Police Branch. Issue no. 2163 Pl. Date of Issue:15.06.49.
10. *Calcutta Police Gazette*, 15th June 1949.
11. *Calcutta Police Gazette* 15th June 1949.
12. Interview with Lila Chowdhury, former assistant commissioner of police, women police, Kolkata Police.
13. As mentioned in the Kolkata Police Museum, Kolkata.
14. *Calcutta Police Gazette*, 23rd August 1949.

15. Interview with Mrs. Lila Chowdhury, former assistant commissioner of police, Kolkata Police.
16. As mentioned in the Kolkata Police Museum on 4th November 2016.
17. When Mr. Sujoy Chakraborty, former Commissioner of Police, Kolkata Police, was interviewed on 22nd April 2010 he said women were never used for searching houses.
18. *Calcutta Police Gazette*, 15thMarch 1960. Also see Calcutta Police Gazette, 23rd March 1960.
19. Krishna Bandyopadhyay, "Naxalbari Politics: A Feminist Narrative", *Economic and Political Weekly,* 63, 15, (5 April 2008), p. 59.
20. Krishna Bandyopadhyay, "Naxalbari Politics: A Feminist Narrative", *Economic and Political Weekly*, 63, 15, (5April 2008), p. 59.
21. After speaking to Asim Chatterjee (popularly known as Kaka). He was actively involved in Naxalite movement in 1970s in West Bengal.
22. When the former Commissioner of Police, Kolkata Police, was interviewed on 22 April 2010 he said in 2003-04 Calcutta Police was renamed Kolkata Police. Whereas another senior police officer in Kolkata Police, when interviewed on 18th May 2012 said on 21st January 2001 Calcutta Police was renamed Kolkata Police. I have not been able to find out which is the case.
23. Sen, Samita. "Towards a Feminist Politics? The Indian Women's Movement in Historical Perspective." *Policy Research Report on Gender and Development.* The World Bank. Development Research Group. Poverty Reduction and Economic Management Network. Working Paper Series No. 9. April 2000.
24. *Calcutta Police Gazette*, 4th February 1982.
25. Letter from Shri. N. C. Chakraborty, deputy secretary to the Government of West Bengal to the commissioner of police, Calcutta.
26. *Calcutta Police Gazette,* 14th July 1982.
27. *Calcutta Police Gazette,* 7th April 1986.
28. *Calcutta Police Gazette*, 11th September 1986.
29. *Calcutta Police Gazette*, 2nd December 1987.
30. *Calcutta Police Gazette*, 9th March 1990.
31. *Calcutta Police Gazette*, 21st August 1990.
32. *Calcutta Police Gazette,* G. O. No. 698 dated 20-08-90.
33. 'Deboshree Chatterjee first woman to head a police station in Kolkata', *The Statesman*, 16th November 2010.
34. 'Kolkata gets its first woman super-sleuth', *The Times of India*, 8th October 2009.
35. 'Cops ignored Rizwanur plea for protection', *The Times of India*, Kolkata, 24th September 2007.
36. 'Streets out of police sight. Rape victim was in car for over three hours and didn't find a cop for help', *TheTelegraph*, Kolkata, 9th June 2012.
37. 'The officer made me feel sick. Battered woman narrates how family assaulted and cops humiliated her', *TheTelegraph*, Kolkata, 27th April 2012.

38. 'Lady stands by torment charge. Explain on TV circumstances that led to discrepancies', *The Telegraph,* 17th February 2012.
39. 'Rape victim loses battle for life at hospital', *The Times of India,* 1st January 2014.
40. 'Kolkata unsafe for woman ?', *The Times of India*, 3rd January 2014.
41. 'City faces shortage of women cops', *The Times of India*, 17th December 2013.
42. Officer of the deputy commissioner (Women Police), Kolkata Police. At present the post of the deputy commissioner of police (woman) is vacant.
43. Office of the commissioner of police, Kolkata Police, Memo No. 5653 / FRC F-1017/09 dated 10th March 2016.
44. Interview with additional commissioner of police, Kolkata Police in 2011.
45. Office of the commissioner of police, Kolkata Police, dated 10th March 2016.
46. 'Women in Uniform.RCP:Donning a new avatar. Its time to change: Proper training and motivation bring out the best in women police officers', *The Kolkata Protector*, Vol. 4, Issue 6. 2014, pp. 12-13.
47. 'City faces shortage of women cops', *The Times of India*, 17th December 2013.
48. 'Lal Bazar Ladies' Special', *The Telegraph*, 4th June 2011.
49. The author had visited the PRB section on June 2014.'An open letter to 'Didi', the CM of West Bengal, on the condition of women in police department'. last accessed 28th October, 2015. See more at: http:// www.merinews.com/article/ an-open-letter-to-didi-the-cm-of-west-bengal-on-the-condition-of-women-in-police-department/15899887.shtml&cp.
50. Daruwala, Maja and Prasad, Devika. *Rough Roads to Equality. Women Police in South Asia.* Commonwealth Human Rights Initiative, Delhi, 2015, p. 47.
51. Mishra, Renuka (ed.). *Compendium on Gender Practices in Police*, SVPNPA Publications, Hyderabad, pp. 96-97.
52. National Crime Record Bureau, Ministry of Home Affairs, Government of India, Crime in India 2014, New Delhi, last accessed 29th October 2015. See more www.ncrb.gov.in.
53. *The Telegraph,* 4th June 2011.
54. As told to the author by deputy commissioner (women police), Kolkata Police.
55. 'RCP: Donning a new avatar', *Kolkata Protector*, Vol. 4, Issue 6, 2014.

11

Understanding Justice Delivery System from the Perspective of Survivors of Intimate Partner Violence in the Context of Protection of Women from Domestic Violence Act 2005

Rupa Biswas

Introduction

Violence against women (VAW) has been defined as "any act of gender-based violence that results in, or is likely to result in, physical, sexual or mental harm or suffering to women, including threats of such acts, coercion or arbitrary deprivation of liberty, whether occurring in public or in private life" (UN, 1993). Despite many decades of women's movement, legal reform and sensitisation around the globe and in India, VAW tends to persist in manifold. While all forms of violence are a matter of grave concern, intimate partner violence is more disturbing as it is perpetrated within the ambit of safest place i.e. homes and by people often related to intimate partners, and/or relatives who are supposed to love and protect women. It takes place in 'private sphere' of home; many cultures have considered the marital relationship in particular and the family in general, as the private area in which others should not interfere with the freedom of the male household head to control events and decisions. Intimate partner violence or domestic violence often regarded as "intimate partner abuse," "battering," or "wife-beating," refers to physical, sexual, psychological, and economic abuse that takes place in the context of an intimate relationship, including marriage. Intimate partner violence can take a number of forms including physical, verbal, emotional, economic and sexual abuse. Intimate Partner Violence (IPV) has been visualised as a pattern of coercive behaviour by a spouse or intimate partner to gain control or power over the other. Common manifestations of IPV like kicking, punching, biting, slapping, strangling, choking, burning with cigarettes, throwing acid, marital rape or forced sex, pushing woman out of house, confining her to home, etc. In many instances, violence becomes more severe like beating women with objects like belts, iron rods, subjecting them to starving for days together, chaining, stabbing and threatening to murder etc. The definition of intimate partner varies between settings and includes formal partnerships, such as marriage, as well as informal partnerships, including dating relationships and unmarried sexual relationships. In some settings, intimate partners tend to be married, while in others more informal partnerships are more common. It leads to violation of human rights and prevents women from enjoying their fundamental freedom such as the rights to life, security, equality, dignity, and self-worth. Moreover, denying their right to live in violence free home. Intimate Partner Violence calls into question the family as a social institution that provides security, protection and affection, as well as the roles and functions traditionally assigned to each of its members. Thus, women are socialised to endure in silence or even rationalise it. Intimate partner violence is the most common form of violence experienced by women and it is estimated that one in three women globally has experienced IPV at least once in their lifetime. Globally rape and intimate partner violence account for about 5% of the total disease burden on women in the age of 15-44 years (World Health Organisation, 2002). Intimate partner violence is widespread in South Asia and yet relatively hidden and ignored. In India, Nepal, Bangladesh and Sri Lanka enactment of several laws to criminalise violence in private sphere over the past decade has taken place. However, the implementation of these laws remains a herculean task and multiple hurdles prevail that impede the implementation of these laws. The present paper focuses on Intimate Partner Violence with special reference to domestic violence and Protection of Women from Domestic Violence Act (PWDVA), 2005 in the district of Barddhaman, West Bengal.

Background of Protection of Women from Domestic Violence Act 2005

Government of India became a signatory to several international and regional conventions and treaties. These include CEDAW (1979), Vienna Declaration and Programme of Action (1993), International Conference on Population and Development (1994), Fourth UN World Conference on Women, Beijing (1995) and UN Millennium Development Goals (2000). After Independence, the steady rise in dowry deaths in India had compelled the government to enact the Dowry Prohibition Act in 1961 to book a person for demanding dowry. The Act, however, was criticised to be theoretical and lacking in clarity. Along with manifold loopholes, this Act excluded presents and the money given to the bride and the groom after marriage from its purview, and it regarded both the giving and the taking dowry as an offence. In the meanwhile mid 1970s the issue of violence in private sphere got attention for the first time in the nation due to the growing incidents of death of young, newly married women. It was on this backdrop with pressure from women's group, the Dowry Prohibition Act 1961 was amended in 1984 and 1986 respectively. Thus, the following Amendments led to the introduction of new Sections in Indian Penal Code (IPC) such as 498A meant for cruelty by husbands and their relatives in 1984 and similarly, Section 304B was introduced in the IPC in 1986 which created a new offence of "dowry death". The 1984 amendment makes dowry a cognizable offence and the meaning of the term dowry has been expanded which included any property given or agreed to be given in connection with a marriage to the bride or bridegroom or any other person is considered as dowry. It is not necessary to show that the same has been given as consideration for the marriage. It also provides for the preparation of a list of presents which are given at the time of marriage to the bride or bridegroom in accordance with the rules made under the Act. Thus, only married women facing violence at the hands of the husbands or their families could claim relief under 498A. A lot of other forms of violence faced by unmarried women, old women could not be brought under this Section. It did not protect women from violence in natal relationships or in relationships that have not received the legal sanction of marriage. The other problematic aspect of this provision was the definition of 'cruelty' itself as it was defined to mean any wilful conduct which could have driven the woman to commit suicide or caused grave injury to her or posed a danger to her life, limb or health (either mental or physical). The definition was worded in such vague terms that it was difficult to bring issues of sexual violence, economic violence or even threats of violence within the ambit of the Section. The experience with using this Section in cases showed that the threshold of the impact of violent conduct on the woman, required to be proved was so high that many forms of cruelty fell through the net. A woman had to prove that she was driven to contemplate suicide, or that her life was in danger before she could access the law. Ultimately, it was on the discretion of the police as to whether the conduct of the husband was of such a nature as mentioned above. The 2nd amendment in 1986, provides that if a woman dies within 7 years of her marriage, due to causes other than natural, her property would be transferred to her children and if she has no children, to her parents. The amendment makes the offence non-bailable. This Section unlike Section 498A can be used only for cases related to dowry. Since no record is maintained and no complaints made at the time of meeting dowry demands while the girl is still alive, it is extremely difficult to prove dowry death under this Section. This Section also presumes that women are harassed for dowry only within the first seven years of marriage. Overall, this Section is not likely to benefit women to deal with intimate partner violence, as violence is not always related to dowry. From the words 'soon before her death' one can infer that it does not take into account the violence committed earlier, or the violence committed on a routine basis from day one, as a valid cause that may lead someone to commit suicide. Thus, abetment to suicide does not come under the purview of this Section. Proof of dowry harassment by the husband or his family is a must for conviction under this Section. What about dowry deaths taking place after seven years of marriage? Hence this Section is also not likely to benefit women in dealing with intimate partner violence. While it was still possible to bring cases of everyday violence against women in the home within the scope of Section 498A, it was not possible to use 304B, if the violence and the eventual death were not linked with dowry. And also, Section 304B came into play only after the woman was dead. These Sections cannot deal with other forms of violence among other members of the domestic sphere. Thus, they have their own limits in defining the scope of intimate partner violence. It is submitted that generally complaints can be registered only after an offence has been committed. But in a domestic situation a woman would need protection even before a crime is committed when she apprehends danger to her life as she is living with her abuser and is also dependent on him. Though, the wife actually musters courage to approach police station, the police would not register a complaint against the husband for assaulting the wife. On the other hand, the police would counsel the women about her role in the family and send her back even without registering a complaint. Thus, making the relevance of law for women facing violence at home is rather limited. Moreover, criminal law itself has little to offer with respect to taking care of the woman's immediate needs of protection, shelter and monetary relief. On the other hand, existing civil law remedies were unable to provide effective and timely reliefs to women facing violence. A persistent problem in cases of violence in marital relationship is that women are thrown out of the homes and then the house is sold or rented to dispossess the women indirectly. Although sometimes, the court can be convinced to give injunction orders to prevent women from being thrown out, proceedings under civil law are slow-moving and time consuming. Even when injunction orders are available, the enforcement is weak due to absence of penalties for violation. Additionally, there is no provision for granting injunction orders or protection orders on an emergency basis, with the result that the women do not have any relief during the course of the proceedings. All these considerations made it imperative to conceptualise a law on intimate partner violence especially domestic violence that would be a combination of both civil and criminal law elements. A civil law that would, on the one hand, restrain the abuser from committing violence, and on the other, provide for the other needs of the woman faced with violence. At the same time, the provisions under criminal law would offer punitive measures to ensure the enforcement of the orders of the courts. So, a special law was the crying need of the hour to protect woman in her own home. It was on this backdrop that the Protection of Women from Domestic Violence Act was enacted in 2005, that came into effect on 26th October 2006. The new law defines domestic abuse or intimate partner violence as any act / conduct / omission / commission that harms or injures or has the potential to harm or injure will be considered 'domestic violence'. The Act recognises four kinds of violence- physical abuse, sexual abuse, verbal and emotional abuse and economic abuse and it also recognises that women's rights are violated not only in their capacity as wives but also as mothers, sisters, daughter, widows and live-in-partners. In that respect, it makes a major breakthrough in recognising the reality of violence which occurs against women within the four walls of home. A woman is entitled to following reliefs under the PWDV Act'05 such as Protection order, Residence order, Maintenance order, Compensation order, Custody order and Interim / Exparte order. The Act has also created windows for two separate machineries i.e. Protection Officers and Service Providers for addressing various needs of survivors of intimate partner violence.

Intimate Partner Violence, Global Scenario

Across the globe intimate partner violence have been exceeding in an alarming proportions. It is estimated that 35 percent of women worldwide have experienced either physical and/or sexual intimate partner violence or sexual violence by a non-partner at some point in their lives. However, some national studies show that up to 70 percent of women have experienced physical and/or sexual violence from an intimate partner in their lifetime. Women who have been physically or sexually abused by their partners are more than twice as likely to have an abortion, almost twice as likely to experience depression, and in some regions, 1.5 times more likely to acquire

HIV, as compared to women who have not experienced partner violence (UN Women). In an another study by World Health Organisation on intimate partner violence revealed the prevalence as such Africa 36.6 % America 29.8%, Eastern Mediterranean 37.0, Europe 25.4, South-East Asia 37.7, Western Pacific 24.6 (WHO, 2013). Forty three percent of women in the 28 European Union Member States have experienced some form of psychological violence by an intimate partner in their lifetime. In a study in USA, on violence against women 21% of the sample report the violence being directed particularly against the female spouses. Statistics reflect that violence against women in Africa is increasingly prevalent and gets manifested mainly in the form of sexual and intimate partner violence. In many places of the continent such incidences of violence is not divulged openly (Cited by Moses et al., 2010). Another study conducted by WHO finds that violence against women spreads in epidemic proportions in several countries in the world. It shows that the magnitude of intimate partner violence varies from country to country. 15% of such incidences reported in Japan whereas 71 percent in Ethiopia. Some earlier researches reflect the cases of intimate partner violence being committed to the extent of nearly 20% in both United States and Sweden, and 23% each in Canada and Britain. Recent regional estimates calculated by the WHO suggest that South Asia has the highest regional rate of IPV in the world, at 43 % (WHO, 2013). Four South Asian countries feature among the fifteen countries with the highest national prevalence of physical intimate partner violence as reported by the Demographic and Health Surveys, with India seventh on the list. In most of the scenarios the crime goes unreported or even unpunished in case it is somehow reported. At least 119 countries have passed laws on domestic violence, 125 have laws on sexual harassment and 52 have laws on marital rape. However, even when laws exist, this does not mean that they are always compliant with international standards or implemented (UN Women).

Intimate Partner Violence, Indian Scenario

Since time immemorial intimate partner violence has been an integral part of the journey of married women in Indian society. As in many other countries in the world IPV in India, is not being recognised as serious issue but also a hidden and ignored form of violence against women and girls. Despite of the fact that IPV is an indelible practice over the ages in Indian society there has been very little or no intensive research among the family researchers towards this phenomenon which is growing unabated in the recent era. IPV deprives women of their fundamental rights like education, employment, equal status, freedom and all that is instrumental for their wellbeing and development. Data shows that large proportions of men and women across the region condone intimate partner violence by husbands against wives (Solotaroff & Pande, 2014). National Family Health Survey-III carried out in 29 states during 2005-06, has found that a substantial proportion of married women have been physically or sexually abused by their husbands at some time in their lives. The findings indicated that nationwide 37.2% of women experienced violence after marriage. Bihar was found to be the most violent, with the abuse rate against married women being as high as 59% and followed by Rajasthan (46.3%), Madhya Pradesh (45.8%), Manipur (43.9%), Uttar Pradesh (42.4%), Tamil Nadu (41.9%) and West Bengal (40.3%). The fourth round of the National Family Health Survey (NFHS) conducted in 2015-16 reported that 30 percent of ever married women aged 15-49 years face some form of intimate partner violence. A study by the International Centre for Research on Women (ICRW) revealed that 52 percent of its female respondents in India had faced some form of intimate partner violence ever in their lives, while 60 percent of male respondents admitted to have perpetrated violence on women (Nanda et al., 2013). The National Crime Records Bureau (2015) estimates IPV as follows:

Table 1: State-wise Reporting of Cases under 304B & 498A of IPC in 2015

State	***304B***	***State***	***498A***
West Bengal	2335	Uttar Pradesh	20169
Rajasthan	1154	Bihar	14383
Assam	664	Madhya Pradesh	11225
Uttar Pradesh	498	West Bengal	8660
Maharashtra	463	Rajasthan	7640

(NCRB, 2015) NCRB data on state-wise reporting of cases under Sec 304B & 498A of IPC in 2015 shows that West Bengal topped as far as reporting of cases under dowry death i.e. 304B which was followed by states like Rajasthan, Assam, Uttar Pradesh and Maharashtra. While it also reveals that Uttar Pradesh has reported highest number of cases under Sec 498A and subsequently followed by Bihar, Madhya Pradesh, West Bengal and Rajasthan.

(NCRB, 2015)

NCRB data on district-wise reporting of cases under Sec 304B & 498A of IPC in West Bengal in 2015 reveals that Nadia district has acquired topmost position as far as reporting of cases under dowry death i.e. 304B which was followed by districts like 24 Parganas South, Murshidabad, Dakshin Dinajpur and Barddhaman. Whereas it also shows that Barddhaman district has reported maximum number of cases under Sec 498A and subsequently followed by other districts like Malda, Nadia, Purulia and Paschim Medinipur.

Table 2: District-wise Reporting of Cases under 304B & 498A of IPC in West Bengal in 2015

District	*304B*	*District*	*498A*
Nadia	69	Barddhaman	795
24 Parganas South	49	Malda	449
Murshidabad	35	Nadia	389
Dakshin Dinajpur	32	Purulia	339
Barddhaman	25	Paschim Medinipur	298

Objectives

The specific objectives of the present study are as follows:

(1) To identify the factors in socio-legal system contributed as hindrances in attaining justice to the survivors.

(2) To examine whether the PWDV Act 2005 can actually prevent, protect and provide relief measures to the survivors.

Methodology: Of late, the State of West Bengal has shown relative rise so far crimes against women are concerned especially in terms of intimate partner violence. Among the districts in West Bengal, Barddhaman is considered as one of the most advanced districts but as per NCRB data 2015, there is high prevalence of intimate partner violence against married women. Thus, the present study was conducted in the rural and urban areas of Barddhaman, district of West Bengal. Descriptive research design was used to analyse quantitative data. The sample selected comprised of married women, survivors of intimate partner violence were in the age group of 20-40 years who had registered cases in the Courts under the Protection of Women from Domestic Violence Act, 2005 was drawn from different socio-economic backgrounds. The sample of 200 married women representing from different castes, religions and socio-economic groups. The sample selected based on simple random sampling technique. A semi-structured interview schedule was prepared for obtaining information from the survivors. The interviews captured data on underlying factors in socio-legal system contributed as hindrances in attaining justice to the survivors and also regarding their experiences with different stakeholders like lawyers, police and judiciary. Besides also aimed at capturing their attitude towards the PWDVA.

Ethical Considerations for the Study

To preserve the rights of the survivors ethical considerations were adhered to such as confidentiality, anonymity, informed consent etc.

Limitations of the Study

Social research is primarily based on human responses and social contexts. Both these aspects are ever changing and hence it would be extremely unwise to generalise the findings as the study was only confined in the Barddhaman district of West Bengal as well as with limited sample. Thus, the findings of the study may not be applicable to the other districts of West Bengal. This study had only accounted the experiences of the survivors of intimate partner violence in this region. The issue of subjectivity remains as the study revolves to understand the experiences of survivors of intimate partner violence who registered cases in Courts. There was hardly any scope for interaction with the perpetrators to understand their perspective. So exaggeration of events by the survivors could not be avoided.

Results

Socioeconomic Profile of the Respondents:

Large proportions (59%) of the married women were in the age-range of 20-30 years and 31.5% hailed in the age group of 31-40 years. Majority (78.50%) of the respondents comprised of Hindu, the remaining were Muslims. With regard to their educational qualifications, 24.50% had completed post graduation, 16.50% were graduates. An equal proportion of 22.50% each completed secondary and higher secondary education, apart from this 11.50% of them found literate and only 2.50% of them found illiterate. While 90.5% of the respondents were housewives, only a handful of them 9.5% were found employed. Majority (53%) of the respondent's belonged to urban areas and the remaining were from rural areas. A large number of the married women 72% represented from joint families, while 28% hailed from nuclear families. Dowry became an inevitable part for their marriage and which was found widely prevalent during the time of survivor's marriage in 87.50% of cases. Only in a handful number of cases marriage took place without dowry which accounted 12.50%.

Factors Instrumental in Underreporting of Intimate Partner Violence: It was found that the majority (63.50%) of the married women did not receive natal family's support and cooperation at the initial stage for registering complaint whereas some (36.50%) of them got natal family's support for it. They cited several reasons for lacking support from natal family like concern for their future (94.49%), financial hardship (74.80%), natal family wanted them to go back to continue the relationship (44.09%) and family honour (0.79%) etc. With regard to awareness on legal safeguards and support services it was seen that 97.50% of the respondents had no and also limited knowledge about legal safety net and other support services available to counter the phenomenon whereas only 2.50% of them were little bit aware about legal safeguards and support services. It was surprising to note that none of them had adequate awareness on legal provisions, support services meant to address the issue. The study revealed that despite of the violence a large proportion of the survivors 40% reported the incidents after 5 years and more while in 27.50% and 20.50% of cases the abuse was reported within 2-5 years and 2 years after marriage respectively. In 9.50% and 2.50% of cases it was reported only after one year and within a year of their marriage.

Cases Registered under Legal Provisions & Nature of Reporting Institutions:

The study reflected that about 44.50% of the survivors a majority of them registered complaint under Sec 498A of IPC followed by the Protection of Women from Domestic Violence Act 2005 (31.5%). The findings had shown that 30% of them registered complaint under both the provisions such as Sec 498A of IPC and PWDV Act 2005. 26.5% of the survivors registered complaint other than the above-mentioned provisions such as 125 Crpc, 302 and 304B of IPC. Among the survivors who registered complaint it was found that majority 56.50% of them registered their complaints in Court followed by police station 52.50%, women's cell 13% and before protection officer under only 12%.

Response of Law Enforcing Machineries:

Police: The role of the police is extremely important in lodging complaints, investigating the matter and filing charge sheet. Data revealed that a major portion of the survivors 41.50% found that police were not supportive in addressing their need whereas 36% of them experienced support from police in addressing their need. In some 9.50% of cases the respondents expected more cooperation than they received. While 13% of the respondents never approached to police. Among the respondents who got support from police also identified its nature which included registering complaints soon 72.53%, followed by providing legal assistance 15.38%, recovering *stridhan* and enforcement of court orders together constituted 2.20% each respectively. Apart from these the survivors received other support in the nature of rescuing them from matrimonial house, submitting charge sheet on time, reconciliation, arresting perpetrators in 25.27% of cases. Whereas the study also indicated the nature of non-cooperation by police and those included: non-registration of complaint 63.86%, followed by delay in registering complaint 60.24%, reluctance in arresting perpetrators 32.53%, receiving threats in order to withdraw their complaints 3.61%. While reluctance in enforcing court orders and not filing charge sheet on time together constituted 2.41% each respectively. Besides other areas of non-cooperation also noted which were asking for bribe, reluctance in recovering *stridhan,* delay in filing charge sheet etc. which accounted 10.84%.

Lawyers: The role of lawyer is crucial in representing their case before court and helping them for getting necessary reliefs. While majority of the survivors 58.50% received support from their lawyers and (41.50%) of them reported non-cooperation from the part of their lawyers. The areas of non-cooperation cited by them as follows like misleading facts (95.18%), nexus with abusers (55.42%), demanding huge money (51.81%), losing necessary documents (26.51%) and delay in filing the case (9.64%).

Judiciary: With regard to Judiciary's role in addressing the issue it was seen that majority of the survivors (84%) expressed their dissatisfaction towards this machinery whereas only 16% of them responded affirmative towards this machinery but at the same time expressed their concern for speedy disposal of cases.

Survivors Experience of Hardship:

The findings of the study indicated that the majority 46% of the survivors had been fighting for getting relief for 1 to 2 yrs followed by 26.5% who had been fighting for 2 to 3 yrs and 17% of them struggling for more than 3 yrs. While 10.5% of them fighting legal battle for less than a year. It was also noticed that most of the married women 49.50% sought monetary relief followed by compensation order (41%), restrain order for not committing violence and for accommodation together constituted (34%) each respectively. Whereas other orders which included custody of *stridhan* 26.50%, punishment of perpetrators 23% and custody of children 6% respectively. Apart from this 28.50% of the survivors sought relief in the nature of interim order, litigation cost, continuation of conjugal life, legal aid, divorce, expenses for children's education, expenses for treatment of survivors and share in husband's property etc. The study found that in majority of the cases 45% of the orders was passed by the Judiciary within 1 to 2 yrs after registering complaint by them. While in 26.25% and 22.50% of cases orders were passed within 2 to 3 yrs and less than a year respectively. In 3.75% and 2.50% of cases the orders were passed more than 4 yrs and within 3 to 4 yrs after registering complaint by them. It is to mention here that the orders which passed within 1 to 2 years after registering the complaint were of interim in nature not the final verdict. The study also identified the factors responsible for delayed judgment and those included delay in Court proceedings 67.74% followed by lawyer's negligence and non-cooperation accounted for (27.42%). Besides survivors also revealed reasons like non-appearance of abusers for hearing contributed to delayed judgment which constituted (46.77%). In majority i.e. 60% of cases no order was passed by the Judicial Magistrates whereas in only 40% of cases orders were issued by the Judicial Magistrates. In most of the cases 53.75% orders were passed under the Protection of Women from Domestic Violence Act 2005 followed by 498A of IPC which constitutes 13.75%. In 1.25% of cases orders were issued under both the provisions PWDV Act and 498A of IPC. Apart from these provisions in a majority of cases, orders were also issued under the provision of 125 Crpc which accounted for (33.75%). As far as nature of orders were concerned, it had been found that maintenance orders issued by the Magistrates in maximum number of time (78.75%), followed by residence order 17.50%, compensation order 11.25%, imprisonment of the perpetrators 8.75% and custody of stridhan 5% respectively. Besides 45% orders issued by the Magistrates were in the nature of interim, exparte, expenses for treatment of child, protection order, provision for litigation cost and reconciliation order etc. As there were only two protection officers who were usually overburdened with huge case load. The absence of registered service provider made the situation even worse.

Strong Indications of Non-Implementation of the Act:

The study revealed that despite of orders issued by Courts a large proportion of the survivors 52.50% were not receiving any reliefs from it. While in 33.75% of the cases the reliefs were not regular to them.

Whereas in only 13.75% of cases the survivors admitted that they were regularly getting reliefs as per the orders issued by Court. The survivors also identified major reasons for not getting relief which included non-compliance of orders by the abuser (80.95%), followed by appeal made by abusers in Sessions and High Court against the order (28.57%) and lawyer's negligence and non-cooperation (9.52%). Besides above-mentioned reasons, the survivors also cited other reasons too which were non-appearance of their abusers during the trial of cases which created barrier for getting relief as they were not aware of the orders passed by the Magistrates. In case of exparte order, it constituted (11.90%). Majority of the survivors 83.50% found that provisions under the PWDV Act were hardly detrimental to combat their issues.

Discussion

The socio-economic background of the married women reflected that variables like residence, age, nature of family, religion, education, employment status of survivors are related to the incidences of abuse. Incidences of violence are more rampant among the survivors from urban area as rural communities are generally considered being more traditional than their counterpart as well as women in villages are less aware of their legal rights and also have lesser access to police stations than women in cities. In addition to that it has been found in the present study that both the women police stations have been located in urban pockets of the district (Asansol and Barddhaman) thus it can relatively influence the degree of reporting. Violence is more prevalent among younger women. It may be due to that young couples are under lot of stress to adjust to new roles, responsibilities. Especially young married women need to struggle a lot to adapt to their husband's families. In addition to that, children's responsibilities put enormous demands and stresses too which often lead to violence. Joint family structure is also related to intimate partner violence and it can be inferred that living in joint households is required to make adjustments with a large number of kin in contrast to those residing in nuclear families. The presence of in-laws in the household may give rise to some conflict and at times they may instigate or provoke their son to commit violence upon their daughter-in-law in case she disobeys their command or found negligent in performing household chores. As far as religion is concerned, this may be explained as Muslims are more likely than Hindus to marry within the kin network, which serves as a protective factor in experiencing violence. In addition to that, socio-economic factors may also contribute for the difference in reporting in different religious groups.

The study also revealed that educated women are more prone to intimate partner violence and the reason behind this is woman with education may start raising questions against the dominant position of their husbands and in-laws, challenge oppression which acts as a potential threat to encounter violence. Subsequently perpetrators resort to violence to retain their dominant position in the family. Besides the study highlighted that majority of the survivors were homemakers, which possess greater risk of encountering violence than who were employed. This is probably because housewives are perceived to contribute less to family subsistence and are valued less than women engaged in work outside. This is due to the fact that household work is largely unpaid. Gradually it enhances their helplessness and dependency upon perpetrators. It may also compel them to live in abusive relationship and also prevent them from taking legal recourse to counter domestic violence further contributing delay in reporting incidents. Employment status may work as a protective shield which provides alternatives and strength to leave abusive relationship, to report their vulnerabilities.

The study revealed that a large proportion of the survivors remained in abusive relationship over a period of time before reporting the incidents to law enforcing machineries and this because of dynamic interplay of social and environmental factors like concern for their children's future, financial constraints, social insecurity, family honour, still loving their abusive spouses, want of accommodation, hope in the relationship etc. Another grave concern that limited and barely any knowledge regarding legal safeguards and support services might contribute delay in reporting the incidents of abuse and also compel them to live in abusive relationship which increases the vulnerability of the survivors. Very often it has been observed that the machineries like police, lawyers which aim to protect them from adversities take the advantage of their ignorance and exploit them by extorting hefty money for arresting perpetrators, filing charge sheet and for issuing orders from court. In addition to that the survivors become dependent upon these machineries that might have nexus with their perpetrators, this too creates hurdles for them in getting relief sooner from court. Majority of them registered complaint under Sec 498A of IPC, although there is a specific law on intimate partner abuse. In this regard their limited knowledge regarding legal safeguards, support services more specifically PWDV Act 2005 influence reporting of cases under PWDV Act. In addition to this most of the time the lawyers make decision in terms of legal matter on behalf of the survivors as they have inadequate knowledge on legal provisions, for which majority of the survivors registered complaint more than one provisions.

There have been many stumbling blocks for the effective implementation of PWDV Act 2005 as the findings revealed non-registration of complaint, delay in registering complaint, reluctance in arresting perpetrators, threats for withdrawing complaints, reluctance in enforcing court orders, recovering stridhan and not filing charge sheet on time by police influenced reporting of incidences and delay in legal proceedings and reliefs to the survivors. There were only two women police stations in the districts and both of them are located in urban pockets further resulting to vulnerabilities to the survivors. The orders mostly passed by the judiciary within 1 to 2 years after registering the complaint were of interim in nature not the final verdict. But the PWDV Act mandates that a Magistrate will endeavour to dispose of every application within 60 days from the date of the first hearing. In these circumstances, deadline is seldom maintained. Thus, it indicates that courts deal with DV cases in the same manner as they would handle other criminal cases. The delay in court proceedings is the result of grave deficiencies in human and infrastructural resources to deal with women's complaints of intimate partner violence. There were only two Protection officers in the district, who had been overburdened with complaints which very often leads to delay in submission of Domestic Incident Report before court. Although there are several reliefs entitled to the survivors of intimate partner abuse under the purview of PWDV Act but in maximum number of time maintenance orders are issued by the Magistrates than other reliefs like residence, compensation, custody of stridhan etc which may raise issue about the apathy of Magistrates on issuing other orders and also their sensitisation about the provisions of the Act. The survivors of intimate partner violence are not only in need of monetary reliefs but also other reliefs. The study also revealed that despite of orders issued by courts a large number of the survivors were not receiving any relief from it. While in some other cases, the reliefs were not regular to them. Majority of the survivors found that PWDV Act is hardly detrimental to combat their complex issues. Inadequate protection officers, service providers, failure on the part of the judiciary and police and lack of basic services and infrastructure are detrimental in executing provisions of the Act. Thus, mere passing orders hardly bring any changes to their lot, unless it has been implemented in true spirit and also needs to address underlying factors for non-compliance of orders by the abusers. The Protection of Women from Domestic Violence Act, 2005 (PWDVA) requires the appointment of Protection Officers, registration of Service providers and notification of shelter homes and medical facilities. As per the information provided by the States/UTs, all the State Governments have appointed protection officers. 25 States/UTs have registered service providers and

21 States/UTs have notified medical facilities and 24 States/UTs have notified shelter homes. According to the latest data with the Ministry of Women and Child Development, the number of States having Protection officers with independent charge, who are key enablers to assess domestic violence, has increased from six to ten (Bihar, Chhattisgarh, Gujarat, Haryana, Kerala, Madhya Pradesh, Rajasthan, Tamil Nadu, West Bengal and Delhi). But in 29 States and seven Union Territories of the country, the number of Protection officers has been reduced by half from 6,279 to 3,145 in the last three years. Figures tell a sorry tale as a state like Maharashtra showed the steepest decline of 33 per cent. "Statistics show an alarming decline in the number of cases registered, an improper budget allocation for the implementation of the Act and a 50 percent decrease in the number of protection officers (Press Information Bureau, GOI, and 11th December 2014). These are serious issues and need to be addressed on a priority basis," Dr Ranjana Kumari, Director, Centre for Social Research (CSR) said. Even though Protection of Women from Domestic Violence Act has been enacted by the Central Government, it is the state's responsibility to implement the Act. All States implement the Act as per their own choice and existing infrastructure. "Each State has a different budgetary allocation to Act. While on one hand Karnataka has been allocated Rs 80 lakh in 2015-16, on the other hand Delhi had been allocated Rs 45 lakh for the implementation of this Act in 2013-14," said Dr Kumari. "All these factors are compounded by neglect on behalf of the State in terms of maintenance of records, leading to inaccessibility of data among the public." While in 2014, NCRB for the first time published data on Protection of Women from Domestic Violence Act, with only 426 cases registered under the Act for the entire year. According to the Economic Survey of Ministry of Finance 2014, the enactment of Protection of Women from Domestic Violence Act remains weak as 19 states have no planned schemes. "No special attention is paid to awareness generation and sensitisation of judicial officers, police and general public. Cases pertaining to domestic violence are often registered under general FIR and not specifically under the Act. Also, a large number of unrecorded cases are also there," said Julie Thekkudan, lead specialist of gender justice at Oxfam India.

Suggestions for Policy Framework

Taking the above issues into account, the following strategies are suggested for intervention:

(a) Appointment of Protection Officers: As the cases of intimate partner violence have been increasing in leaps and bound in the region so protection officers with independent charge needs to be recruited to expedite the processing of domestic violence complaints.

(b) Appointment of Service Providers: In absence of registered service provider in the region contributed to miserable situation for the survivors. Drive needs to be taken to register service providers under the PWDV Act. Appropriate assistance to be provided to them to carry out duties.

(c) Awareness and Sensitisation on PWDV Act: It is utmost important to generate mass awareness about the law and women's entitlements under the Act as most of the survivors were actually not aware of the provisions of the Act. The list of Protection Officers, addresses of the units of the Protection Officers and details of Service Providers should be readily available and posted widely so that women have easy access to it.

(d) Women's Cells in Police Stations/ Setting up Women Police Stations: All Women Police Stations are more innovative creations. This is to mention here that there are only two women police stations in the Barddhaman district. It is an urgent need to set up such cells/police stations in all the urban and rural pockets with adequate funds, staff support and powers.

(e) Setting up Separate Courts for Addressing IPV: Proper attention has to be given by the appropriate authority for establishing a separate Court where only the offences related to intimate partner violence can be tried and it should be made mandatory that every official of this Court would be female (Judges, Advocates, Clerical staffs, etc.).

(f) Gender Sensitisation for Law Enforcement Machineries: Even today, violence in the private sphere is usually treated as a minor issue by the law-enforcement machineries in our country, whether it is the police, the judiciary and lawyers. It is the need of the hour to sensitise them to the gender issues, particularly to intimate partner violence against married women. A module on gender sensitisation should be incorporated in all the training programmes for the police, judicial magistrates and lawyers. The police, lawyers and judges at all levels of hierarchy needs to be exposed to the gender equality education which would enlighten them on existing assumptions and myths. This process in the long run helps the criminal justice system to be more responsible and sensitive to the survivors of IPV.

(g) Setting up More Family Courts: It is to mention here that family courts in the district were defunct and which leads many women to seek police help and exploit sec 498A of IPC. In order to get away from this practice, more family courts that provide early reliefs to the survivors needs to be set up.

(h) Setting up More Family Counselling Centres: The Central Social Welfare Board has assisted voluntary organisations to set up Family Counselling Centres in each State through the State Social Welfare Advisory Boards. The counsellors, who are trained in Social Work/ Psychology etc, work towards reconciliation in order to maintain the institution of the family. More and more FCCs need to be set up to deal with the issue as there was only one FCC in the region.

(i) Partnership with Different Stakeholders: Partnership with various stakeholders can function on several levels. Within the local community, a partnership needs to be promoted with religious leaders, community-based organisations, panchayats and municipalities. Within civil society, the range of partners includes women's self help groups, NGOs, the media, academia, etc. At the State level, strategies must be devised in building partnership with the different machineries of criminal justice system like the judiciary, the police, legal aid and lawyers. Besides, partnership needs to be developed with the healthcare system.

(j) Role of Non-Governmental Organisations (NGOs)/Voluntary Organisation (VOs): NGOs/VOs have to work in partnership with government agencies and international organisations to provide a diversity of services like education, legal literacy, health services, counselling, legal aid, employment opportunities and advocacy to the survivors. They can play pivotal role in bringing pressure on governments to ratify or withdraw their reservations to the international human rights instruments such as the UNDHR, CEDAW, UN Declaration on the Elimination of Violence against Women, the Vienna Declaration and Programme of Action and the Beijing Declaration and Platform for Action, etc.

(k) Support to NGOs/ Voluntary Organisation: Recognising the potentialities of these organisations for generating public response to violence and social mobilisation much greater support should be provided to the voluntary sector by the Central and the State Governments. The existing schemes of assistance to NGOs/VOs should be modified to include a specific component for combating atrocities against women.

(l) Services Under Single Roof: One-stop crisis centre for the survivors of IPV needs to be set up in the district so that they are likely to receive different services at a time under single roof like provision of medical services, legal information, shelter, counselling services and vocational training, etc.

(m) Judgment to be Delivered within Stipulated Period of Time and its Enforcement: Attention has to be given by the Judiciary to deliver the final verdict of the cases within stipulated period of time as mentioned in the specific legislation to avoid unnecessary delay and to ensure relief to the survivors. In case of failure of proper investigation to be made by the appropriate authority for which provision of penalty should be there. An effort has to be made by the appropriate authority for making accountable Judiciary in order to avoid unnecessary delay in Court proceedings and also to improve the status of pending cases. In this connection it's worth mentioning that there is a provision under the PWDV Act that the cases have to be disposed off within a period of 60 days of first hearing. Mere passing orders cannot minimise the sufferings of the survivors unless it is enforced in its true spirit. In this regard there is an urgent need of strong networking among different machineries in the region like police, Judiciary, protection officer, legal aid, medical personnel, family counsellor, shelter home, short stay home, swadhar home etc. These machineries have to work closely in order to address manifold need of the survivors in the region.

References

Agarwal, et al. (2016). 'Women Courts an Alternative Justice System for Women', *Indian Journal of Social Work*, 77 (1), 53-66.

Chaudhary, Sudha (2013). 'Domestic Violence in India', *Journal of Indian Research h*, 1(2), 146-152.

Implementation of Protection of Women from Domestic Violence Act 2005: *Press Information Bureau, Govt. of India*, 11th December 2014, available online at www.pib.nic.in (Accessed on 22nd July 2017).

India: Ministry of Home Affairs, 2015: Crime in India 2015, New Delhi: *National Crime Records Bureau,* available online at http://ncrb.gov.in/ (Accessed on 22nd July 2017).

Jaising, Indira (2009). "Bringing Rights Home: Review of the Campaign for a Law on Domestic Violence", *Economic & Political Weekly* 44 (44), 50-57.

Jejeebhoy et al. (2014). "Violence against Women in South Asia: The Need for the Active Engagement of the Health Sector", *Global Public Health*, 9 (6), 678-90.

Kambli, Tejashri D, et al. (2013). "Study to Assess Determinants of Domestic Violence Among Women in Urban Slum of Mumbai", *IOSR Journal of Dental and Medical Sciences*, 8 (4), 18-22.

Kavitha, VRS (2012). "Spousal Domestic Violence of Married Women in India", *Journal of Sociology and Social Anthropology*, 3 (1), 7-13.

National Family Health Survey (NFHS-3), 2005-2006 available at online rchiips.org/nfhs/NFHS-3%20Data/.../Chapter%2015%20-%20Domestic%20Violence%.. (Accessed on 22nd July 2017).

National Family Health Survey (NFHS-4), 2015-2016 available at online rchiips.org/NFHS/factsheet_NFHS-4.shtml (Accessed on 22nd July 2017).

Nithya, NR (2013). "High Literacy and Mounting Violence: A Case of Women in Kerala, India", *International Journal of Scientific and Research Publications*, 3 (9), 1-9.

Panicker, Lalita (1999). "Cruelty within Walls: Legal Redress for Domestic Violence". *Legal News and Views*, 13 (7), 16-17.

Purushotham Naidu, T (2013). "Domestic Violence against Women in India: A Human Rights Violation". *Asia-Pacific Journal of Social Sciences*, 5 (1), 135-151.

Rasheed, D (2015). "Domestic Violence and Women's Health", *Indian Journal of Social Work* 76 (3), 461- 480.

Sabarwal, Shagun, et al. (2013). "Determinants of Marital Violence: Findings from a Prospective Study of Rural Women in India", *Economic & Political Weekly* 48 (16), 41-45.

Solotaroff, J. L., & Pande, R. P. (2014). "Violence against Women and Girls: Lessons from South Asia". Washington, DC: World Bank.

United Nations Women 2012. *Progress of the World's Women: In Pursuit of Justice.* New York: United Nations Entity for Gender Equality and the Empowerment of Women.

World Health Organisation, the 2002. *World Report on Violence and Health*, Geneva.

World Health Organisation (2012). *Understanding and Addressing Violence Against Women: Intimate Partner Violence.* Geneva: WHO.

World Health Organisation (2013). "Global and Regional Estimates of VAW: prevalence and health effects of IPV and non-partner sexual violence". Geneva: WHO

World Health Organisation: Intimate Partner and Sexual Violence against Women. 2016 available online at http://www.who.int/mediacentre/factsheets/fs239/en/ (Accessed on 22nd July 2017).

List of Contributors

1. **Asha Mukherjee** is a Professor and Head, Department of Philosophy and Comparative Religion and former founder Director of Women's Studies Centre, Visva Bharati, Santiniketan, West Bengal.
2. **Chandreyi Alam,** an eminent Lawyer of Kolkata High Court and a Social Worker.
3. **Himadri Lahiri** is former Professor, Department of English and Culture Studies, University of Burdwan, West Bengal.
4. **Anindita Bandyopadhyay** is Professor in Bengali in the University of Burdwan.
5. **Amitayu Chakraborty** is working as Assistant Professor of English at Durgapur Women's College, West Bengal.
6. **Debayan Deb Barman** is Assistant Professor of English at THLH Mahavidyalay (University of Burdwan), West Bengal.
7. **Rakesh Chandra** is a Professor and Head, Department of Philosophy, University of Lucknow, Director, Institute for Women's Studies.
8. **Dr. Urmimala Das** is presently the Director of Women's Studies Research Centre, Odisha.
9. **Dr. Tumpa Mukherjee** is working as Assistant Professor in Sociology, Women's Christian College, Kolkata.
10. **Dr. Rupa Biswas** is an Assistant Professor of Sociology, St. Xavier's University, Kolkata.
11. **Dr. Shehnaz Begum** is Assistant Professor of English, Purnidevi College, Bolpur.

Index

K

L

M